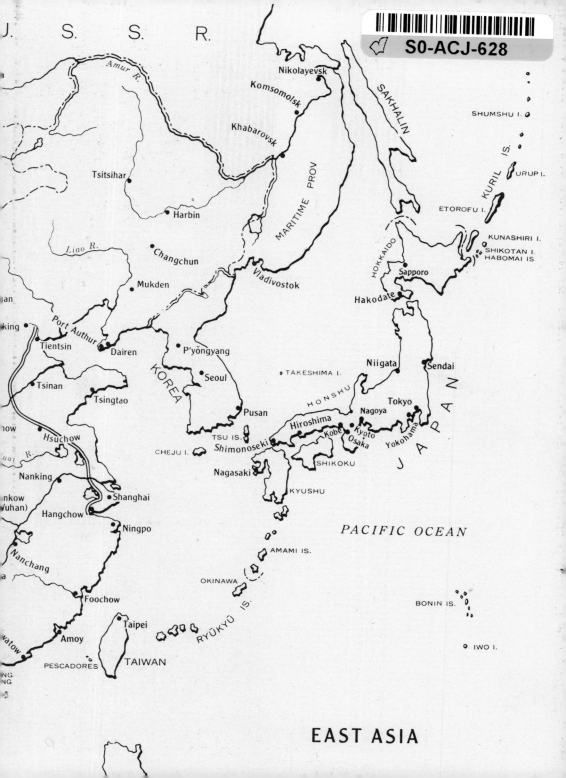

U. S. S. R.

Amur R.

Nikolayevsk

Komsomolsk

SAKHALIN

SHUMSHU I.

Khabarovsk

KURIL IS.

URUP I.

Tsitsihar

ETOROFU I.

MARITIME PROV

KUNASHIRI I.

Harbin

HOKKAIDO

SHIKOTAN I.
HABOMAI IS.

Liao R.

Changchun

Vladivostok

Sapporo

Mukden

Hakodate

Port Authur

Tientsin

Dairen

P'yŏngyang

Niigata

Sendai

TAKESHIMA I.

Tsinan

KOREA

Seoul

HONSHU

Tokyo

Tsingtao

Pusan

Nagoya

Hsuchow

Hiroshima

Kobe

Kyoto

Yokohama

JAPAN

TSU IS.

Osaka

Nanking

CHEJU I.

Shimonoseki

SHIKOKU

nkow
(Wuhan)

Shanghai

Nagasaki

Hangchow

KYUSHU

Ningpo

PACIFIC OCEAN

Nanchang

AMAMI IS.

OKINAWA

BONIN IS.

Foochow

Taipei

RYŪKYŪ IS.

Amoy

IWO I.

PESCADORES

TAIWAN

EAST ASIA

Modern Japan's Foreign Policy

MODERN JAPAN'S FOREIGN POLICY

by

MORINOSUKE KAJIMA

CHARLES E. TUTTLE COMPANY: PUBLISHERS
Rutland, Vermont & Tokyo, Japan

Representatives

Continental Europe: BOXERBOOKS, INC., *Zurich*

British Isles: PRENTICE-HALL INTERNATIONAL, INC., *London*

Australasia: PAUL FLESCH & CO., PTY. LTD., *Melbourne*

Canada: M. G. HURTIG LTD., *Edmonton*

Published by the Charles E. Tuttle Company, Inc.
of Rutland, Vermont & Tokyo, Japan
with editorial offices at Suido 1-chome, 2–6
Bunkyo-ku, Tokyo, Japan

© *1969 by Charles E. Tuttle Co., Inc.*

Library of Congress Catalog Card No. 75–77124

Standard Book No. 8048 0658–6

First edition, 1969
Third printing, 1970

Book design by Keiko Chiba

PRINTED IN JAPAN

Table of Contents

Preface

IN MY PREVIOUS book, *A Brief Diplomatic History of Modern Japan* (Tuttle, 1965), I surveyed Japan's foreign policy from a historical standpoint.

I am, therefore, very happy that in this book I am able to supplement the historical background of Japan's diplomatic policy with a collection of my articles pertaining to Japan's contemporary foreign policy and its future trends.

In 1966 I published *Nippon no Gaiko Seisaku,* the only comprehensive book of its kind relating to Japan's diplomacy. At that time I was chairman of the ruling Liberal Democratic Party's Foreign Relations Research Committee and, therefore, had a hand in guiding the course of Japan's foreign policy. This book represents the essence of my thirteen years of exhaustive study of Japan's external relations while holding the above position besides acting as chairman of the Foreign Affairs Committee in the Upper House of the Japanese Parliament.

The present publication is actually a condensed English version of *Nippon no Gaiko Seisaku.* From the original Japanese text I have selected a number of significant facts that relate to Japan's foreign policy. At the same time, I have also included a number of essays which I contributed as leading articles to the journal *Kokusai Jihyo* (International Current Review), an organ of the Kajima Institute of International Peace, of which I am president.

7

In order that foreign readers will not naïvely misconstrue events in this country, I think it is relevant to point out that there is a disproportionately large number of leftists in Japanese journalistic circles who would lead us to believe—quite erroneously, of course—that their views reflect the majority of Japanese public opinion.

It is now common knowledge that through their concerted efforts, actual conditions in Japan have often been deliberately falsified, giving an exaggerated impression of the strength of the so-called leftist intelligentsia and their effort to influence Japanese national opinion.

Consequently, the author hopes that this book will serve to give foreign readers a deeper insight into the core of Japan's foreign policy as it is pursued by the Japanese government and ruling Liberal Democratic Party, a policy based on harmony and moderation.

At a time when so much is expected of Japan's foreign policy contributing constructively toward the consolidation of world peace, especially peace in Asia, it is my fervent wish that this book may reach a wide section of the people in the United States and in other countries who are observing Japan's role in world affairs with sympathy and understanding.

In closing, I should like to add my expression of sincere gratitude to Messrs. Yuichiro Isobe and Makoto Momoi to whom I entrusted the translation of *Nippon no Gaiko Seisaku,* and to Mr. Seiichiro Katsurayama for his counsel and assistance. I am also grateful to Mr. Charles E. Tuttle for having undertaken the publication of this book.

Tokyo   Morinosuke Kajima

~~~~~~

CHAPTER 1

Neopacifism

REARMAMENT and peace were major topics discussed heatedly during the campaign for the October, 1952, general election. Indeed peace has become an increasingly important issue of today. More important, however, is to ponder this issue in a political perspective against the background of the international situation we face today.

This we must do, though or rather because there are gaps in the concept of peace among politicians, philosophers, and men of religion. There are also varied opinions on how to keep peace. Some argue for "renouncement of armaments" or "arms reduction." Others call for "expansion of arms." These statements reflect both the international situation and the environment in which a country is placed. There can hardly be a single, clear-cut royal road to peace.

For Japan today, the renouncement of her self-defense capability does not spell a guarantee of peace. Neither does arms expansion lead to peace if it lowers the people's living standard. My "neopacifism" is designed to suggest basic concepts and solutions to various problems of peace.

Contemporary Pacifism

The late United States President Franklin D. Roosevelt quoted in his *On Our Way*—a book on his political achievements in the first year of his presidency—the words of a Greek wise man: "Creation is the victory of conviction and not of power." Roosevelt believed these were "words of permanent truth." And he stressed that his new policies would seek such a victory.

Mere diplomatic technique is not enough to bring permanent victory to the policy of peace. The policy should be supported by people's conviction in peace. Positive pacifism, I believe, is the single practical policy for Japan today, when she can gain no profit but destruction from wars. World War II had gone beyond the picture drawn from our experience of World War I. By the same token, and because of the progress in fighting techniques—in particular atomic bombs and aircraft—the next global war will doubtless surpass our imagination based on the experience of the last war.

On the other hand, pacifism today is full of many, vital defects. First, it is impolitic; its leaders are mostly too imaginative. Few of them are politicians in the true sense of the word. Thus contemporary pacifism tends to be too religious and moralistic; it remains apart from political reality. Many of the pacifists, therefore, do not face squarely the reality of Japanese and international situations. No wonder they start from wrong assumptions and reach wrong conclusions.

Second, pacifists today have no sense of limitations. They see to stages of progress. In achieving their goal, they attempt to obtain everything and lose everything. Third, they are too idealistic; even when their objectives are reasonable, their means are irrational. They place too much hope on the future and remain undaunted while leaving present realities to the mercy of those who act against pacifist idealism.

Finally, pacifism lacks planning. Its leaders are preoccupied with struggles and antiwar campaigns and pay little attention to well-organized planning. Their objectives might be sophisticated but their activities are disorganized. Thus pacifism today seldom becomes a center of political planning, and remains an outsider.

Coudenhove-Kalergi, an Austrian nobleman, a son of a Japanese mother, and world famous proponent of Pan-Europeanism, once said: "The greatest enemy of peace is pacifism." It is extremely interesting to hear from this enthusiastic disciple of pacifism such words of derision of European pacifists or dreamers who try to influence their community by words not deeds. They preach on the fear of war. But they lack the courage and spirit of self-sacrifice of statesmen and soldiers. In speeches and articles, many talk about the danger of war and call for the prevention of war. But few dare to offer their lives or even pay material sacrifice for their cause.

Not fighters but preachers, they let others struggle and expect only to reap the dividends and the prizes. In short, Japan's pacifism remains a religious, ethical movement—far from a creative, positive, and political pacifism. Wars are condemned by religious pacifists as immoral and by political pacifists as useless and only harmful. For the former, wars are evil and for the latter, stupidity. The religious pacifists thus try to eliminate wars by remolding human beings and the political pacifists by perfecting a viable peace mechanism.

Essentials of Neopacifism

A new age by nature requires a neopacifism. Japan's religious pacifism should be replaced by realistic pacifism, and dreamers by statesmen. Fighters—and not dissidents—should join the ranks. Only genuine pacifists who face the reality squarely can command popular respect. Only heroic pacifism can lead a nation.

To say "another war is impossible" is no less right than to argue "another war is inevitable." Whether the possibility of war might lead to actual war depends on the foresight, perception, and, above all, deeds of true pacifists, because war and peace are not natural but artificial phenomena. As such, peace is man's objective attainable only by stages. Neopacifists set such stages or limits for their activities and toil toward the ultimate goal—peace—by attaining each stage step by step, because they believe a step forward in a real world is far better than a thousand steps in dreams. A limitless number of plans attract only dreamers and keep realists away. But a single fighter-realist can contribute to peace far more than a thousand dreamers.

Pacifists can achieve their goals successfully only when they are prepared to offer their lives for the cause of peace. So long as the pacifists are looked down upon as cowards and those who sacrifice lives for ideals worshiped as heroes, the public inevitably is impressed by war rather than by peace. But the pacifists can impress people strongly if they give up their roles as preachers and prize seekers and become fighters, disciples, and martyrs of their ideals.

War and Arms

Japan's current state of disarmament and defenselessness does not necessarily spell a contribution to peace. Because peace calls for an arms reduction under one situation and a defense buildup under another.

If Great Britain and Belgium, for instance, had had armaments strong enough at least not to be belittled by Germany in 1914, the Germans would have almost certainly accepted the peace offer made by Great Britain, then on the verge of catastrophe. And World War II might have been prevented if, immediately prior to its outbreak, France and the Soviet Union had been a little better prepared than they actually had been against German blitzkrieg operations.

Furthermore, the current Korean War would never have occurred, if the United States troops had not withdrawn from South Korea or if South Korean troops had been made strong enough to counter the North Koreans and had been given a U.S. guarantee following the U.S. withdrawal. All this is a good lesson: if a nation, preoccupied with pacifism, neglects her armament, while her neighbor is looking for a chance for aggression, she is merely courting war—not peace.

On the other hand, she invites not peace but aggression, if her rearmament or arms expansion designed to secure peace leads to an arms race with her peaceful neighbor.

Every issue of peace must be treated individually. Japan, therefore, cannot adopt a single, uniform policy of peace toward all foreign nations. With a nation which is stable in her policy and respectful of her treaty obligations, Japan can maintain peace through a peace mechanism. Against an aggression-oriented country in the midst of revolution and chaos, peace can be secured only by a superior military might—the combined capability of Japan, her allies, and protectors.

Neopacifism and True Patriotism

If amplified, in its interpretation, a war can be conducted not only with arms but also with economic and cultural means, including economic boycott, blockade, and propaganda. China, for instance, had won in the political struggle against Japan with a boycott; Gandhi resorted to hunger strikes in his successful campaign to liberate India. Recently Iran and Egypt were trying to achieve independence not through arms but through political struggles based on people's movements.

Around the corner will be an era when nationalist struggles will be staged not with swords and bullets but with spiritual weapons. Nations then might replace the arms race with diplomatic, economic, scientific, technological, and cultural competition. They might even compete in legal, social works. People's health and art might even become instruments of national competition.

At any rate, a sense of competition, which creates and maintains the culture of mankind, will be here to stay. The elimination of all forms of struggles and the warlike nature of human beings might lead to the end of culture and progress. The objective of neopacifism too is not to eliminate the struggle, but to refine, purify, and modernize the means of competition.

A renovation of patriotic ideal under neopacifism can be a strong weapon in dealing with reactionaries, because nothing will be more attractive to the public than patriotism. This follows that neopacifism must be based on purified patriotism. Pacifism, if too cosmopolitan and unpatriotic, instantly becomes illusionary and loses its supporters. After all, a degree of patriotism is in itself an indicator of a people's nationalistic sentiment. Neopacifists should, therefore, beat reactionaries in competition over patriotism.

For this purpose, neopacifism must liberate patriotism of a sterile type and remold it into a neopatriotism consistent with modern ethics. Once and for all, we must replace the physical and materialistic patriotism of the past with a new spiritual and moralistic patriotism.

In practice, the nation should offer its due respects to the souls of those who had sacrificed their lives for the country in the battlefields and should extend every possible protective hand to the bereaved families of the war dead. At the same time, relief measures should be adopted for the soldiers who had fought bravely for their motherland and for the repatriates who had worked overseas in economic and cultural fields.

It is also necessary for the nation to recognize that those who were purged because they had worked for the country in ideological, journalistic, political, and economic fields deserve far greater respect than those who had done nothing or little for their motherland.

Patriotism, above all, must not be monopolized by a single political party or circle. He who tries to prevent his nation from being involved unconsciously in the catastrophe of war is no less patriotic than one who attempts national expansion through victories in war.

Not only that, there are quite a few nations in the world where it is more risky for one's life and social position to work for peace than to support wars. In these countries, disciples of peace require far greater courage than disciples of war. In my belief all those who sacrifice their self-interest for national ideals are patriots without exception. The greater their sacrifices, the greater their patriotism. (November, 1952)

CHAPTER 2

Revision of Japan-United States Security Treaty

Opinion Favoring Extension of Security Treaty Gaining Ground

THE CURRENT Japan-United States Security Treaty has a ten-year term. After the ten years, the treaty can be abrogated anytime on a year's notice. The term of the existing security treaty expires in 1970. Opinion favoring the extension of this security treaty is fast gaining ground among members of the ruling Liberal Democratic Party these days.

The climate surrounding the security treaty being such, Prime Minister Sato's statement in the Upper House Budget Committee on March 8 this year attracted attention. Sato said in reply to an interpellator: "The defense structure must be built on a long-term basis. Therefore, it is necessary to take appropriate steps to give longevity to the Japan-United States Security Treaty when the ten-year term expires." On the next day, March 9, Sato elaborated on this remark and said: "It is possible that Japan and the United States will agree that neither country will give notice of abrogation. It is also possible that a new security treaty exactly the same as the existing one will be signed." Sato thus referred in a concrete way to the steps that might be taken when the ten-year term is up and promised to conduct further studies on the matter.

It is still fresh in our memory that the so-called renovationist forces, such as the Japan Socialist Party, Sohyo (General Council of Labor Unions), and the Japan Communist Party, organized a furious struggle to block the revision of the security treaty and created large-scale disturbances six years ago. These renovationist forces are now joining hands to organize a vigorous struggle to abrogate the security treaty with 1970 as the target year. We cannot remain idle spectators.

Needless to say, various preparations are now being made by certain people in the Liberal Democratic Party to organize a national movement to counter the renovationist struggle against the security treaty. The fact that the issue of extending the treaty has recently become a matter of public debate is to be greatly welcomed. Particularly am I overjoyed at Prime Minister Sato's previously mentioned statement in the Diet.

Suggestion for Extending the Security Treaty Until 1980

I have long felt the need for extending the term of the current security treaty. I have long believed that the Foreign Affairs Study Council of the Liberal Democratic Party, of which I am chairman, must take the initiative in creating among the members of the government party a climate favoring the extension of the security treaty. Unless something is done to frustrate the renovationists' move to oppose the extension of the treaty, there is a possibility of great confusion being fermented as the year 1970 approaches. It is feared that this confusion, if ever created, might far surpass in scale the anti-security treaty disturbance of 1960. And we must expect the confusion to continue even after 1970. The possible result is a cold war within Japan, with the whole country thrown into turbulence similar to a civil war. In order to avoid the so-called 1970 crisis, some steps must be taken before it is too late.

I, therefore, took the floor in a plenary session of the Upper House on January 28 last year and asked the government if there was any possibility of the term of the Japan-United States Security Treaty being extended by another ten years until 1980. Prime Minister Sato said in reply that it was essential for Japan to retain the security treaty but that he had no intention of revising the treaty just to extend its term, because the term can be extended even under the existing agreement.

According to newspaper reports, this statement by Prime Minister Sato was the first official manifestation of the Japanese government's intention to maintain the Japan-United States Security Treaty. I would like to add here that even at the time of the 1960 treaty revision, I had advocated that the treaty be made operative to 1980. In view of the fact that the Japan-United States Security Treaty is a counterbalance to the Sino-Soviet alliance, I insisted that its term should be extended to 1980, which is the year when this treaty expires. The late Kichisaburo Nomura, former Japanese Ambassador to the United States, was the only person who supported my suggestion. Some people even said that making the term up to 1970 was too long and they advocated a five-year treaty instead. If the term of the treaty had been put at twenty years at the time it was revised in 1960, there would be no need for any fuss today.

The reason why Japan signed a security treaty with the United States in September, 1951, simultaneously with the signing of the Peace Treaty, was that the Soviet Union and Communist China, in February, 1950, concluded a military alliance, with Japan as their hypothetical enemy, and that the Korean War broke out shortly afterward. The security treaty was absolutely necessary to guarantee the peace and security of Japan. In short, the security treaty was the inevitable product of the balance of power principle in international politics. International peace has been maintained on this "balance of power" principle almost since the 15th century. A study of the history of foreign relations provides good examples such as the Triple Alliance among Germany,

Austria, and Italy and the Triple Entente among Great Britain, France, and Russia before World War I as well as the Japan-Germany-Italy Axis Treaty and the alliance among the United States, Great Britain, France, and the Soviet Union before World War II.

The Soviet Union and Communist China have concluded a mutual assistance agreement to aid North Korea, whereas the United States has concluded mutual defense pacts with the Republic of Korea and Taiwan. Now that Communist China is proceeding vigorously with the development of its nuclear power amidst the current turbulent Asian situation, nothing is more dangerous for Japan than to make the mistake of abrogating the Japan-United States Security Treaty and of disregarding the "balance of power" principle.

Fallacious Argument of Japan Socialist Party

It may be natural for the Japan Communist Party to demand immediate abrogation of the security treaty and advocate the so-called unarmed neutrality of Japan. But why does the Japan Socialist Party share this view? How does the socialist party think Japan can maintain its peace and security? It seems that the Japan Socialist Party advocates the establishment of a collective security system involving Japan, the United States, Communist China, and the Soviet Union, to replace the existing Japan-United States Security Treaty. Is such a system possible in the present state of the international relations?

The social democratic party in any West European country thinks the best guarantee of national interests is to prevent communist aggression. Why is the Socialist Party of Japan obsessed by the illusion that the Soviet Union and Communist China are "peace forces?" I believe that the unarmed neutrality advocated by the Japan Socialist Party will create a power vacuum in Japan, lead to increased military pressure on Japan from Communist China and Russia, and encourage their indirect invasion of Japan. If the Japan Communist Party should ever succeed in carrying out a *coup d'état,* Mao Tse-tung's policy of playing up the Japan Socialist Party as a "direct allied force" will be justified.

The Road to a New Locarno Treaty Setup

Despite what I have said, I think that the Japan-United States Security Treaty can be abrogated, if changes in the future international situation should cause Communist China and the Soviet Union to scrap their alliance. It probably will become possible then for Japan, the United States, Communist China, and Russia to set up a collective security system such as advocated by the Japan Socialist Party. If the Japan-United States Security Treaty is extended until 1980, it will expire in the same year as the Soviet-Communist China alliance. Probably by that time, the United States and the Soviet Union will have much closer relations than today, while Communist China may have abandoned its present militant policy and switched to a peaceful coexistence policy. If so, the Socialist Party's proposal of a collective security system involving the above-mentioned four countries will no longer be a castle in the air. If such changes should take place in the international situation, it will mean the end of the cold war between the East and the West, and the emergence of a "new Locarno Treaty system" in Europe and the Atlantic area under the United Nations, with the North Atlantic Treaty Organization (NATO) and the Warsaw Treaty Organization joining forces. Nothing can be better, if a Far East version of this new Locarno Treaty system could be established in the Asia-Pacific area.

In this connection, I remember the days when Japan scrapped the Anglo-Japanese Alliance. The Anglo-Japanese Alliance served as a strong prop, back-stopping Japan in its rise in the world through the Meiji and the Taisho eras. The alliance, however, was abrogated when its third term expired in 1921. The Anglo-Japanese Alliance was replaced by the London Naval Reduction Treaty, a treaty concerning the defense of the Pacific islands as well as by an agreement among Japan, the United States, Great Britain, and France concerning the maintenance of the *status quo* of the Pacific islands, and the Nine Power Treaty concerning China. Nothing would be more desirable, if the Japan-United States Security Treaty could be replaced by a supraparty peace setup after it is scrapped in 1980.

Compared with Anglo-Japanese Alliance

I want to say a few more things about the Anglo-Japanese Alliance. One of them is that the Japanese people had no inferiority complex with respect to the British Empire, then at the height of its glory and prosperity, and concluded the alliance with proud assurance. In those days, the national power gap between Japan and Great Britain was far greater than that between Japan and the United States today. Yet, both the government and people of Japan welcomed the Anglo-Japanese Alliance wholeheartedly. Nobody expressed fears that Japan might be made an agent or a colony of Great Britain. It is deplorable, therefore, that the Socialist Party and a group of so-called progressive intellectuals today criticize the Japan-United States Security Treaty as depriving Japan of independence and autonomy and as making Japan a colony of the United States. Such criticism is nothing but a servile argument.

The Japan-United States Security Treaty aims at the mutual defense of Japan. Under the treaty, Japan is obligated to offer land, facilities, and service, while the United States is obligated to dispatch armed forces. It is wrong for us to argue about "autonomy" or "equality" in the case of an agreement like the Japan-United States Security Treaty which pledges cooperation between countries sharing the same interests in international politics. This treaty should rather be considered disadvantageous to the United States in that the treaty concerns the defense of the territory of Japan. The true significance of this type of treaty lies in the mutual benefits derived from each other's strong points and the supplementing of each other's shortcomings.

Secondly, it must be noted that the Third Anglo-Japanese Alliance concluded in 1911 was re-revised in the sixth year before the ten-year third term expired. The alliance had been renewed twice before. Thanks to the repeated renewals, the Anglo-Japanese Alliance remained in force even during World War I, much to the advantage of Japan. I earnestly hope that the existing Japan-United States Security Treaty will be extended to 1980 at the earliest possible date so that the unnecessary friction within Japan will be minimized.

Today, the Soviet Union is advocating peaceful coexistence and is at odds with Communist China. Yet, there has been no change in the Soviet Union's ultimate objective of winning Japan into the communist camp. Exposed to nuclear threats from Communist China, Japan has no alternative but to rely on U.S. nuclear protection for its safety and security. This is why Japan has to extend the Japan-United States Security Treaty to be assured of continuing peace and security. (March, 1966)

CHAPTER **3**

Collective Organization for the Pacific Region

Pan-Asia Ideal and Pacific Collective Organization

I HAVE advocated the formation of Pan-Asia as the paramount goal of Japanese diplomacy for many years. This ideal, however, could not be realized because of the arbitrary pressures exerted on Japan's foreign policy following the outbreak of the Manchurian Incident and up until the end of the Pacific War.

At the same time, the Pan-Europe movement of Count Coudenhove-Kalergi of Austria which had fired my imagination as a youth also went through a similar experience. It had won the hearts of many shortly prior to the 1930's, but received a serious setback when the dark curtain of German Nazism and Italian Fascism fell over the European continent.

With the end of World War II, the movement was revived, culminating finally in the formation of the EEC (European Economic Community) in 1957. This event, regarded as an important turning point in world history, has subsequently inspired the EEC to advance with giant strides from an economic union toward political unity.

Owing to the phenomenal development of science and technology and the resulting progress in the fields of transportation and communication, the world is becoming smaller and relations between the individual nations much closer. In such circumstances, in order to strengthen cooperative re-

23

lations and adjust their relations, it is a matter of urgent necessity for these nations to join in a regional collective organization for the adjustment of their interests as well as for the promotion of peace and prosperity.

At present there is the United Nations in which member nations share a common membership, but within it they have formed racial groupings. Thus, it is my belief that the formation of a regional collective organization serving as an intermediate body between the United Nations Organization and its various groupings is a dictate of history.

As is known, in Europe EFTA (European Free Trade Association) is already in existence, following the formation of the EEC, and elsewhere the nations have launched similar projects such as LAFTA (Latin American Free Trade Association), CACM (Central American Common Market), UAMCE (L'Union Africaine et Malgache de Coopération Economique), and the Arab Common Market.

In addition, there are broader regional collective organizations such as NATO (North Atlantic Treaty Organization), OAS (Organization of American States), OAU (Organization of African Unity), OCAM (L'Organisation Commune Africaine et Malgache), and the Arab League. Similar bodies in the Soviet bloc include COMECON (Council for Mutual Economic Assistance) and the Warsaw Treaty Organization.

It is apparent, therefore, that Asia, despite its poverty, is lagging behind in the formation of regional collective organizations. This is especially true in the region neighboring Japan. While plans are afoot to set up the OAEC (Organization of Asian Economic Cooperation) under ECAFE (Economic Commission for Asia and the Far East) and the OPEC (Organization for Pacific Economic Cooperation) under the aegis of the Japan-Australia Joint Economic Committee, it will take some time before they become a working reality. Efforts to organize ASA (Association of Southeast Asia) are still in a state of suspension.

In the meantime, the early attainment of my ideal of Pan-

Asia has become extremely difficult because of the control of the Chinese Mainland by the communist regime. As an alternative, I am endeavoring to realize the establishment of a Pacific common market or Asian-Pacific community within the framework of the United Nations as an initial step.

As explained in Chapter 8, the concept of an Asian-Pacific community would embrace Japan, Southeast Asian countries, Australia, New Zealand, the United States, and Canada in a system binding them politically, economically, and culturally. It is a matter of deep satisfaction to know that both in Japan and in the countries concerned there are positive signs that the time is ripening to move positively toward its materialization.

Interpellations in the Diet and the Government's Attitude

I should like to refer to my emphatic appeals in the National Diet on a number of occasions for the establishment of a Pacific common market or an Asian-Pacific collective organization.

On June 15, 1960, at the time of the revision of the Japan-United States Security Treaty, my interpellations in the Upper House Special Committee on the Japan-United States Security Treaty and other related questions were focused on the operations of the treaty. Although I directed my questions to economic cooperation between Japan and the United States, I did take the opportunity then to propose the formation of a Pacific common market, emphasizing "the need of promoting economic cooperation among the countries in the Pacific region, namely, Canada, Central and South America, Southeast Asia, Australia, and New Zealand."

While alluding to the opening paragraph of the Root-Takahira Agreement concluded between Japan and the United States in 1908, stipulating that "it is the wish of the two governments to encourage the free and peaceful development of their commerce on the Pacific Ocean," I called on the government to realize the urgent need of not only promoting commerce on the Pacific Ocean, but also of the necessity to establish at an early date a Pacific common market, particularly at a time when the EEC was making rapid progress and the ideal of the Atlantic community was gaining strong support.

Referring to the thesis written by the one-time Foreign Minister Katsuo Okazaki, entitled "The Past, Present and Future of Japan's Foreign Policy," suggesting that Japan's future diplomatic goal should be the formation of an Afro-Asian common market, I proposed for government consideration the establishment of a Pacific common market as a more realistic goal.

Replying for the government, Prime Minister Kishi pointed out that, in view of the great economic disparity between industrial Japan and the agricultural countries of Asia and Africa, there were many obstacles in the way of an early establishment of the common market. After stating that the situation in Europe among the EEC nations was entirely different, Mr. Kishi agreed that since the countries surrounding the Pacific Ocean, except for Communist China, were members of the Free World community, efforts should be directed toward the formation of such an organization.

Later on March 6, 1964, I reiterated the importance of realizing an Asian-Pacific collective organization in my interpellations in the Budget Committee of the Upper House. I seized the opportunity to point out that at the three-power summit meeting attended by the leaders of Malaysia, the Philippines, and Indonesia in August, 1963, an agreement on a federation plan, forging for the first time in history 150 million people of Malay origin, was signed, symbolizing the concept of Maphilindo. I also added that President Sukarno of Indonesia, in response to the cheers of the populace, declared: "Maphilindo is the first step toward our goal. Asia is one!" Moreover, I affirmed my strong belief that I did not believe that Prime Minister Ikeda's visit to the countries of Southeast Asia and the western Pacific in the autumn of 1963 was merely for the solution of problems between Japan and these countries, but was rather intended as a first step toward building up a structure of prosperity, unification, and pacification yearned for by the people of Asia for many years.

Prime Minister Ikeda replied that during his tour of the western Pacific, President Diosdado Macapagal of the Philippines had expressed his wish to see the islands of the western Pacific—Japan, the Philippines, Indonesia, Australia, and New Zealand—which God had abundantly blessed, strengthening their friendship and promoting their mutual prosperity. The Japanese Prime Minister was sincerely happy to know that such feelings were rising high in the nations of the western Pacific.

Touching on the subject of Japan's policy toward Southeast Asian countries, Prime Minister Eisaku Sato, who succeeded the late Hayato Ikeda, stressed that Japan should not only strengthen her ties of friendship with these countries individually, but should also work toward the creation of a collective organization covering the entire region.

It is interesting to note that Mr. Walt W. Rostow, Counselor and Chairman of the United States State Department's Policy Planning Council, who visited Japan at the invitation of the Japanese Committee for International Goodwill, delivered a speech in Tokyo in which he stated that in his exchange of views with leading Japanese personalities he had gained the impression that there was a feeling of regionalism rising in Asia. He felt that this spirit of regionalism in which the Asian countries constituted a single region could be the basis for their maintenance of independence and cooperatively promoting economic development. Mr. Rostow underlined the necessity of interdependence, giving as an example the "Alliance for Progress" between the United States and the countries of Central and South America. This partnership, he stressed, is the pursuance of common objectives while respecting the existence of different national interests.

I wish to emphasize here the importance of regional collective organizations from the standpoint of national security. Needless to say, apart from the old system of treaty negotiations or treaties of a purely military nature, national security must now take into account economic and ideological factors. In other words, with the widening scope of national security, it has become necessary to consider, besides the conventional military alliances, a regional collective organization or a common organization embracing economic, social, educational, and other aspects. I believe that there is a pressing need for an intermediate body between the world organization like the United Nations and individual regional security arrangements such as a regional collective organization. As for Japan, it is imperative for her to have a Pacific or Asian-Pacific collective organization in the interests of her national security.

OAEC and OPEC

Let us consider what progress has been made by the conception of OAEC (Organization of Asian Economic Cooperation) of ECAFE (Economic Commission for Asia and the Far East) and OPEC (Organization of Pacific Economic Cooperation) of the Japan-Australia Joint Economic Committee.

Asian regional economic cooperation, discussed at the 16th assembly of ECAFE in the spring of 1960, took positive shape with the proposition to establish OAEC by Mr. U Nyun, the Secretary General of ECAFE, in January, 1962. However, most of the countries in the ECAFE region received the proposal with reservation, pointing out that the formation of such an organization should be preceded by full discussion of fundamental questions regarding regional economic cooperation.

An economic commission composed of seven economic experts from member states of ECAFE, the Philippines, India, Iran, and New Zealand, as well as nonmembers, Great Britain, France, and Mexico, was subsequently set up under the sponsorship of Secretary General U Nyun to look into the concrete proposals for economic cooperation within the region.

In December, 1963, the seven-man commission of experts submitted a report which, though incomplete, drew the following conclusions: separate expert committees should study further the questions of liberalization of trade within the ECAFE region; the adjustment of development projects and promotion of industry within the region; the establishment of a regional development bank, and the question of cooperative organizations.

It was agreed that priority should be given to the establishment of a regional development bank.

After preparatory meetings were held in Bangkok and Manila for the establishment of the Asian Development Bank, government representatives of twenty-eight countries in October, 1965, agreed on the statute of the said bank. Then at the end of November at the Second Ministerial Conference of Asian Economic Cooperation of ECAFE in Manila, the capital of the Philippines was chosen as the site of the headquarters of the bank. The conferees also signed the Agreement for the Establishment of the Asian Development Bank. Following the ratification of the agreement by the countries concerned, a third regional development bank, similar to the ones in the Americas and Africa, will come into being toward the end of 1966.

The decision to choose Manila as the site for the headquarters of the Asian Development Bank came as a shock to Japan inasmuch as it was optimistically predicted that Japan's strenuous efforts to have the headquarters located in Tokyo would be rewarded. The reasons for Japan's failure to win the site may be attributed to the fact that both the first and second ministerial conferences were held in Manila, the president of the Philippines was personally active in efforts to win the headquarters for his country, the United States was backing the Philippines' objective, and despite the fact that Japan had publicly pledged $200 million, the highest sum along with the United States, the Philippines' catch-phrase "the Asian Development Bank should be located in an underdeveloped country" was irresistible.

In the wake of her failure to have the headquarters of the bank in Tokyo, Japan should also ponder over the repeated criticisms heard abroad that Japan, as an industrially advanced country, lacks sufficient sense of international responsibility toward the underdeveloped nations of the world. For instance, Japan's aid toward the underdeveloped countries in 1964 was only 0.44 per cent of her national income, a markedly low rate compared with the average of 0.95 per cent for the member states of DAC (Development Assistance Committee) of the OECD (Organization for Economic Cooperation and Development). Japan also lags behind the United States and West Germany in bilateral aid agreements with Asian countries. I firmly believe that Japan should step up her economic cooperation in the region on a substantial scale through the medium of the Asian Development Bank.

The interests of the countries in the ECAFE region being highly complex, the path lying in front of the bank will be far from smooth. There also remain many unsolved questions, such as the liberalization of trade and adjustment of industrialization projects requiring mutual cooperation within the region, not to speak of the time required before the OAEC can become a reality.

The concept of OPEC (Organization of Pacific Economic Cooperation) was publicly announced in May, 1963, in a statement entitled "The Goal of Pacific Economic Cooperation" by the Japan Economic Research Council, consisting of four economic organizations, including the Japan Federation of Economic Organizations and the Japan Chamber of

Commerce. In order to cope with the new world economic development such as the EEC, it was suggested that the aim of OPEC should be to hold a round-table conference once a year on a government level, attended by the delegates of such Pacific nations as Japan, the United States, Canada, Australia, and New Zealand, to discuss the promotion of trade, economic cooperation, economic development, and cultural exchange.

Although there are the Joint Japan-United States Committee on Trade and Economic Affairs and the Japan-Canada Economic Ministerial Conference on a governmental level as well as the Japan-United States, the Japan-Canada, and the Japan-Australia joint economic committees on a nongovernmental level, it is desirable for these separate bodies to be coordinated into a multipurpose economic organization such as the OPEC.

It was significant, therefore, that at the Second Japan-Australia Joint Economic Committee meeting held in Canberra in September, 1964, Australia proposed the establishment of a new organization to promote economic cooperation among the five nations bordering the Pacific Ocean. The participants agreed to study the methods for the setting up of the organization.

The reason for initially confining the OPEC scheme to the five nations is due to the fact that whereas these nations bordering the Pacific are industrially advanced nations, the others are developing countries. Secondly, it was felt that it would be inadequate to merely abolish trade barriers among these countries or to develop new markets in the member countries in order to promote economic relations between the industrially advanced and the developing countries. It was necessary for the advanced nations to cooperate in consolidating the social basis for the promotion of economic development of these developing countries.

It was from this standpoint that the industrial nations of the Pacific which had hitherto been left out of regional arrangements, such as Japan, Canada, Australia, and New Zealand, had moved toward the formation of a collective organization linked with the United States. Faced with the possible future entry of Great Britain into the EEC and the end of the preferential treatment accorded to British Commonwealth nations, Australia and New Zealand are keenly aware of the need to form some kind of a regional collective organization.

Later in May, 1965, the Third Japan-Australia Joint Economic Committee meeting held in Tokyo decided to establish "The Joint Committee Relating to the Pacific Regional Economic Cooperation Organization" and made the following decisions:

1. To promote the establishment of a cooperative organization with the Japan-Australia Economic Joint Committee as its nucleus.

2. To invite financial representatives of the United States, Canada, and New Zealand to attend the Fourth Japan-Australia Economic Joint Committee as observers.

3. To take up as the first project of the said cooperative organization the joint development of Papua and New Guinea.

Hitherto, the lack of enthusiasm on the part of the United States was one of the biggest obstacles to the realization of the OPEC. However, lately the United States has begun to show increasing concern for the economic development of Southeast Asia as shown in President Johnson's billion-dollar development plan for the region and in the recognition of the important role which Japan can play in Southeast Asian development.

If the United States should attend the Japan-Australia Joint Committee meeting at the end of 1966, it would be of great significance, marking the first time in history for the financial representatives of the five nations to meet to discuss regional economic cooperation. Should the outcome of the meeting result in the inauguration of the OPEC, even on a nongovernmental basis, there is every likelihood that the various governments concerned will eventually participate in the project.

Expansion of Foreign Ministry Structure Desirable

In Southeast Asia itself, the region was not without some moves toward the formation of a regional collective organization. For example, in January, 1959, the Prime Minister of the Federation of Malaya, Tunku Abdul Rahman, and the President of the Philippines, Carlos Garcia, in a joint statement called on Southeast Asia to form ASA (the Association of Southeast Asia). With only Thailand responding to the call, the three countries, namely, Malaya, the Philippines, and Thailand in July, 1961, set up the association with the aim of promoting cooperation in the economic, social, cultural, scientific, and administrative fields. With the formation of Malaysia, however, their joy was short-lived as the Philippines, laying claim to sovereignty over Sabah, refused to recognize the new state.

Even the federation plan of the so-called Maphilindo, comprising Malaya, the Philippines, and Indonesia, met with failure when the dispute between Indonesia and Malaysia became seriously aggravated. In addition, the separation of Singapore from the Federation of Malaysia in August, 1965, further weakened the federation system of Malaysia.

A number of recent developments have revived hopes in the concept of Maphilindo, i.e., the military *coup d'état* in Indonesia on September 30, 1965, which radically reduced the influence of communism, the endeavors of Malaysian Prime Minister Tunku Rahman to come to terms with the Philippines on the question of Sabah, and the mediation efforts of the Philippines to try to resolve the dispute between Indonesia and Malaysia.

Although the independence of Singapore was due to the

inability of the Chinese to cooperate with the Malay population, it would be a severe blow to the island republic if the
Malaysian common market were to be abolished. There is
still hope that trading prospects will help toward bringing
about a reconciliation between the two parties.

Before leaving Tokyo in July, 1965, to attend the Fourth
Joint Japan-United States Committee on Trade and Economic Affairs to be held in Washington, Japanese Foreign Minister Shiina revealed plans for a Southeast Asia Development
Ministerial Conference, the aim of which was to discuss
among the countries concerned the promotion of economic
development in Southeast Asia. After repeated postpone-
ments, the conference was finally held in April, 1966, in
Tokyo, attended by the ministers of Thailand, the Philippines,
South Vietnam, Laos, Singapore, and Malaysia. Burma was
absent from the conference, but observers were present from
Indonesia and Cambodia.

Meanwhile, the Japanese Ministry of Foreign Affairs has
been maintaining a lukewarm attitude toward the conception
of an Asian-Pacific collective organization. Despite the passage of a number of resolutions by organs of the Liberal Democratic Party, namely the Foreign Relations Research
Committee, the Economic Research Committee, and the
Overseas Economic Cooperation Committee, for the adoption
of an all-around Asian policy especially in the economic field,
they have always met with a negative response from the
Foreign Office. Apparently the ministry is so preoccupied
with day-to-day affairs that it is unable to give any thought
to any new projects.

In view of these circumstances, Japan's diplomatic policy
can hardly be expected to take a forward-looking approach.
Although the Finance Ministry is quick to carry out retrench-
ments, I believe that the structure of the Ministry of Foreign
Affairs should be expanded, enabling it to meet the absolute
requirements in various countries overseas. At the same time,

a system of having more than one Minister of State in charge of diplomatic affairs should naturally also be considered.

In the latter half of the 20th century, it is undeniably necessary for Japan to work for the realization of the idea of a Pacific collective organization. Without such an objective, there is very little future hope for Japan's diplomacy. (January, 1966)

CHAPTER 4

Question of Recognition of Communist China

Obstacles to Recognition of Communist China

IT IS BEYOND dispute that the question of Communist China is of such importance that it affects the very existence of Japan. To make matters worse, there are, under the present circumstances, no perceptible signs that Japan could consider the normalization of her relations with Communist China.

Among the obstacles to normalization of relations is Communist China's pursuance of a chauvinistic and militant policy, aimed not only at so-called United States imperialism and Soviet revisionism but also even at the United Nations, and her rejection of the principle of peaceful coexistence, unsatiated ambition to communize the world, and choosing to advance along the path of nuclear armaments.

We should not lose sight of the fact that Communist China has been laying greater emphasis on her theory of the people's liberation war, advocating it more insistently in an effort to capitalize on the unsettled conditions in Asia. This theory of arming the entire population and laying stress on guerrilla warfare was clearly outlined in an old treatise written by Chairman Mao Tse-tung entitled *The Problems of Guerrilla Warfare and Strategy in the War of Resistance Against Japan.*

This theory was revived when Lin Piao, the Minister of Defense, adapted it from a new angle in world strategy in his article, *Praising the Victory of the People's Liberation War,* pub-

36

lished in commemoration of the 20th anniversary of the war against Japan on September 3, 1965. In his article, Marshal Lin Piao stressed that the "seizure of power by armed force is the main purpose and highest form of revolution." Pointing out that "the Yenan strategy of encircling the urban centers from the rural areas should be expanded on a world scale," he likened North America and Europe as the "urban centers" and the rest of the world as the "rural areas."

Imbued with this theory of forming a people's front, Communist China is utilizing it in consolidating its position against so-called United States imperialism. Not only is Communist China calling on its own people, but is also endeavoring to extend its "study" throughout the world, hoping to apply it in practice.

In spite of the fact that sixteen years have passed since the Communist Chinese established their regime in Peking, the majority of the world's nations—67 out of 117 members of the United Nations—have yet to recognize it. In addition, its failure to receive the approval of the United Nations for membership is due to its aggressive and militant attitude.

However, since it is a fact that Communist China is in effective control of the Chinese Mainland with a population of 700 million and is a nuclear power, it is dangerous to permanently disregard its existence. As a matter of fact, there is a growing opinion in the world that Communist China should be brought into the international society of nations and be seated at the table of the disarmament conference.

This issue has taken on added significance since January, 1964, when President de Gaulle of France extended his country's recognition of Communist China. Moreover, despite the refusal of the 1965 session of the United Nations General Assembly to pass the resolution for Communist China's entry into the world body, the narrowing gap in the voting is bound to create a more favorable atmosphere in the future for the Peking regime to become a United Nations member.

For example, compared with the previous voting in the

United Nations on the resolution to have the issue of Chinese representation designated as an important question in 1961 which was 61 in favor, 34 against, 7 abstentions, and 2 absent, the latest voting was 56 in favor, 49 against, 11 abstentions, and 1 member failed to take part in the voting. Furthermore, whereas those who voted previously on the resolution to seat Communist China and expel Nationalist China in 1963 were 61 for, 57 against, 12 abstentions, and 1 absent, the latest figure found the pro and con equally balanced at 47, with 12 abstentions, 2 failing to participate, and 1 absent.

On the other hand, the Japanese Socialist Party and other leftist groups have earlier been calling for the recognition of Communist China, but the government and the majority of the people of Japan, in view of the existence of the Japan-United States security system and the relations with the Nationalist government of Taiwan, believe that the time is still premature to extend recognition to Communist China.

When France recognized the Communist Chinese government, both Prime Minister Hayato Ikeda and Foreign Minister Masayoshi Ohira took the position that Japan's attitude would be determined on the basis of a rational solution reached at the United Nations and in accordance with the overwhelming world opinion. Later, replying to a question in the Lower House, Foreign Minister Ohira declared that "should a situation arise in which Communist China becomes a legitimate member of the United Nations with the blessing of its members, Japan will have to consider normalizing diplomatic relations with Communist China."

It is not at all surprising that Prime Minister Sato, in referring to the question of Communist China in the 50th extraordinary session of the Diet, warned that "judging from the nature of the Peking regime, its possession of nuclear arms poses a threat to the security of Japan," and "in face of China's high posture diplomatic policy, Japan has no intention of kowtowing for the purpose of improving Sino-Japanese relations."

Preconditions for Recognizing Communist China

Communist China's Marxism-Leninism and Mao Tse-tung's so-called revolutionary line are incompatible with Japan's liberal democratic principles. However, the people of our country and of China, a country separated by only a narrow strip of water, are of the same racial stock and share a common script. As our relations have been inseparably linked from time immemorial, politically, economically, and culturally, it is unnatural and intolerable not to recognize Communist China permanently.

Nevertheless, it is my earnest desire that Japan should approach the issue of recognition with resolute subjectiveness from her own standpoint. Taking into consideration the statement by former Foreign Minister Ohira that "should a situation arise in which Communist China becomes a legitimate member of the United Nations with the blessing of its members, Japan will have to consider normalizing diplomatic relations with Communist China." I believe that in her own national interest Japan should work out a solution to this question, cautiously and calmly and without adapting herself only to the trend of the times or from an impassioned stand against communism.

On the basis of this belief, I urged, during my general interpellations on Japan's foreign policy in the Budget Committee of the Upper House on March 6, 1964, that Japan should take steps in the direction of recognizing and normalizing relations with Communist China, provided that the latter accepts the following four preconditions:

1. Recognition of the Japan-United States Security Treaty.
2. The Japan-Republic of China Peace Treaty to be respected.
3. Renounce all rights to claim reparations from Japan.
4. In accordance with the principles of noninterference in

internal affairs, promise not to engage in communist subversive propaganda or to undertake indirect aggression against Japan.

Not only did the then Prime Minister Ikeda declare that he held views similar to those that I had expressed, but public opinion generally appeared to uphold this stand.

When the present cabinet of Prime Minister Sato took over the reins of government, I asked for its confirmation of the views I had earlier expressed on January 28, 1965 in the plenary session of the Upper House. After expressing respect for my views, the Prime Minister added that "as to how the points will be concretely taken up are problems which must be left to the future." There being no opposition by the Liberal Democratic Party, I believe that Japan should consolidate her policy toward Communist China on the basis of these four preconditions.

In view of their importance of the preconditions, I should like to deal with them separately, pointing out their significance and the prospects for the future.

1. Recognition of the Japan-United States Security Treaty.

The Socialist Party in Japan, waging a tireless struggle aimed at abrogating the Japan-United States Security Treaty, has described the demand that Communist China recognize the said treaty as unjustified, but it should be remembered that when Japan restored diplomatic relations with the Soviet Union the latter, though reluctantly, recognized the said treaty. The Japan-United States Security Treaty being a counterbalance to the Sino-Soviet Treaty of Friendship, it is natural for Communist China to recognize the treaty in question not only from the standpoint of the balance of power in international politics, but also for at least as long as the Sino-Soviet Treaty of Friendship remains in force.

It is worth noting that Premier Chou En-lai, in an exchange of views with Mr. Tokutaro Kitamura, former

Finance Minister who led a party of Liberal Democratic Party members to Peking in April, 1964, declared that "we do not think that Japan should immediately break off relations with the United States and promote Sino-Japanese ties. Japan-United States relationship may remain unchanged, while Sino-Japanese relations are gradually normalized through the so-called piling-up method."

Later in October, Premier Chou reportedly expressed willingness to Mr. Narita, head of the fourth Socialist Party mission to Communist China, that should relations be normalized with Japan his country would be willing to conclude a nonaggression pact with Japan without affecting the validity of the Japan-United States Security Treaty.

2. The Japan-Republic of China Peace Treaty to be Respected.

There are many reasons for Japan's insistence on the above precondition, not the least of which is Japan's feeling of indebtedness to Generalissimo Chiang Kai-shek for having issued a proclamation to "repay enmity with virtue" at the time of Japan's surrender, for safely repatriating more than two million Japanese soldiers and civilians from the China Mainland, and for having renounced all rights to claim reparations from Japan. Even in the event of Communist China becoming a member of the United Nations, Japan opposes any move to strip Nationalist China of her seat in the world body. It is as clear as day that any attempt to unseat one legitimate member (Nationalist China) of the United Nations and replace it with a regime (Communist China) that is antagonistic to it will unnecessarily heighten tension in the Far East by overturning the present blance of power on which the peace and security of the region depend. Accordingly, Japan should maintain her present Japan-China relations based on the Japan-Republic of China Peace Treaty.

This view was confirmed by Prime Minister Sato in his affirmative reply in the Budget Committee of the Lower

House to Mr. Eiichi Nishimura, a Democratic Socialist Member of the National Diet, who had stated that "in accordance with the interests of the Japanese people and international behavior, I believe that the peace treaty concluded with Nationalist China will continue to be remain in force in the future as well."

3. Renounce All Rights to Claim Reparations from Japan.

On concluding the peace treaty with Japan, President Chiang Kai-shek renounced all rights to claim any reparations from Japan. Consequently the latter assumes the question as having been settled, but Communist China neither recognizes Nationalist China's right to speak on its behalf nor even the validity of the Japan-China peace treaty.

Earlier in July, 1955, Premier Chou En-lai asserted that "Communist China reserves the right to claim reparations from Japan because the people of China cannot forget the destruction and sufferings at the hands of the Japanese militarists." Although Premier Chou did not mention any specific sum, the amount reportedly being considered by Communist China is said to be in the neighborhood of $50 billion, an astronomical figure that could cripple the Japanese economy.

Communist China's reservation on the issue of reparations is a powerful trump card in her hands in any dealings with Japan. At the same time, it is feared that this stand is also a stumbling block to any move to normalize relations between Japan and Communist China.

4. In Accordance with the Principles of Noninterference in Internal Affairs, Promise not to Engage in Communist Subversive Propaganda or to Undertake Indirect Aggression Against Japan.

This precondition provides that Japan and Communist China will respect each other's position, with the latter making a solemn pledge not to behave in any manner that may be construed as interfering in internal affairs, such as engaging in

Communist subversive propaganda or undertaking indirect aggression against Japan. This entails Communist China renouncing the extremist teachings of Marxism and wholeheartedly accepting the principle of so-called peaceful coexistence.

At the present time, Communist China is maintaining an arrogant posture on this question. As a result, the United States feels that it has no alternative but to wait until a new generation of Chinese leaders, more amenable to accepting the principle of peaceful coexistence, assumes power in mainland China. The Soviet Union, on the other hand, appears to entertain some hopes that a change will come as Communist China advances to a higher level of national construction. In any event, any solution to this vital question will require a long-range view.

It is clear from the chain of events in the Afro-Asian countries, among them the Algerian *coup d'état,* the Indo-Pakistan dispute, and the Indonesian revolution, that the Communist Chinese policy toward the nations of Asia and Africa has been dealt a severe blow. If Communist China fails to heed the lessons of these events and frantically attempts to resort to roll-back tactics, she must expect to receive even more bitter reverses.

Communist China's Policy Toward Japan

While I believe that Japan, from the standpoint of her national interest, should firmly adhere to the four preconditions for the recognition of Communist China, it is important that Communist China's policy toward Japan should be carefully examined.

Communist China regards United States imperialism as the foremost and most powerful enemy within the framework of her world policy objectives. In seeking a relentless showdown with America's Far East and world policy, the fact should not be overlooked that Communist China in any move regards Japan as an integral part of her world policy.

Thus, the Communist Chinese aim to weaken the Japan-United States security system to a point where it becomes a dead letter and simultaneously to isolate Japan by driving a wedge between Japan and the United States. In other words, Communist China's ultimate goal is to make Japan impotent as well as harmless, for a powerless Japan can best serve the cause of Communist China's ambition to communize Asia and the world.

To attain this objective, Communist China is giving strong support and direction to the Japanese Communist and Socialist parties and other leftist organizations, hoping to step up the anti-American struggle and to form a united front against the United States and the Japanese government. Strenuous efforts are being made to muster what is called the Mao Tse-tung's "direct allied forces."

What must not pass unnoticed is the fact that Communist China regards the Japanese Socialist Party, unlike other Social Democratic parties in Western Europe which have divorced themselves from Marxism, in a special light, treating them as "direct allied forces" of Communist China. Communist China is well aware that the Japan Socialist Party, supported not only by the main current faction of Sohyo (General Council of Labor Unions) but also by the wide masses of the working class, is a major opposition party in the National Diet with incomparably more power to influence the general public than the Japanese Communist Party.

Communist China, realizing that conservatism is still a potent force in Japan, is making powerful appeals to conservative elements in Japan's political and financial circles, as well as all strata of Japanese society, with offers to promote Japan-Communist China friendship, expansion of trade, and normalization of relations, all aimed at encouraging the growth of procommunist elements in Japan, that is, the so-called Mao Tse-tung's indirect allied forces.

In the face of these moves, we must be vigilant in dealing with Communist China's call for "Japan-Communist China friendship," as their real aim is not genuine friendship for the Japanese people. Whereas the Japanese people desire nothing more or less than friendly relations with the people of China, the leaders of Communist China regard "Japan-Communist China friendship" as merely a tool in their fight against United States imperialism and its so-called followers, Japan's conservative forces and monopolistic capital. Anyone disagreeing with these communist aims is not really interested in Sino-Japanese friendship according to their line of thinking. The Communist Chinese have imported their policy into Japan and are attempting to impose it on the Japanese people. Thus, they are using the Sino-Japanese friendship as a camouflage to mount their political and ideological struggles in Japan.

Moves in the Mass Communication Field

Communist China today is actively maneuvering to undermine the solidarity of the conservative forces in Japan and to win the uncommitted section of the population to their side, paying particular attention not to drive them into the camp of the enemy. To achieve its aims, it is of deep interest to note that they are utilizing Japan's mass communication media to the maximum.

For example, despite strict Communist Chinese censorship, Japanese newspapermen stationed in Peking are allowed more frequent press interviews with leading officials than correspondents of other countries. Special facilities are also offered in gathering information and in transmitting news. News is provided with due consideration being given in Peking for articles appearing in either the morning or evening editions of Japanese newspapers.

At the same time, Communist Chinese correspondents in

China, are adroitly currying the favor of Japan's most influ-ential newspapers, attempting in every way to get the most favorable and fullest coverage for Communist Chinese news with the desired slant.

Whenever Communist Chinese delegations visit Japan, they make the fullest use of Japan's mass communication media. This was especially true in the case of the Economic and Goodwill Mission headed by Mr. Nan Han-chen which visited Tokyo in April, 1964. Mr. Nan lost no opportunity to hold exclusive interviews with members of the editorial staff and editors of Tokyo newspapers, appeared in television programs, and did everything possible to implant the policies of Communist China into the minds of the Japanese people through the media of mass communication. Likewise, most Peking delegations make it a point to visit various places in Japan, hold interviews with local pressmen, and energetically expound Communist Chinese propaganda in regional news-papers.

The overwhelming majority of the people of Japan lean on the side of anticommunism, but they are not altogether im-mune to certain forms of persistent Communist Chinese subversive propaganda. The Japanese people undeniably have a sentimental feeling of affinity for the people on the Chinese Mainland, based on tradition, centuries-long rela-tions, and the sharing of a common script. Because of these sentiments, many people hold erroneous ideas about the Chinese revolution, viewing it with a detached feeling as an Oriental or purely Chinese affair and dissociating it from the Russian revolution which was marked by untold cruelties.

It was probably for these reasons, according to a student of Communist China, that reports of the suppression move-ment of counter-revolutionaries by the Communist regime for several years after it was installed in power in October, 1949 had not been widely publicized in the Japanese newspapers. He further asserts that the Japanese press had practically ignored the tragedy of the century that had followed in the wake of the Communist Chinese seizure of the Chinese Mainland. According to the official report published by the Communist Chinese authorities, the number of people killed in the mass purge had exceeded 1,170,000 in the first year alone.

Although the toll of deaths from 1951 to 1952, the years during which the movement to liquidate the counter-revolutionaries reached its peak, have not been officially revealed, an unimaginable blood bath had taken place. However, instead of reporting this grave historical fact, Japanese journalism appeared to be more interested in writing about whether there were or were not any flies in Communist China.

At present Japan is striving to promote an economic and cultural exchange on a nongovernment basis with Communist China, guided by the principle of separating politics and economics. But with the intensification of the Sino-Soviet rift and the so-called 1970 crisis looming ominously ahead, Communist China's cultural and propaganda campaign is bound to grow more complex and sophisticated.

In these circumstances, I earnestly hope that those people connected with the media of mass communication will take appropriate measures to deal with the Communist Chinese maneuvers from the standpoint of genuine national interests. (December, 1965)

CHAPTER 5

The Need to Re-examine "Tokyo Trial"

The Motion Picture *Greater East Asia War and International Tribunal*

THE PICTURE that has impressed me most recently was Shin Toho's *Greater East Asia War and International Tribunal,* the target of severe criticism from various circles because of its "anti-American" theme. It was also criticized for its treatment of war criminals as heroes.

The United States Embassy here reportedly issued an informal warning to American residents "not to take roles in a movie film which overtly incite the national sentiments of the two countries."

American extras in fact refused to perform. In every respect it was a film that caused an international controversy.

The United States reportedly questioned four points:

1. Japan was provoked and decided to attack (Pearl Harbor) by the memorandum of the United States Secretary of State Cordell Hull dated November 26, 1941.

2. The Pearl Harbor attack was not a surprise raid but a by-product of the delay at the Japanese Embassy in Washington to translate the Japanese ultimatum.

3. The attitude of defense attorneys at the international military tribunal were really commendable, particularly those who defended Tojo.

4. Japan's dream of establishing the Greater East Asia

Coprosperity Sphere is gradually coming true now that Asian nations are gaining independence.

Narrations to these effects, American authorities seemed to have worried, "might be construed as nothing but a means to justify Japanese actions."

Furthermore, the film was criticized for "lack of fairness" in presenting, "defense councils' rebuttals more than prosecutors' views" during the scenes of the Tokyo trial. Faced with this and other criticism, Shin Toho finally was obliged to insert three extra scenes.

Among the scenes added was the testimony which made the defendants' case worse. It was made by Professor Masajiro Takigawa, dean of the Kyoto University Law Faculty, who said "the war has been an aggressive one since the Sino-Japanese Incident."

Other testimonies included the Manchurian Emperor's words that "our country was subjected to Japan's aggression" and General Ryukichi Tanaka's statement that "before the war ended I had believed we were taking a self-defensive action which I now think was an aggressive war after all."

Nevertheless those who actually saw the film must have agreed with an *Asahi Shimbun* movie critic who wrote on January 8, 1959: "From the scenes, one may get an impression that Professor Takigawa and other witnesses who accuse the defendants look more disgusting than the accused . . .

"Thus viewers may unconsciously think the defendants are heroes who fought against foreigners making egocentric and self-righteous harangues . . ."

Undoubtedly Shin Toho tried to present a fair picture of the Tokyo trial. But today and for us, the film is impressive only because it looks as if the trial itself were tried. After watching this movie, I myself keenly felt the need to review the Tokyo trial.

Verdicts and Minority Opinions

Following V-E and V-J days, the victors held international military tribunals in Nuremberg and Tokyo to probe into war responsibilities and to punish war criminals. Throughout the trials, numerous diplomatic and other secret documents were made public. And so were diaries and memoirs of statesmen, diplomats, military and business leaders, just as it was done after the end of World War I. In tracking the causes of and the responsibilities for wars, there was a certain dissimilarity between 1919 and 1945. In the latter, the international military tribunals were held for this specific purpose. The verdicts given to punish the war criminals sounded as if the real causes of and responsibility for the war had been thoroughly clarified.

But now the time seems to have come for us to review whether such judgments were fair and proper. After World War II, Germany and its allies refuted the so-called guilt or responsibility clause of Article 231 of the Versailles Treaty under which they were held solely responsible for the war. The refutation was for their own political and economic interests, and Japan's political and economic interests today are doubtlessly to refute the verdicts of the Tokyo trial.

During the trial, disputes among judges were conspicuous to say the least. The court was virtually split into majority and minority groups. Their differences were so wide that French, Dutch, and Indian judges—from the minority—had to give very long opinions to refute the majority verdict. In fact, their opinions were longer than those of the majority group. Furthermore, the minority views impressed the United States defense council so strongly that American attorneys sent General Douglas MacArthur a letter vehemently criticizing the unfairness of the court.

The letter pointed out, among others, that "the trial was unfair" and "not based on evidence," that there was reason to "suspect" the defendants' guilt but that was all that the court had found and that "the verdicts will by no means enable the allies to achieve their objectives."

These points were exactly what the three judges insisted in their presentation. The British newspaper, *The Times,* then carried an editorial titled "Unfairness in Tokyo." On January 11, 1949, *The Washington Post* argued in its editorial to the effect that it had become increasingly clear that not only American reputation but also justice itself had been damaged by the Tokyo trial. Bases and procedures of the trial were illegal, uncertain, and disadvantageous to the defendants, as Judge Pal of India pointed out.

Toward the end of his book, the Indian judge says to the effect that only after time meliorated zeal and prejudice and only when rationality unmasked deception, the goddess of justice, holding a balanced scale, will demand many of the past records of guilt and innocence be altered.

Indeed the time is ripe for us to review the verdicts of the Tokyo trial.

Studies of the Causes of and the Responsibilities for War

Last autumn, Minister Otaka, senior diplomat in the Foreign Office published a book *On the Responsibility for World War II.* In its preface, he writes: "As a question of history, the responsibility for declaring war is an extremely important issue . . . intimately related to people's ethics and honor." And he goes on to say: "In the United States . . . the study of the declaration of war became necessary . . . In 1946, the United States Congress set up an *ad hoc* investigation committee to conduct a final examination of the issue." The study revealed the fact that President Roosevelt had planned a war against Japan earlier than the Pearl Harbor attack and that neither Congress nor the public was informed of this secret U.S. war plan.

Thus Minister Otaka implies that the study of the causes of and the responsibilities for the war is now in a new stage. After quoting *War Against Japan,* published in 1957 by Major General W. Kirby of the British Army who criticized the Hull note, Minister Otaka concludes: "Similar books exist in England, Germany, and France . . . but an individual cannot collect and analyze them all . . . the Japanese government must be responsible for carrying out such study as an official work to keep the record of history straight."

I myself believe the government should not only collect such books and documents as historical references but carefully review and completely correct the verdict of the Tokyo trial, as the German government once did. Or it should at least revise the guilt or responsibility clause imposed on Japan.

Such action by the government will doubtlessly serve Japan's political and economic interests and provide a moral basis for Japan's reconstruction. A similar view is expressed by Dr. Masajiro Takigawa who said in his book *A Trial of the Tokyo Trial:* "It is up to the historians of the future not the victors of the past to judge whether the war Japan fought was an aggressive action or a war of self-defense.

"Japan will not rise again as a full-fledged nation-state so long as the people are obsessed with the idea that they are the 'criminals of the world' who started a war of aggression . . .

"The Tokyo trial made us suffer spiritually on top of our human and material sacrifice in Hiroshima and Nagasaki. . . . We must tell the world how we suffered so that those who desire justice then could think sincerely about what justice really means. By so doing, we can contribute to permanent peace on earth . . ."

The Soviet Union and Its War of Aggression

A Russian judge sat through the Nuremberg trial. This apparently made the court reluctant to provoke his wrath or to disagree with him. Thus prosecutors mercilessly attacked Germany's aggressive acts, whereas they made no reference at all to the fact that the Soviet Union broke neutrality and nonaggression pacts in invading Poland, Finland, and Baltic nations. The court indeed gave its verdicts without mentioning a word about Soviet aggressions.

Exactly the same procedure was repeated at the Tokyo trial. Either because of Russian objection or deterred by a Russian judge, the court also gave its verdict accusing Japan alone as an aggressor, disregarding completely the fact that the Soviet Union unilaterally broke the Russo-Japanese nonaggression treaty and invaded the then Japanese territories.

The tripartite alliance excluded the Soviet Union specifically under its Article 5. The alliance did not cover Russia. Nevertheless, the military tribunal in Tokyo ruled in its verdict that the Japanese-German-Italian treaty was planned and concluded to carry out an aggressive war against the Soviet Union. The verdict explained in length how Japan followed Germany's suit in breaching nonaggression pacts and invading the Soviet Union. It then said: "This court holds the view that a war of aggression had been planned throughout all the period examined by this court . . . that this war of aggression was one of the major factors of Japan's national policy and that its purpose was to occupy those parts of the Soviet Union in the Far East."

The court refers little to the conclusion between Japan and the Soviet Union of a neutrality pact, except that "Japan was not sincere in concluding the neutrality treaty with the Soviet Union. . . . It seems," the court merely adds, "Japan regarded her pact with Germany more important than the treaty with the Soviet Union which Japan signed only in order to make her attack against Russia easier."

This statement completely disregards the fact that Japan had resolutely and repeatedly rejected German requests that Japan should attack the Soviet Union. Nevertheless, an

American judge supported the verdict containing such a statement. Unless and until the Japanese government refutes it with an effective counterstatement, the Russians naturally would continue to claim their rights over the entire Kuriles including the Kunashiri and Etorofu islands.

If Japan wants to re-claim the southern Kurile Islands, the government must first of all devote every effort to set the historical fact straight that Japan did not start a war of aggression against the Soviet Union. To meet this pragmatic objective, too, a review of the Tokyo trial is urgently needed.

If one objectively studies prewar, wartime, and postwar records of World War II, one may find a number of acts of the Russians, Americans, British, and their allies which should have been condemned—more or less in a similar manner to those condemned at the Nuremberg and Tokyo trials.

The verdicts at the trials, however, never referred to such acts of the victors. In this respect alone, they cannot escape serious charges.

The Versailles Treaty:
Its "Guilt Clause" and Germany

After World War I, Germany and her allies were held solely responsible for the war under the so-called guilt clause of Article 231 of the Versailles Treaty. Germany devoted her entire national effort in refuting the clause. A review of how she did so is certainly useful for Japan and her allies to refute the Tokyo trial which held Japan and her allies solely guilty of starting the war.

At the Versailles Peace Conference, the victors forced Germany to accept the so-called guilt or responsibility clause under the famous Article 231 concerning the responsibility for the war. Germany protested against this clause, but finally signed the treaty. Since then, debates on the responsibility of war have become important political issues.

At the Weimar Constitution Conference in June, 1919, German legislators unanimously adopted a resolution against the guilt clause. Again in September, 1926, when Germany joined the League of Nations, her Foreign Minister Gustav Stresemann declared to the world the German denunciation of the clause.

Later in June and July, 1932, or at the Lausanne Conference, Germany so strongly reiterated her demand to annul the clause that the conference itself was plunged into chaos. Thus the German government had never abandoned its firm stand that it could by no means tolerate the guilt or responsibility clause.

Under Article 231 of the Versailles Treaty, Germany was ruled not only ethically guilty but financially responsible. She had to pay reparations. Thus to refute the verdict was to her of political, and hence practical, interest. If the verdict was eliminated or modified, she could not only redress her national honor but terminate or at least reduce reparation payments.

Germany first published the so-called *Kautsky Papers,* the diplomatic papers written prior to and at the time of Germany's declaration of war, and later other diplomatic documents from 1871 till the outbreak of war. Her government then set up as its public relations offices, a German Organizational Activities Committee (Arbeitsausschuss Deutscher Verbände) and a Central Institute for the Studies of Causes of War (Zentralstelle für Erforschung der Kriegsursachen). Through these organizations, the German government launched a world-wide campaign claiming that the guilt or responsibility clause was unfair, unjust, and historically unfounded. The campaign steadily gained substantial support in Austria and Hungary, and successfully overthrew a common belief about the Versailles Treaty in England and Italy.

The German campaign also affected seriously the activities of the Neutral Committee for the Studies of Causes of War set up by the Swiss, Scandinavians, and Dutch. In the United

States also, Germany found a number of sympathizers. These American sympathizers started the so-called Revisionalists Movement supported by Professors Burgess, Beard, Burns, Cochran, and Schevill, and former Senators Owen and Knox. Even in France, where few, except Georges and Démartial, had any doubt of Germany's sole responsibility, many started to wonder.

Thus a common belief that Germany and her allies alone should be held responsible for the war was gradually overthrown. This fact, I believe, should be recalled clearly in contemporary Japan. If we try hard, it would not be impossible to alter or at least modify the verdict of the Tokyo trial.

Historical Facts and Verdicts of Tokyo Trial

My study on the causes of and the responsibilities for World War I was published in my book *The Study of Causes of World War I*. In it, I singled out the alliance-entente system as an indirect cause of the war: "A theory that the responsibility for World War I lies in the international political system itself is gradually accepted in many countries. . . . And argument which holds Germany alone responsible or, on the contrary, acquits her of any charges, is considered as an extremely unscientific, historically groundless, political, and emotional theory debated only between ex-belligerents." By exactly the same token, defects of international political systems were indirect causes of World War II. Never should Germany, Italy, and Japan alone be held fully responsible for war.

I wrote in my book that "it is not proper at all to argue that the war was caused by either tradition or ambition of a nation, statesman, or military leader. . . . Because none of the German, Austrian, and Russian statesmen and military leaders, who were blind to dangers and deaf to advice, did actually want a war at the last moment. . . . The real sources of catastrophe should rather be found in the fact that Europe, governed by the principle of balance of power since the 16th century, was divided into two camps—the tripartite alliance and tripartite entente through a series of secret alliances and ententes since 1871.

"A conflict, originally limited between Serbia and the Austro-Hungarian group, was not settled by the two parties but eventually was participated in by world power. This," I pointed out, "was basically because of the then existing alliance-entente system which reflected the balance of power in Europe."

Just as in the case of World War I, no statesman or military leader in Germany, Japan, the United States, and Great Britain wanted war at the last moment before the outbreak of World War II. The source of catastrophe can be located in the confrontation and showdown between the two camps, the Japanese-German-Italian and Anglo-American-Russo-Franco alliances.

Such division of world powers followed the same pattern observed before the outbreak of World War I. To repeat, the basic cause of the failure to settle local conflicts in Central Europe and Asia and to keep world powers from participating in the conflicts was the alliance-entente system which represented the then balance of power. Clearly European and Pacific wars would provide world powers with chances to achieve certain gains they wanted. However, none of them resorted to war deliberately just for such gains. No nation actually wanted war.

In the case of World War I, Germany tried hard to limit the war between Austria and Serbia. Before World War II, she again wanted to localize the conflict with Poland only. Japan too adopted a policy of not expanding the conflict in the Asian continent in an effort to prevent the outbreak of an all-out war. This today is a widely accepted historical fact.

All the heads of state and politicians knew too well that an all-out war was uncertain in its political consequences and huge in its loss of lives and properties. Nevertheless the war broke out. Why?

Because political and military leaders had done something which led to the mobilization and declaration of war. Or they failed to do something which could have prevented their nations from mobilizing their armies and declaring war. In this sense, world powers were more or less responsible for the war. The guilt clause of the Versailles Treaty was unjust. So were the verdicts of the Nuremberg and Tokyo trials which held Germany, Japan, and their allies alone responsible for the war.

The verdicts were imposed on the vanquished by the victors. They were the victors' judgments, no longer supported by almost all the influential historians and diplomatic commentators. Just as in the case of World War I, the theory of divided responsibility is replacing that of single responsibility. This is the contemporary trend concerning war responsibility.

But how to divide such responsibility among the nations is a still unsettled issue. Some argue they could divide it mathematically by a certain ratio. Others attempted to set an order of responsibility. But a calculation of such a complex issue by precise formula is neither easy nor possible, because the issue is too delicate to be defined by a black-and-white formula. At any rate, it is clear beyond any doubt that the verdicts in Nuremberg and Tokyo, which condemned Japan and Germany alone as guilty and responsible for the war, were unfair and unjust. (February, 1959)

CHAPTER 6

Japan-United States Economic Collaboration and Implementation of New Security Treaty

A Record of Interpellations in the Upper House Ad Hoc Committee on the Japan-United States Security Treaty, June 15, 1960

THERE was no clause concerning Japan-United States economic collaboration in the original treaty drafted by the Foreign Office while it was negotiating with the United States, whereas specific clauses on economic aid and cooperation were found in the Sino-Soviet pact, NATO, and SEATO documents. I pointed out this fact to Prime Minister Kishi, Foreign Minister Fujiyama, and others, calling for the insertion of such a clause in the new treaty. I also asked economic and financial leaders for their cooperation.

As a result, a new stipulation on economic cooperation was inserted in Article 2 of the new treaty, and reconfirmed in a more concrete form by a Kishi-Eisenhower joint communique. The clause and communique, I believe, are the very bases for Japan to prosper economically, stabilize her national living standard, and take part in aid programs for developing nations, one of the central issues of the contemporary world.

I, therefore, had no doubt that the clause would be warmly welcomed by everyone in this country. Nevertheless, to my great disappointment, the question of economic collaboration was scarcely discussed in the process of the Lower House deliberations of the new treaty. Worse yet, some even implied that the clause was inserted to disguise the military nature of the treaty. This was indeed an extreme case of ignorance.

The security pact originally was a product of shock and fear over the conclusion of the Sino-Russian alliance treaty and the outbreak of the Korean War that immediately followed. It, therefore, contained military elements. But never in the past has it been actually employed. Neither will it be in the future unless, as Prime Minister Kishi put it, Japan is threatened by an aggressor. But the pact should also be implemented in the fields of economic and political cooperation if it is to be cherished dearly by our people and is to survive as long as possible.

It follows then that the pact must be implemented with a long-range and overall vision, not only as a military treaty but as a superpolitical arrangement covering politics, economy, and culture. The recent revision of the pact, therefore, should be based on such a basic understanding.

Indeed economic cooperation has become a superpolitical issue, not merely a purely economic question such as expansion of trade, acceptance of foreign capital, or technological cooperation, particularly after Soviet Premier Nikita Khrushchev adopted a new policy called "peaceful coexistence and competition." In the following interpellation, I referred to not only economic issues but my views on the employment of the pact and Japan's future course of diplomacy. To my great pleasure, I found that the views of Prime Minister Kishi and Foreign Minister Fujiyama completely coincided with mine.

Chairman Ryuen Kusaba: We shall now resume discussion on three subjects concerning the Japan-United States security pact. I recognize Mr. Morinosuke Kajima.

1. Japan-United States Economic Collaboration

(a) On the Import of the Economic Clause
Morinosuke Kajima: Thank you, Mr. Chairman. It has been

my long-cherished wish to insert a clause concerning economic aid and cooperation in the new treaty. Accordingly, whenever possible, I have urged Prime Minister Kishi, Foreign Minister Fujiyama, the Liberal Democratic Party, and financial leaders to consider such a clause. It is, therefore, my great pleasure to find the clause in the pact at last.

In the process of the Lower House deliberations, however, we have not heard any thorough discussion on the economic issue. Newspapers, magazines, radio broadcasts, and public opinion in general seem to have paid little attention to the issue. This I regret a great deal.

I am convinced the economic clause is the very factor which will genuinely stabilize the people's living, consistently improve economic life, and increase social welfare after this pact is ratified and put into effect. Furthermore, we must recall that since Soviet Premier Khrushchev advanced his new policy of peaceful coexistence and competition, this economic issue has become an important one in the international political scene.

Even President Eisenhower regretted he was a bit slow in noting the importance of this issue. Two years ago, the President, in his State of the Union message, referred to the military deterrent and added his remarks on an entirely different kind of war we were already confronted with—a gigantic economic offensive which communist imperialists had launched against free nations. He said something to the effect that the communist imperialist regimes had recently met major failures in their attempts to extend their influence by direct, armed means. Consequently they shifted their efforts of political control to economic infiltration into developing nations.

Should we underestimate their nonmilitary activities, Eisenhower warned, they might be able to beat free nations, our military might notwithstanding. Many of us, however, either avoid or fail to recognize such a possibility. This fact itself, the President added, increases the danger of the new communist offensive. We must admit that the majority of us did not anticipate the psychological shock which the launching of the first Soviet satellite gave to the world. Lest we should fail to anticipate a far more severe shock the world might receive from the Soviet economic offensive, we must never commit a similar error in another field, the President concluded.

At about the same time, Vice President Richard Nixon pointed out as follows in connection with the importance of nonmilitary elements: "Unless we can deal with a threat in the nonmilitary field where communism has achieved some results in the past, we may not be able to save American freedom even with the mightiest power in the world. And if we Americans should take a shortsighted view of the communist challenge, reduce our foreign aid, cripple mutually beneficial trade, and ignore propaganda planning, we would simply be throwing a huge sum of money for missiles, aircraft, and submarines into ditches."

In Great Britain, too, the importance of the economic issue has by no means been overlooked. Harry Welton, a Sovietologist, for instance, published a book, *The Third World War* with a subtitle *New Battlefields—Trade and Industry*. His subtitle reflects the degree of attention he pays to Khrushchev's new declaration of economic war. In fact, he emphasizes a need for us to find out precisely and in time the real Soviet intention, facts about international communism and its subversive acts, and the real nature of the Russian trade offensive, because, in his view, World War III has already broken out between two economic systems and in the battlefields of trade and industry.

If defeated in this war, Great Britain and other trading nations will immediately face an economic catastrophe. In Japan, however, little attention is paid to the importance of the economic issue in securing peace and safety. I do not know a better example of ignorance.

I, therefore, would like to raise a few questions mainly on

the economic issues and implementation of both the preamble
and Article 2 of the new treaty as well as of the Kishi-Eisenhower joint communique.

(**b**) Cases of NATO, SEATO, and United States-Republic
of China Pacts

In the morning, an honorable member of the committee,
Mr. Nagano, referred to the economic question—mainly as
a domestic issue. My question deals with the economic issue
in the context of international economy and competition. I
would like to direct it at Foreign Minister Fujiyama, hoping
to hear supplementary remarks, if any and if necessary, from
the international trade and industry minister and other gentlemen.

First of all, Article 2 of the new security pact, stipulating
Japan's economic collaboration, seems to be common in principle with Article 2 of the North Atlantic Treaty, Article 3
of the Southeast Asia Treaty, and Article 3 of the Mutual
Defense Treaty between the United States and the Republic
of China. Are there any differences in the economic clauses of
the four pacts? I would appreciate your view on this point.

Foreign Minister Aiichiro Fujiyama: Economic clauses similar
to the one in the new security pact can be found, as pointed
out by Mr. Kajima, in Article 2 of NATO, Article 3 of
SEATO, and Article 3 of the United States-Taiwan pact.
Virtually the same expression is used in SEATO and the new
security pact. Article 3 of SEATO refers to technical aid.
The United States-Taiwan pact mentions nothing about the
difference in international economy between the two nations,
whereas the new security pact does refer to such a point.
This is because the relationship between the United States
and Japan is between two nations advanced both politically and industrially. So is the relationship among NATO
member nations.

This is how we interpret the principle of the treaty and
our interpretation is supported by the fact that it stresses
economic aid less than it does economic collaboration between

the two parties. This point, I believe, represents a difference from other pacts.

Morinosuke Kajima: Could you tell us how the NATO, SEATO, and the United States-Taiwan pacts are implemented?

Foreign Minister Aiichiro Fujiyama: At the beginning, when NATO was set up, its founding fathers were preoccupied with coordination and buildup of military establishments. Little attention was then directed at how to make the best use of the economic clause in the treaty. But with the military establishment gradually built up, the treaty organization began to deal with a wider spectrum of problems related to intra-organizational cooperation within the Atlantic community. All this started at the 7th NATO Council meeting in September, 1951 in Ottawa.

An immediate result then was the announcement of the so-called Ottawa Declaration into which were embodied recommendations by a committee, consisting of ministers from Belgium, Canada, Italy, the Netherlands, and Norway, to the council calling for a closer, economic, financial, and social collaboration within the treaty area. Also in a committee report, NATO ministers stressed liberalization and expansion of trade activities as well as closer cooperation with OEEC (Organization of European Economic Cooperation).

Later in May, 1956, the promotion of common interests among the Atlantic Community was placed high on the agenda at the Paris conference. It was then agreed that regular studies should be made of the political side of economic problems, and efforts must be made to remove gaps in international economic policies among the NATO member nations. The conference also adopted a decision to set up a cabinet ministers' committee to study and compile a report on nonmilitary cooperation in general under Article 2.

The report was submitted to the Paris conference in December, 1956 by the committee composed of delegates from Italy, Norway, and Canada. The report in essence called for (a) international and individual actions to build a sound and developing economy, (b) maximum freedom possible in trade payments, and the flow of labor and capital, and (c) economic aid to underdeveloped nations.

During the NATO meeting last December, as the honorable gentleman may recall, economic problems were major topics and from these discussions developed a question of economic aid for developing nations. The central issue of this collaboration in SEATO is less intraorganizational collaboration as in NATO than aid for underdeveloped nations. The United States, of course, does not limit its aid programs to member nations in SEATO, but she is apparently doing her best in the treaty area. Australia, too, is providing SEATO nations with aid. In August, 1959, a SEATO technical school was set up in Bangkok, and is still operated under the joint management of the United States, Great Britain, and France.

The SEATO Council is advised on economic affairs by its committee of economists. As to your last question, the United States-Taiwan Treaty, we have so far received no information about its economic clause and actual implementation.

(c) Article 2 and MSA (Mutual Assistance Agreement)

Morinosuke Kajima: I would like to hear your views on the relationship between Article 2 of the new treaty and the MSA agreement. The article, in my understanding, stipulates nonmilitary aid, whereas the agreement defines military aid. An MSA-type clause on military aid can be found in NATO and SEATO. My question is why the MSA clause was not incorporated into the new treaty.

Foreign Minister Aiichiro Fujiyama: I do not see why there should be any specific relation between the MSA agreement and Article 2. In fact, a few words and phrases in the treaty were quoted or referred to in the MSA agreement. To avoid misunderstanding, the agreement has a stipulation governing how such words and phrases should be interpreted. But there is nothing else which indicates a relationship between the two. I rather believe it is better not to identify the implementation of military aid in the MSA with a question of providing a basis for peaceful economic cooperation.

(**d**) Japan-United States Economic Collaboration

Morinosuke Kajima: This question might be too comprehensive and broad for you to answer briefly, but could you give us an outline of the current situation of economic collaboration between the United States and Japan?

Foreign Minister Aiichiro Fujiyama: The question of economic collaboration, or economic relations in general, between the two countries has two aspects, as explained by the prime minister: a bilateral aspect between the two governments and a multilateral phase or economic collaboration by the two nations for other countries.

In the former, efforts are directed at increased cooperation through negotiations in order to expand trade activities and settle conflict of interests between the two nations. We are doing this despite various domestic problems, particularly those related to trade and commerce, in each country. The second phase, or the United States-Japan economic aid for developing nations in Southeast Asia and other areas, is one of the problems the two nations are deeply concerned with. One can never overemphasize the need to deal with this important issue through close cooperation and collaboration of the two countries.

However, Japan is yet to recover her economic potential, though it has grown gradually so far. This has doubtlessly deterred her from actively participating in the economic aid program. Of course, Japan will double her effort to rebuild her economic potential and accordingly to contribute to such a program. But so far, we must admit, our economic condition has kept us from actively contributing to the Japan-United States aid program for other nations.

Now that Japan's economic potential is about to grow, she should actively cooperate with the United States in the aid program—a countermeasure against the nonmilitary offensive launched by our potential enemies who have gradually replaced their military cold war tactics with an economic race or competition, as the honorable gentleman pointed out.

Such cooperation by Japan is, I believe, very important in Southeast Asia where there exist certain misunderstandings about the United States economic aid "with strings attached" and Japan's economic activities reminiscent of her past record is gradually disappearing. As I mentioned the other day, Japan's economic cooperation in developing India's iron-ore industry, for instance, is also strongly supported and welcomed by the United States government. I have no doubt that Japan and the United States can collaborate closely in such fields, and continue their joint efforts in carrying out projects under the Colombo Plan and other international programs.

The two nations also face another important issue in the field of economic cooperation and collaboration: their policies toward the European Common Market and the Outer Seven. Such an economic trend in Europe might in future lead to the birth of a European economic sphere which would doubtlessly affect free trade and economic activities in non-European areas.

Such a possibility remains a matter of common concern of the United States and Japan. It is then natural for the two nations to take joint action to deal with such a possibility, if necessary. One form of such action could be Japan's participation in either a conference, organization, or agreement, when set up, to coordinate economic activities of Atlantic nations. For such a purpose, I believe, Japan must ask the United States for her collaboration.

Morinosuke Kajima: I understand a "passive attitude" on the part of the United States has made it difficult for the two nations to set up an economic committee. Could you tell us the real reason? The United States and Canada regularly hold a joint ministerial economic committee meeting. Some argue a similar body should be set up between Japan and the United States. Do you mind telling us your reaction to such a proposal?

Foreign Minister Aiichiro Fujiyama: Bilateral economic cooperation has, in principle, been conducted and problems have been settled through normal diplomatic channels all over the world in general. The committee was set up to solve problems of capital flow and other special economic issues inherent to the geographical fact that the two nations have a common national boundary.

In most multinational treaty organizations such as NATO and SEATO, committees on economic affairs are set up. But no such committee exists in a bilateral organization. But as pointed out by Committeeman Nagano in the morning session, it is necessary to strengthen economic collaboration between the United States and Japan if they are to cooperate closely in their overall relationship. Such collaboration, I agree, can be more effectively achieved not by a normal diplomatic route or a regular or permanent committee meeting but by an exchange of opinions among ministers of the two governments. This I will certainly take into consideration in the future conduct of our foreign policy.

(e)   A Demand for a Pacific Common Market

Morinosuke Kajima: I believe Japan should not only be satisfied with economic collaboration with the United States, but promote similar cooperation with nations in the Pacific area including Canada, Central and South America, Southeast Asia, Australia, and New Zealand. What would your reaction be to a concept of setting up a Pacific common market? In 1908, Japan concluded with the United States the Root-Takahira Agreement which stipulated "freedom of trade and commerce in the Pacific Ocean."

I think we should work for this ideal. But now that the European Common Market has developed rapidly, along with the general acceptance in Europe of the concept of an Atlantic community, I am convinced we should not only be content with increasing freedom of trade and commerce in the Pacific area but should try to create a Pacific common market. I wonder whether you would agree with me. I would also be greatly obliged if I could hear opinions of the prime minister, foreign minister, international trade and industry minister, and economic planning agency director on this proposal, one of my long-cherished ideals.

Foreign Minister Aiichiro Fujiyama: We also share such an ideal in general terms. By general, I mean an ideal of Pacific nations creating cooperative relations, particularly in the economic fields, with the Pacific Ocean as a sort of catalyst. To share such an ideal is one thing. Quite another is to believe such relations can be created at the present stage. I doubt that the basic conditions which created the European Common Market exist in similar degree in the Pacific area.

Australia and New Zealand, for example, are still members of the Commonwealth. As such, I wonder if they could freely establish relations with other Pacific nations completely independent of their ties with the Commonwealth, which in the future, I believe, might change particularly in the economic field. At least at this moment, a completely free association with the Pacific nations remains a difficult proposal for the two Commonwealth nations. Take, for another example, the United States and Central and South America. For us in the diplomatic field, their present relations do not seem to indicate any possibility of creating a Pacific common market including all these countries.

But these and other countries under different economic conditions could join, even today, a system of exchanging opinions with the Pacific Ocean as a catalyst to deepen mutual understanding. This issue is so complex and delicate that a proposal of a common market with insufficient regard to specific and basic conditions of each country concerned might not be considered feasible. With this point in mind, however, we believe there is room to consider the proposal seriously.

Prime Minister Nobusuke Kishi: The foreign minister has just explained his basic concept. Generally speaking, I agree with him. I do not think historical, political, and economic basic conditions similar to those which gave birth to the European community exist among the nations around the Pacific Ocean. But these Pacific nations, excluding Communist China, today belong to, and have a common ideal with, the Free World. Recently they have stepped up their economic exchanges. Japan also is keenly interested in the economic development of the Southeast Asian nations and Central and South American countries. To help them raise their living standard is also our great concern, which, I am convinced, is shared by the United States, Canada, and other industrially advanced nations. Under such circumstances, it seems to be very difficult to attempt immediately the creation of a common market in this area. We had better try to organize the existing and ever deepening economic relations among the Pacific nations. For that purpose, I believe Japan should actively participate in an international conference or other systems for exchange of opinions. To repeat, I do not consider that the basic conditions to create a community exist at this stage.

State Minister Hayato Ikeda: I would like to answer the interpellation by pointing out a difference between the European Economic Community (EEC) and the European Free Trade Association (EFTA) which along with economic cooperation in Central and South America has become a central topic since the birth of the European organization. First of all, the six EEC nations have very identical economic potential and a common interest in the concept, advanced by Robert Schuman, that they should eventually be united politically.

But the other countries which belong to EFTA have no such economic and political common ground. I am pointing out this fact to explain that when we speak of a Southeast Asian or Pacific economic community, we should bear in mind the prerequisite that each country possesses an identical economic potential. To meet this prerequisite, therefore, we must first of all help developing nations to acquire substantial economic potential through either the Colombo Plan, a second World Bank, or an Asian OECD (Organization for Economic Co-operation and Development). Japan should cooperate with other nations in such programs, and if and when she acquired sufficient capital she should also undertake her own aid programs in view of her special relations with the developing nations in Asia. Throughout the Meiji, Taisho, and Showa eras, Japan's economic potential grew so large that she annually invested fairly large amounts of capital in Korea, Taiwan, and Manchukuo. Our capital also went to Southeast Asia in 1930 and 1931. Seven or eight years later the annual capital investment overseas amounted to ¥100–¥200 million ($28.4–$56.8 million). This is indeed a considerable amount in view of the then high yen value.

I therefore believe it is quite possible for Japan today to take the initiative in helping Southeast Asia as she strengthens her own economic potential. Japan, for instance, can introduce a yen foreign-exchange system or set up a rice bank, a system under which Japan invests her capital in buying Burmese rice and transporting it to India or Indonesia where rice is scarce. This system will be much better than for Japan to purchase rice and store it as surplus in Japanese warehouses. Only after such unique Japanese aid programs have been initiated can Southeast Asian nations possess identical economic potential and eventually join a common market in the area. I, of course, understand the ideal the honorable gentleman proposed. But in reality, his proposal will become more feasible and practical if Japan collaborates with other nations in helping underdeveloped countries and joins the United States in assisting these nations with United States capital.

State Minister Wataro Kanno: The prime minister and two senior members of the cabinet have already explained their views on a Pacific common market. In most parts, I agree with them. I believe it may be a little premature to create a common market in the Pacific area. First, I believe, Japan must liberalize trade and foreign exchange. Then it may not be too late to think of the common market.

Morinosuke Kajima: Today, in the nuclear and space age, it will be anachronistic to believe Japan, as a sovereign nation, can be completely independent of economic relations with other nations and be self-sufficient. Japan's economic activities cannot and should not be confined within her territory, but must be extended to a wider economic sphere. Concerning this point, I found a brilliant expertise in an article written by Katsuo Okazaki, former foreign minister, on the past, present, and future of Japan's diplomacy. In it, he calls for a concept of an Afro-Asian common market. He argues Japan's future diplomacy must include such a big dream. I believe a Pacific common market is far more realistic than the Okazaki plan. I would appreciate if Minister Fujiyama would reveal his opinion as to which proposal is more practical, either an Afro-Asian common market or a Pacific counterpart.

Foreign Minister Aiichiro Fujiyama: As I understand, the Afro-Asian group referred to here includes Southeast Asian countries, Near and Middle Eastern countries, and newly independent African states. These nations have a certain common denominator in their economic conditions. They are in fact identical in the stages of their economic developments, the degrees of their economic managements, and even in the production processes from primary or agricultural to industrial products.

In this sense, we can safely say they are economically identical. However, with their current economic conditions, they are bound to clash with each other simply because they produce similar primary products and compete in the sales of the same merchandise manufactured under economic environments still not completely free from colonial economy. Of course, one can argue that the very possibility of such a conflict makes it more important to set up a common market for better coordination. But even in that sense, the new system inevitably differs substantially from the European model.

In the Pacific area, we find various nations in varied degrees of economic development. Indonesia, the Philippines, Australia, New Zealand, South American nations, the United States, and Japan are all different. Of course, there may exist certain identical factors. But there exists a big gap between the nations in the degree of their industrialization.

A greater gap can be found in the basic economic condition on which each of these nations stands. The honorable gentleman asked me which is easier to create, an Afro-Asian or a Pacific common market. I must admit this is a very difficult question to answer. Frankly, I have neither ability nor expertise to judge which is easier to create.

(**f**) Problems Between Japan and the United States

Morinosuke Kajima: The Kishi-Eisenhower joint communique says to the effect that Prime Minister Kishi stressed the importance of continuous consultations on economic problems in which both Japan and the United States are mutually interested and that the President expressed his complete agreement to what the prime minister proposed. I wonder if the prime minister would be kind enough to explain to us precisely what economic problems he meant, and also reveal his view on the possibility of including the question of a Pacific common market in the continuous consultations he referred to.

Prime Minister Nobusuke Kishi: The joint communique was announced after the conference with President Eisenhower. What I stressed in my statement was the need of a continuous consultation on economic affairs of common interest to the two nations. By such economic affairs, I meant two things: an economic exchange between the two countries—such as trade, capital flow or exchange of technical know-how, and joint economic aid to underdeveloped nations. The latter should be designed, I believe, for raising the people's living standard which in turn will eventually lead to their own welfare and development of prospective markets. A higher living standard will also contribute a great deal to world peace because it will assure the people in such nations of a more stabilized economic life. Japan and the United States have so far collaborated with Southeast Asian nations in this field. But I believe we should do more and carry out the aid program more effectively.

It is not a matter of principle. Rather it needs to be executed as a practical proposal or project. Furthermore, I think it is important to maintain a continuous channel of dialogue with the United States in settling problems as they arise. I do not believe either a normal diplomatic channel or an *ad hoc* meeting of officials concerned is enough to meet such problems. My idea is not to deal with the problems after they arise, but to prepare to meet them before they come up. For this purpose the continuous consultations I referred to in the communique will help, for instance, the Japanese side to know in advance any problems arising on the American side and to consult about the means to deal with it. I think I had explained this point this morning when Committeeman Nagano asked me a similar question. Both Mr. Nagano and Mr. Kajima proposed a United States-Japan economic committee. There are, I believe, a few things the two nations should agree on before they set up such a committee. At least I think we should first of all set up a system under which the two nations can continue their dialogue. This was what I stressed during my meeting with President Eisenhower who then agreed with me completely. Thus, the real intention of the communique is for the two nations to jointly examine the economic problems on a continuous basis.

(**g**) Aid to Developing Nations

Morinosuke Kajima: What exactly did you mean by the underdeveloped nations referred to in the joint communique? I presume Southeast Asian nations fall under this category, no doubt. But are Central and South American states included in the same category?

Foreign Minister Aiichiro Fujiyama: Generally, or should I say commonly, an underdeveloped nation is one whose major economic activity is agriculture, a primary industry. But this definition contradicts the fact that Australia, which is an agricultural country, is far from being an underdeveloped nation. I think the definition is not easy. But the United Nations defines it as a nation where the per capita annual income is below $150. Under this definition, all the Asian countries, except Japan, Near and Middle Eastern countries except Israel, African states except the Union of South Africa, most of Central and South American countries, and part of Europe are underdeveloped. All these underdeveloped nations occupy nearly two-thirds of the world's population.

Morinosuke Kajima: Is Brazil included [in the category of an underdeveloped nation]?

Foreign Minister Aiichiro Fujiyama: Yes, she is, I presume.

Morinosuke Kajima: Aid to underdeveloped nations is a matter of greatest concern for the world. Its impact on international politics is serious. Could you tell us the scope, policies, and current state of Japan's aid programs to underdeveloped nations?

Foreign Minister Aiichiro Fujiyama: As you are well aware, an underdeveloped nation is generally dependent on agricultural products and lacks industrial potential. Therefore, such a nation might need Japan's help in industrializing itself to the extent that she can produce her own daily consumer goods. This reminds us of the import of technical cooperation, including both technical assistance and technical plus management cooperation. At the same time, the underdeveloped nation, still in the early stage of economic development, needs either private or state capital investment. To assist her in this field, Japan must invest more in overseas projects, I believe. All this is what I meant by our policy of foreign aid.

Morinosuke Kajima: The joint communique also says to the effect that the President specially referred to the fact that Japanese people are playing an increasingly bigger role in the economic development of Free Asia. But, in my view, a major bottleneck for Japan to play such a role lies in the absence or defects of treaties of commerce and navigation with Asian countries. Are you in favor of and prepared to conclude such treaties immediately?

A company in which I am directly involved undertook the construction work of a power plant in Burma, as the first case of Japan's payment to Burma of war reparations. For five years, we had no trouble at all thanks to cooperation extended by the Burmese government and private quarters. Everything went on smoothly until the work was completed. The following day, every one of us had to leave Burma, not because the Burmese wanted us to leave, but simply because we had no right to reside there after the work was completed, since there was no treaty of commerce and navigation between the two nations. We thus had to sacrifice our friendship with the Burmese people we had cultivated in five years, and to give up various business offers. All this reminded me of the possibility that if the current situation should continue, our aid program to underdeveloped nations might end with the completion of our payment of war reparations. I, therefore, strongly suggest that the government should immediately conclude the treaties with Asian countries, and I hope the foreign minister will devote his energy to this after the security pact is approved by the Diet. Could I have your reaction to my suggestion?

Foreign Minister Aiichiro Fujiyama: We have been trying hard to conclude treaties of commerce and navigation which are indispensable for Japan to extend economic aid and promote trade. However, most of the Southeast Asian countries have just recently become independent. The treaties are extremely complex and closely and delicately related to domestic laws. It follows then that the newly independent Asian nations, still not fully experienced in such legal matters, need time before they can make the necessary adjustments between international obligations and domestic laws. It also takes time for them to be fully equipped to conclude the treaties and implement them efficiently.

Of course, they are doing their best in this respect, but not enough yet. But the prospect is bright. With Thailand, for instance, we have already revived the prewar Treaty of Commerce and Navigation. With India and Malay we have concluded treaties of commerce with almost the same effect as a treaty of commerce and navigation. Peace treaties with Indonesia and Taiwan include stipulations governing commerce and navigation. We are also about to conclude a treaty of commerce and navigation with the Philippines. As you perhaps know, a Philippine mission is already here to negotiate with us. Similar negotiations are scheduled to take place with Pakistan very shortly. We in the government thus are trying our best to conclude the treaties with Asian nations— without unnecessary trouble.

2. Implementation of the Security Treaty

Morinosuke Kajima: The Upper House, by its very nature, debates the security treaty whose passage is a foregone conclusion. This does not follow that the debate of the pact itself is unimportant. But I think the real value of the pact depends on its implementation after it is put into force. I would like to express my hopes on three issues concerning the treaty implementation. Answers by the prime minister or foreign minister would be greatly appreciated.

(**a**) As a High-Level Political Pact

First of all, the existing security pact is a product of fear and shock over the Korean War. If the new pact is to be cherished by the people and is to survive long, it should be supported by practical—economic and political—measures. The treaty, therefore, should be implemented with a long-range, comprehensive view not as a mere military pact but as a high-level political treaty covering military, economic, and cultural fields.

This is my hope. In fact the North Atlantic Treaty is implemented with such a comprehensive view. The treaty organization has recently published a three-man committee report, a document on nonmilitary collaboration compiled by Italy's Martino, Norway's Lange, and Canada's Pearson. Its Clause 15 reports on the implementation of NATO as follows: "Since the establishment of NATO, defense cooperation has been the foremost and most urgent function of the treaty. But such function has proved insufficient. After the treaty was signed, it has been recognized that national safety requires more than just a mere military measure. Political consultation, encouragement of economic collaboration, development of resources, advancement of education, and public understanding are equally or more important than construction of warships or military equipment for the protection of a nation's safety or alliance."

Clause 36 further states: "As predicted by the founders of the North Atlantic Treaty Organization, the development of political, economic, and military mutual dependency among nations requires gradual steps concerning international solidarity and collaboration. Some nations, if situations turn favorable, can enjoy certain political and economic independence. But no great power can guarantee her safety and welfare by her own action alone."

All this, I believe, shows clearly that NATO is put into effect as a high-level political treaty. The security treaty we have before us should also be implemented in such a manner. Could you give us your opinions?

Prime Minister Nobusuke Kishi: As pointed out by the interpellator, Article 2, the political and economic clause, of the new security pact clearly shows that the new pact must play the important role of meeting its new and vital significance. I have just heard a very valuable opinion on the actual implementation of the pact. Indeed, defense cooperation is its function—military in its nature and necessary when the situation requires. But preventing such a situation from arising,

I believe, is the very objective of the treaty. This deterrent effect is the significance of the treaty itself. Article 2, however, stipulates how the two nations should implement the pact in peacetime and on a permanent basis for closer bilateral relations, economic development, and national welfare.

The interpellator has just pointed out the significance of the NATO pact committee report and other related matters concerning nonmilitary collaboration of NATO members. I believe the new pact we have before us must be implemented with emphasis on economic collaboration and closer bilateral ties in the political and social fields.

(**b**)   Multilateral Security System

Morinosuke Kajima: My second hope is that friendly relations should be promoted with not only free nations but also nonaligned countries and communist states, including the Soviet Union and Communist China, so long as such relations will not run against the principle of the new security pact. We should not be satisfied with and must never rely exclusively on the new pact for our national security. Rather we should actively contribute to peace in the Far East by abiding by the spirit of the ten principles of the Bandung Peace Declaration adopted by both communist and noncommunist nations, including Japan.

Here I would like to explain my interpretation of the alliance-entente system which, as a scholar, I have studied for nearly ten years. There are two ways to establish an alliance-entente. Prince von Bismarck, for instance, adopted a multilateral alliance-entente system by concluding the Germany-Austria-Italy tripartite alliance, a reassurance treaty with Russia and in addition the Mediterranean Sea treaty with Great Britain. After Bismarck's fall, Kaiser Wilhelm II streamlined the system. For him, Bismarck's policy was too complicated. He thus renounced the reassurance treaty with Russia after declaring that only a genius like Bismarck could juggle three or four balls simultaneously and that such magic was beyond his capability. His policy was succeeded by both

Chancellors von Bülow and von Bethmann-Hollweg who led Germany into the war in 1914.

I believe a single alliance or entente system itself is one of the causes of war. Japan's great statesmen, Komura, Katsura, and Ito, adopted a series of multilateral alliance-entente policies. Altogether they concluded Anglo-Japanese alliances three times, and Russo-Japanese ententes five times during the latter part of the Meiji era.

Japan's national security was further strengthened by American-Japanese and Franco-Japanese ententes. History shows clearly that such a multiple or multilateral system secures peace far more effectively than a single one.

The security treaty we are discussing here is a start not a goal, as Prime Minister Kishi puts it. I know well you have many plans to make the best use of the pact. I only wish that you will advance a policy of friendship and peaceful relationship with not only free nations but also nonaligned and communist states so long as such a policy does not run counter to the spirit of the pact. I do not believe the new pact will ever contradict the ten principles of peace adopted by the Bandung Declaration. I trust that you could be as deft as Bismarck in making the best use of the pact to bring peace to Japan and the world.

Prime Minister Nobusuke Kishi: Japan's foreign policy is based on pacifism and its keynote is diplomacy for peace. Japan therefore is firmly committed to remain a free nation and abide by democracy. However, outside Japan, differences of policies are reflected in the division of the world into the Western and Eastern camps. Nevertheless, between the two camps, communications, economic exchanges, and friendly relations are not completely cut off. The security treaty, for instance, does not contradict the ten peace principles of the Bandung Declaration. Neither does it run counter to the spirit of the Russo-Japanese joint communique. It is quite natural and proper for us to conclude the pact, the means to secure our peace and safety and to prosper in peace, and at the same time to cooperate and promote friendly relations with nations of different national policies and ideology. I believe we can do this if we understand and respect each other's stand and never trespass on respective rights.

To repeat, the conclusion of the security treaty in no way contradicts the Russo-Japanese joint communique. On the contrary, we want to expand trade with the Soviet Union under a Japan-Soviet trade agreement. We also believe that improvement of communications between the two countries will result in better understanding, which in turn will create a climate of mutual trust and cement friendly ties. Thus our diplomacy will take multiple courses. A single security treaty is not and shall never be our exclusive choice. It is important, I believe, for us to promote friendly relations with communist nations by first clarifying where we stand. We have done just that in the past and will continue to follow this line of foreign policy.

(**c**) Defensive Nature

Morinosuke Kajima: I would like to refer to my third and last hope. In my view, a local conflict escalates into an all-out war because of the existence of an alliance-entente. But the new treaty is a system consistent with the principle of our Peace Constitution, and consequently defensive in nature. Extra precaution and consideration are, therefore, imperative on the part of the government lest our country should be directly or indirectly involved in a conflict which might break out in an area where we have no special interests.

The Lower House, as I understand, seemed to have focused its attention on Quemoy and Matsu. In my view, however, these islands are only one of the potentially dangerous areas of the world where a local conflict might lead to a global war. Japan should be careful so as to avoid involvement in a local conflict in such dangerous places, including Berlin, the Near and Middle East.

World War I started with a local conflict in Serbia. German Chancellor von Bethmann-Hollweg then tried to limit the conflict between Austria and Serbia—in vain. In the face of Russian opposition this actually resulted in a war between Russia and Germany.

The war inevitably involved France, who was then allied with Russia, and Great Britain, who had an entente with France. Great Britain's participation in the war brought Japan, the then alliance partner of Britain, into the war. By the same token, World War II involved Japan in the global struggle mainly because of and after she had concluded the tripartite alliance. This is what I call the dangerous nature of the alliance-entente system.

Today, with the United Nations as a world organization, the situation is much different from prewar days. But I still insist the government cannot be too cautious in seeing to it that Japan does not become involved in a distant, local conflict because of the security pact. I would appreciate your comments on this.

Prime Minister Nobusuke Kishi: I can see a clear-cut, basic difference in international relations, particularly in the use of force, between the prewar and postwar periods. In accordance with Article 51 of the United Nations Charter, the security pact remains strictly defensive by nature and will never be evoked unless Japan is attacked by an armed aggressor. I was impressed by Mr. Kajima's expertise on the history of past alliances and ententes which, as he pointed out, resulted in wars.

But I do believe contemporary alliances are different from the prewar counterparts in that today they represent purely and strictly defensive measures as stipulated in Article 51 of the United Nations Charter. Our security treaty, too, is strictly defensive, but not in an abstract sense. Under this pact and in accordance with Article 51 of the United Nations Charter, Japan will use force—but only—to remove an aggressor who attacks her. Such use of force falls under the category of collective or individual self-defense.

And Japan's defensive action, if taken, will be immediately

reported to the United Nations and will continue until the world organization takes some appropriate counteractions. Under this pact, therefore, we do not have to worry about Japan's involvement in a conflict not directly related to her own national interests or not involving Japan in a use of force. The situation today is entirely different from that in prewar years, I believe. I can understand what you theoretically meant by the danger of an alliance-entente system. But we are here talking about not a theoretical case about a treaty, an article in the United Nations Charter, or a purely academic hypothesis, but the new security treaty as a practical measure of national defense.

Of course, we must be careful of and pay due attention to the danger, even a theoretical one, of an alliance system. But I am sure that danger can be avoided, and Japan will not be involved in a war not directly related to our national interest. I can assure you that we will be very careful about that.

3. New Course of Japan's Diplomacy

Morinosuke Kajima: Lastly, I would like to refer to a new course of our diplomacy. Today we are in a nuclear-space age. And perhaps we need a diplomacy to meet the requirements of such an age. Late in 1957, the Soviet Union launched two artificial satellites. Since then the missile age has been with us. Military experts say that a conflict might not be confined to the earth but extended to an altitude several thousand miles in space. All this makes it necessary for us to think of every affair on this earth in terms of space.

Immediately after the Russians launched their first artificial satellite, British Prime Minister Harold Macmillan raced to Washington to confer with President Eisenhower. On his return to London, Macmillan told Parliament that he believed "without any hesitation" the world was facing the true historical turning point. Never before, he was quoted to have said, had Russia and Soviet communism been so "threatening as today." He also said that Americans were convinced that even a big power like the United States could no longer secure its survival without an alliance. They also believe, he added, that an ideal they must protect cannot survive without an alliance.

After this homecoming address, Macmillan set a new course for his foreign policy on the concept that self-reliance and self-sufficiency is anachronistic, that free nations can secure their progress and safety only by truly cooperating with each other and that Great Britain should collaborate with the United States and coordinate the efforts of other free nations.

From this historical lesson, we should learn that after the ratification of the new treaty, Japan, the United States, and other free nations should cooperate in economic, scientific, technological, cultural, and every other field imaginable. Only by so doing can we secure our absolute safety and progress.

As pointed out by my colleague, Mr. Nagano, this morning, Article 5 of the Sino-Soviet friendship pact stipulates that the two nations must cooperate in the economic field with whatever means necessary. Article 2 of our treaty refers to economic cooperation only in a very general, rather roundabout way. Though it certainly can be made best use of in the actual application of the treaty, I still consider it necessary for the government to take necessary steps, as complementary measures, in economic, scientific, propaganda, and intelligence fields. It is also imperative, I am convinced, for the government to launch active policies of friendship in its diplomatic approaches to nonaligned and communist nations.

That, I believe, is the new course of our diplomacy. I wonder if the prime minister would care to comment on this.

Prime Minister Nobusuke Kishi: I think I have already answered, to a certain extent, to the spirit of Article 2 of the new pact with the United States: to repeat, Japan will remain a free nation under any circumstances. This, I believe, is our firm commitment and our basic national policy. It then follows that it is quite natural for Japan to collaborate in every field with the free nations who share a common ideal with Japan, as the honorable gentleman aptly pointed out.

As I understand it, the gentleman further suggested that we had better conclude an agreement on specific scientific cooperation to meet the requirement of the scientific age. We in the government sincerely appreciate your opinion and will study further the means necessary to promote and cement scientific and technological ties between the two nations.

As I have already explained, Japan will do her best to strengthen cooperation with the nations who share a common ideal with us. This is the basic stand of our foreign policy. We will never deviate from this basic line. But at the same time, we should promote friendly relations with those countries whose national policies differ from ours and those of the free nations—within an overall framework of our peaceful diplomacy.

In doing so, we hope they would understand that the best way to promote friendship and peace is to respect each other's stand and never meddle in the other party's business. In other words, a true mutual understanding is the very basis on which we can promote peace and friendship.

Morinosuke Kajima: With sincere appreciation, let me conclude my interpellation. Thank you.

CHAPTER **7**

New Security Treaty: Its Revision and Implementation

A Record of Interpellations in the Upper House Foreign Affairs Committee, September 1, 1960

Morinosuke Kajima: I understand Foreign Minister Kosaka is scheduled to attend the 15th United Nations General Assembly meeting shortly, and is to confer with Secretary of State Christian A. Herter, Deputy Secretary of State Douglas Dillon, and other American leaders on the United States-Japan economic cooperation during his stay in the United States.

I would be greatly honored if the foreign minister could clarify his views on the implementation of the new security pact and on the United States-Japan economic collaboration, particularly economic aid to developing nations in Southeast Asia. First, let me tell you about my aspirations on these issues.

1. As a High-Level Political Treaty

As you are well aware, the new security treaty stipulates, in its preamble and Article 2, the basic principle on economic cooperation which was further confirmed in the Kishi-Eisenhower joint communique. During the meeting of the Ad Hoc Committee on the Security Treaty of this House the other day, I made certain recommendations to Prime Minister Kishi

86

and Foreign Minister Fujiyama on the implementation of the pact.

I then stated that the old security pact was born from fear and shock of the Korean War, that the new pact should be acclaimed by the people and should survive not just as a military arrangement but as a high-level political treaty covering all the fields of military, economy, and culture. It should also be implemented from a wider viewpoint. To this hope of mine, Prime Minister Kishi at that time expressed his complete agreement. But unfortunately the Kishi Cabinet resigned before it was given a chance to actually implement the pact.

Thus the implementation of the pact is left entirely to Prime Minister Ikeda and Foreign Minister Kosaka. I sincerely hope the two gentlemen will consider my points in actually implementing it. To repeat, the new pact must be applied as a high-level political treaty and not as a mere military measure. It must be put into practice from a wider viewpoint and cover the political, economic, and cultural fields. Above all, I hope the government will encourage economic collaboration under the new pact. I would be obliged if you could comment on this and other related matters.

Foreign Minister Zentaro Kosaka: Let me answer the interpellation by first expressing my respect and admiration to the honorable gentleman's deep concern for the newly revised security treaty and his expertise just explained to this committee.

As pointed out already, the pact is defensive in nature. In the ultimate form of international relations, we envisage a world where peace prevails without any fear or suspicion among the nations. That will be the time when the security pact will no longer be needed. And that will be the ultimate goal of the pact itself.

In this sense, I completely agree with the interpellator that we should not only implement the pact militarily but make the best use of it in the economic and cultural fields, as stipulated in the pact itself. During my forthcoming visit to the United States, I am planning to exchange views on political issues with Secretary Herter and on economic problems with Deputy Secretary Dillon. Throughout these conferences, which I presume might last more than one hour each, I would like to express my opinions and listen to theirs on mutual economic prosperity between the two countries. I believe that through mutual economic prosperity of the two nations, we could most effectively contribute to world peace.

In the cultural field, the United States government has been very enthusiastic. Its leaders are known to have a deep concern about polio, for instance, and have already sent to Japan a number of iron lungs and packages of polio vaccine. This alone, as so aptly reported by Welfare Minister Naka-yama at the cabinet meeting the other day, clearly indicates the fact that cultural relations between the two countries have been cemented by the security pact. In this sense, I must admit I was greatly impressed by the opinion expressed by the honorable gentleman.

2. Aid to Underdeveloped Nations

Morinosuke Kajima: Newspapers report that the foreign minister will deliver a speech at the United Nations mostly devoted to political affairs, particularly East-West relations, disarmament, and African problems. In other words, he might give less emphasis to economic issues than political problems in his address, according to the report. There is, of course, no question about the importance of these political problems.

But economic issues, particularly development aid to about 100 underdeveloped nations, comprising nearly 1,250 million people, are the greatest concern of the world today. Without a solution of this problem the world as a whole will be deterred from achieving a general economic development. Japan is by no means an exception.

All the great statesmen of the world have made clear their stands on this issue. Eisenhower, for instance, said that the world could build a new order under which it can enjoy safety, freedom, and peace only if industrially developed nations actively cooperate with the countries placed in unfortunate circumstances. "We are facing a big turning point in history," he said. And he added: "The die has already been cast."

Khrushchev asserted that it is a duty of the United Nations to contribute as much as possible to the economic development of newly independent nations now struggling in the vestiges of colonialism. Such a duty, he said, can be performed only by large-scale economic aid.

France's General de Gaulle stated that it is the duty of big powers enjoying economic prosperity to help the poor and unfortunate. Great Britain's Macmillan labeled the improvement of living conditions in the world's underdeveloped nations one of the greatest missions of the world.

I am convinced that Japan, too, through the mouth of Foreign Minister Kosaka, should clarify her attitude toward this greatest mission of the world.

I now recall Japan's proposal to provide Southeast Asian developing nations with a $4 billion economic aid program. The proposal was made by former Prime Minister Yoshida in his address at the National Press Club about six years ago, or more precisely, on November 8, 1954.

In his speech, the former prime minister also said that if Communist China's economic development should exceed substantially those of her neighboring nations in a few years, China's pressure on these nations will be too strong for them to resist. He predicted that these nations would then succumb to communism easily.

In fact, Communist China's capital investment to increase her economic potential has been so formidable that it is now at least double the average per capita investment in Southeast Asia. To meet this Chinese challenge in time, external powers should help these Asian countries where development funds are always insufficient. True, there are several agencies specializing in the supply of capital to underdeveloped nations. But these agencies altogether annually provide Southeast Asia with only about $400 million, or less than 10 per cent of the amount necessary to compete with Communist China.

This means that the capital supply by government and international agencies should be expanded to a much larger scale. We Japanese will not and should not spare our efforts in leading such a capital supply program to a big success.

He insisted that we might lose in an economic race with Communist China unless we act determinedly and carry out the program on a larger scale than I have just mentioned. We are racing against time. Immediate action is wanted.

This address by former Prime Minister Yoshida was enthusiastically welcomed in the United States. Mr. Sato, now present in this room, then expressed great praise for the Yoshida address. I still remember the words of praise Mr. Sato spoke in this very room of the Upper House Foreign Affairs Committee six years ago. Soon afterward, Mr. Yoshida resigned. Gone with him was the grand concept of Southeast Asian development. This, I believe, Foreign Minister Kosaka, who was then a member of the Yoshida cabinet, still remembers quite well.

In six years, since 1954, the world has undergone considerable changes in the political field. The death of Stalin was followed by the rise of Bulganin and then of Khrushchev. After Khrushchev secured his position in the Kremlin, he launched a series of new policies, including proposals of disarmament, arms abolishment, peaceful coexistence, and economic competition.

All this shows clearly that the real threat of communism in Asia is less military than economic. Today nobody would doubt that the free and the communist nations are confronting each other in a showdown over their economic aid race in underdeveloped countries. The race is conducted over a vast area—from Korea to Africa and Latin America. The Congo and Cuba are not excluded from the race. I, therefore, must call your attention to the fact that the Yoshida proposal made six years ago is not only still valid but desperately needed.

The new pact clearly stipulates the terms of economic collaboration between the United States and Japan. Therefore, the two parties are free to negotiate on their aid program simply as an integral part of the treaty arrangement. In other words, United States-Japan negotiations on aid programs are much easier now than in the Yoshida days.

Japan has earmarked ¥5 billion ($13.9 million) as a fund for economic aid to underdeveloped nations, particularly those in Asia. But this amount is outrageously small. In view of the contemporary international situation, I must insist that the amount should be drastically increased, though I know well the financial limit to which Japan can go in performing her duty of providing foreign aid. But I still believe Japan should go farther and help Asian nations more in the economic field, along the basic principle so aptly set forth by former Prime Minister Yoshida. I trust the honorable gentleman on the government bench will consider my proposal most sympathetically.

I am firmly convinced that a program designed to stabilize and improve living conditions of a few 100 million people suffering from poverty in Asia is the most supreme diplomatic policy action consistent with the principle of humanism and national interests.

Foreign Minister Zentaro Kosaka: My address for the United Nations is now being drafted. And I must study the draft carefully before I can complete the final version. But I can tell you this much: the economic issue is what I am determined to stress most strongly in my address.

In fact I am planning to submit my proposals to the United Nations on both political and economic issues. In my proposals, I would like to emphasize a need for all the powers to consider more seriously capital supply to the underdeveloped —or developing—nations. Formerly all these nations were called backward. But I now believe they had better be called developing countries since most of them no longer remain backward or underdeveloped but are actually "developing."

As you are well aware, there exists an international organization called DAG, D standing for development, A for assistance, and G for group. This was organized after the Paris Conference on Economic Affairs of the Atlantic Nations held in January this year.

The conference adopted three resolutions on aid to developing nations, coordination between the Atlantic Community and EFTA, and reorganization of OEEC. The resolution reflected international agreement over the establishment of a new world organization designed to deal with aid programs and trade of the Atlantic nations.

The result was the proposed creation of a new organization called OEECD (Organization for European Economic Cooperation and Development). If actually set up, the new organization will be the first and most important committee of DAG.

Japan was admitted to DAG formally after the other countries recognized her past and potential contribution to foreign aid programs. Other DAG members include the United States, Canada, Great Britain, France, Germany, Belgium, Italy, Portugal, and the Netherlands. In addition to these nine countries, the European Economic Community (EEC) joins the organ as a corporate member.

The DAG first met in Washington last March and later in Bonn last July. The third meeting is scheduled for October in Washington. The purpose of DAG is to exchange information, consult on and coordinate problems of capital and other aid programs to developing nations. I know some complain that foreign aid is essentially a charity program of a millionaires' club. I believe such criticism is groundless. The common ideal of world powers, I am convinced, is to balance the economic potential of world nations if they are to coexist peacefully.

From this viewpoint, I think I must urge the United Nations' members for better and more effective economic collaboration.

The honorable gentleman referred, in the latter part of his interpellation, to the Yoshida concept first made public in the National Press Club in Washington six years ago. Today everybody recognizes the need of increased economic aid to Southeast Asia.

The recent establishment of a second World Bank no doubt reflects such global recognition. Aid programs through the bank now are being extended over a wider area in Southeast Asia. But to my regret, the programs are not in an optimum shape. They should be stepped up, if not strictly then roughly, along the basic line proposed by former Prime Minister Yoshida six years ago. It is also our sincere desire to do our best in supporting such programs.

Here I would like to point out that since former Prime Minister Yoshida first proposed an active aid program six years ago, the global cooperative system has greatly improved and undergone considerable changes. It is now firmly established and functioning quite effectively.

And we now face choices: establishment of a new aid organ or more active cooperation with the existing aid organization. I do not rule out the import of a bilateral program. But we must admit an aid program with "strings attached" is bound to be hated, to be frank.

I thus prefer personally a multilateral concept to an independent, new organization. That is why I just explained about existing world organizations. As to the amount of Japan's foreign aid program, I must express my complete agreement to what has been pointed out. This is exactly the problem whose solution needs your assistance. I, myself, am still a novice and inexperienced in obtaining a large slice of the budgetary pie. I, therefore, beg you, the honorable gentlemen of the committee, to help us in the government to receive more appropriations for our foreign aid program.

How can the amount available for aid be increased? I

personally believe the Export and Import Bank's fund should first of all be increased. The bank charges very low interest for its export finance. This, I believe, is a world-wide trend. Nevertheless I have recently heard an argument that the interest rate could and should be raised.

A higher rate for export financing would be extremely embarrassing for those of us in charge of economic cooperation. I repeat my request that the gentlemen assist us by not approving any step which might ultimately deter us from taking an active part in economic aid and collaboration.

Thank you.

CHAPTER 8

A Role Japan Should Play in International Affairs as an Advanced Nation of the Free World in Asia

IN MAKING any frank assessment of Japan's foreign policy at the beginning of 1966, the fact must be recognized that the world is still in an extremely fluid situation and that acute dangers lurk in almost every corner of Asia. Although Japan is holding high her principle of "love for freedom and total dedication to peace," it is a principle that meets with no objection from the Japanese people. It is an affirmation that Japan is a free and democratic state and wishes to remain so forever.

However, owing to the antagonism between the Free World and communist bloc, the world today is precariously maintaining peace on the balance of power between the two, or more appropriately on the basis of the preponderance of power of the free nations. While a peace dependent on the balance of power is both regrettable and undesirable, yet this being the cold reality of our times, I earnestly hope that Japan will take an unshakeable position as a member of the Free World community. To sway like grass either to the East or West at the mercy of the wind is not only likely to lead to a loss of international confidence, but endangers the national existence of Japan.

Needless to say, it is impossible for any nation to live in peace by itself in the present-day world. Most of the nations, whether of the Free or the Communist World, are members of

95

a collective security system of one form or other, and Japan also concluded a security pact with the United States. While Japan is thus ensuring her own security, she is also at the same time discharging her duties as a member of the Free World community in Asia. Since she is the only developed nation in the region, the United States and other free nations lay great store in Japan's role. On the other hand, there is also strong dissatisfaction that Japan's efforts in this regard have not necessarily been adequate.

In these circumstances, the Socialist Party and other leftist elements have been calling for the renunciation of the Japan-United States Security Treaty on the ground that the treaty not only intensified tensions in the Far East but also threatened to involve Japan in America's military actions. They assert that the United States might use this treaty to employ her armed forces in Japan for the purpose of "ensuring international peace and security in the Far East," but it can only be said they are mistaken in thinking that the security treaty is for the purpose of war and the employment of an armed force. They forget that the objective of the treaty, whether it is the United Nations security system or security treaties in general, is to prevent the situation envisaged in the treaty from arising.

The use of the United States armed forces stationed in Japan for the maintenance of "international peace and security in the Far East" is limited to justifiable cases, such as under the resolution of the United Nations or the invocation of another security treaty to which the United States is a party. Moreover, even if this were the case, Japan is not obliged to join in a common action.

Nevertheless, Japan for her part, should be prepared to exert her utmost for the sake of preserving peace in the Far East. Only by doing so will Japan be able to fully ensure her national security as well as the peace of the Far East. Since we are living in an age of collective security, the fact that

Japan is a member of the Free World community should be more deeply and more widely recognized by the people.

In addition, genuine peace is still an unattained ideal, but positive efforts should now be made for its realization. However, in a section of our country there is a negative trend to simply shout "defend peace." Consequently, in any international conflict, an impression exists that it is praiseworthy not to assist either of the contending sides. Far from offering support to either of the parties, this ambiguous behavior is more apt to have a detrimental effect than to lead to a just settlement.

Be that as it may, Japan of today can no longer remain an idle onlooker when it comes to the question of peace. Although Japan cannot get militarily involved, in view of her Peace Constitution, there are many ways in which she could contribute in the political, economic, and cultural fields.

Strengthening of the United Nations and the Peace Constitution

While the necessity to strengthen the United Nations for the attainment of genuine peace is not denied, Japan should make every possible effort to consolidate the Organization's peace-keeping machinery. If she is elected in the near future as a nonpermanent member of the United Nations Security Council, she must assume greater responsibilities.

For the United Nations to fully carry out its peace-keeping functions, there is an urgent need for it to establish a standing army under its Charter. With East-West relations as they are, this force is unlikely to come into being in the foreseeable future. As an alternative, the conception of a United Nations stand-by force is taking concrete shape under the sponsorship of Canada, the North European countries, Holland, Great Britain, and New Zealand. Japan, too, has indicated her support for such a conception, but whether she can actually participate in such a plan is questionable in the light of her Peace Constitution.

Under Article 9 of the Constitution which renounces war and the use of force, the dispatch of the self-defense force overseas is prohibited. This fact has been affirmed in a resolution by the Upper House. Under existing laws relating to the self-defense force, the force may only be ordered into action during such emergencies as national defense, maintenance of public security, and natural disasters. For fear that they might become involved in an unforeseen war, the force cannot be dispatched overseas for purposes other than those mentioned.

Leaving aside the question of the United Nations stand-by force, could Japan justify her hesitance to participate in a standing force in case the United Nations should in the future establish such an army? It is true that Article 9 of the Constitution states that Japan "forever renounces war as a sovereign right of the nation and the threat or use of force as means of settling international disputes." However, in case the role is that of a United Nations standing force to police law and order, by willingly participating, would not Japan be truly fulfilling the spirit of Article 9 which "aspires sincerely to an international peace based on justice and order?"

The aspirations for world peace cannot be attained merely by Japan shutting herself up in the shell coated with Article 9 of the Constitution. In order to strengthen the peace-keeping machinery of the United Nations, Japan must in the future search untiringly for positive means to contribute toward that end.

Nuclear Arming by Communist China and Asian Security

Admittedly it is no exaggeration to say that the proliferation of nuclear arms constitutes the gravest threat to the world of today. Japan, as the sole country to have suffered from the destructive atomic bomb, has a particularly strong fear and deep concern when it comes to nuclear weapons. For the prevention of the proliferation of nuclear arms, while the key to the solution is to enlarge the present partial test ban treaty, steps are now being taken within a limited sphere to make inspections based on the advances made in detection technique and carried out by the International Atomic Energy Agency (IAEA).

On the other hand, the fact that Communist China, disregarding world public opinion, has carried out two nuclear bomb tests and is actively engaged in nuclear arming has acted as a brake to nuclear proliferation. Regarding the effects of Communist China's nuclear arming as extremely grave, the French nuclear weapons expert General Gallois says that the important thing is not the scale or effectiveness of the nuclear weapons but the reality of the possession of such weapons changing the entire aspects of Asian diplomacy. The general asserts that the "greatest untoward event in the Far East" would occur when the Communist Chinese leaders link their vast territory and massive population to their nuclear arms under ethical principles.

In the face of this Communist Chinese nuclear threat, Japan's security is guaranteed by the Japan-United States Security Treaty, but other Asian nations are not sufficiently safeguarded.

The question of the security of these nonnuclear powers in Asia thus poses a serious problem. The British Labor Party government of Harold Wilson was quick to realize the importance of this problem. When the British Foreign Minister Michael Stewart visited Japan in October, 1965, wide publicity was given to the statement of the Japanese Prime Minister Eisaku Sato who joined him in declaring that "some measures should be considered to remove the feeling of insecurity among the nonnuclear powers of Southeast Asia." In this connection the British newspaper, *The Times,* pointed out that Europe had NATO, and Asia which was faced with a nuclear vacuum was becoming acutely aware of this fact.

Meanwhile, the United States Vice President Hubert Humphrey in an interview with Japanese newsmen in America recently said that the time has come for the United States to associate friendly nations in the formulation of her nuclear war potential and nuclear policy. This did not mean that nuclear arms would be transferred to these countries, but inferred that Japan as a major power should be able to participate in the deliberations.

Secretary of State Dean Rusk later told newsmen that it was the policy of the United States government to welcome Japan to talks on the nuclear problem. He further revealed that discussions on this problem had already taken place with America's allies, including Japan, and that these talks had touched upon nuclear strategy.

This crucial problem was also discussed in December when Lord Chalfont, Great Britain's Minister in Charge of Disarmament, visited Japan. It is logical for Japan to be prepared to positively discuss the problem of security in the Asian and Pacific region which is menaced by nuclear annihilation.

Economic Cooperation with Southeast Asian Countries

For the peace and prosperity of Asia, since the cooperation of industrialized Japan is indispensable, Japan includes the question of assistance to the underdeveloped to be among her important obligations. This is a matter that should take precedence if we are to remove the causes of disputes in Asia and strengthen the foundations of peace.

It will be recalled that in April, 1965, President Johnson, who has been drawn into the morass of the Vietnam war, called for unconditional discussions that will lead to a peaceful settlement. The fact that he also announced a development plan costing $1 billion for Southeast Asia is nothing less than a recognition of the necessity to extend assistance to the under-developed countries as an intergral part of the settlement of the Vietnam problem.

While the Second Afro-Asian Conference to be held in Algiers had to be indefinitely postponed on November 2, 1965, the speech by the Japanese delegate at the conference of foreign ministers, emphasizing the importance of economic development, was warmly received. One of the notable characteristics of this conference was the shift of emphasis from such purely political slogans as anti-imperialism and anti-colonialism to economic cooperation as the basis for Afro-Asian solidarity. Besides Japan's representative, the delegates of Tunisia, Iran, Senegal, and the Philippines expressed similar views at the Afro-Asian Foreign Ministers Conference.

Japan's assistance to underdeveloped countries mainly involves the region of Southeast Asia, but it is obvious that assistance is not uniform in character. For example, countries like Thailand and the Philippines rely on Western countries for aid; India and the United Arab Republic look for assistance from both the East and the West; a third group follows the policy of self-reliance advocated by Communist China. In any case, it is incumbent on Japan to foster enthusiasm among the peoples of the region for national development and to render economic assistance that is in keeping with local conditions.

In more specific terms, the words "Asian poverty" highlight the critical need to close the gap between the increasing population and lagging agricultural production. The success achieved by Thailand in corn cultivation is a good example. Imports of Thai corn amounted to 720 thousand tons (valued at $45 million) in 1965, a threefold increase over the figure of 230 thousand tons in 1964. The profitable results far outweighed the costs of Japan's technical guidance in the field of agriculture and the training and exchange of agricultural experts.

It is quite natural for Japan to have developed its own methods of technical training not only in agriculture, but in industrial construction as well. Along with managerial and technological knowledge in the field of large industrial enterprises, Japan also has had abundant experience in the field of small and medium enterprises. Japan is also able to contribute its talents in the drafting of national economic plans for agricultural and industrial development and to offer guidance in the execution of these plans.

Needless to say, Japan should also extend financial assistance within the limits of her economic power. Japan's economic assistance on a government basis to Southeast Asia has recently become more active, but its scale and method still lag far behind those of other highly industrialized countries. In addition, there has been a marked tendency in recent years for private investments to decrease, due to many hazards facing investment aid, not to speak of technical aid. For this reason, it is highly desirable that increased use be made of overseas economic cooperation funds and that the overseas investment insurance system be further improved.

In March, 1966, the Ministerial Conference for Southeast Asian Development was convened in Tokyo under the auspices of the Japanese government, providing a suitable opportunity for Japan to re-examine her entire economic cooperation policy.

Formation of an Asian-Pacific Collective Organization

Lastly, in order to make such an economic cooperation more effective, it is to be strongly hoped that an Asian-Pacific economic collective organization will be formed as quickly as possible by Japan, countries of Southeast Asia, Australia, New Zealand as well as the United States and Canada. Being a long-time advocate of the Pan-Asian ideal, I can hardly repress my feelings of great joy to see Japan's political and financial circles determinedly moving in the direction of its realization.

However, it is erroneous to regard this project as being aimed at forming an anticommunist organization. The objective of this project is the same as that of the EEC, the European Economic Community, which has achieved such outstanding results. For instance, West German Foreign Minister Gerhard Schroeder has described the purposes of the EEC as follows: "The aim of establishing the EEC was to contribute to the peace and stability of Europe by removing economic rivalries and differences among the member nations, and not as a confrontation against or the isolation of the East European bloc."

Actually, the formation of the EEC has led to a rise in the prosperity of this vast market, expanding demands for commodities from other countries, including the East European bloc, and greatly increasing trade between the EEC countries and the other countries of the world, both East and West.

I firmly believe that if an Asian-Pacific economic community can be organized as an Asian model of the EEC, such projects as President Johnson's Southeast Asian Development Plan, international regional development schemes undertaken by ECAFE (Economic Commission for Asia and the Far East), and the Colombo Plan, as well as other national development programs will produce more effective results. On the other hand, it is true that from an ideological point of view the relations between the members of the community and Communist China will present some difficult problems. This fact was poignantly referred to by the late President Kennedy of the United States who said: "The isolation of the people on the Chinese Mainland and the peoples of the Pacific region is a great world tragedy of our times, and the United States deeply desires that this state of affairs should be only a passing phenomenon."

The world of today sees the Soviet Union turning to peaceful coexistence, gradually showing an enthusiasm to adjust relations with the Free World. The so-called American-Soviet peaceful coexistence is said to have taken ten years to take definite shape. Japan with the United States should work patiently for the future when they, together with Communist China and other countries of Asia, the Pacific area, and the entire world will be reunited in friendship, cooperation, and freedom. (November, 1965)

CHAPTER **9**

Japan's Asian Diplomacy

The Long Dark Shadow of Communist China

IT IS INDEED a source of deep anxiety that international tensions should be building up in Asia, a region which constitutes the basis of Japan's diplomacy. Although I have dealt with Japan's policy toward Communist China in Chapter 4, every major problem confronting turbulent Asia is being influenced by the dark overhanging shadow of Communist China. These include the problems of the Vietnam war, Asian security, assistance to underdeveloped countries as well as the questions of Korea and Taiwan, the questions of Laos and Cambodia, the Indonesia-Malaysian dispute, and the controversy between India and Pakistan.

I should like to limit myself here to the present-day conditions in Communist China and her world policy. My other earlier writings and the chapter mentioned above provide much of the background material. In addition, the question of nuclear power development by Communist China will be taken up separately at a later date.

In an editorial carried in the 1966 New Year edition of the Communist Party organ, the *Peking People's Daily,* an appeal was made to the entire nation under the title of "On the Occasion of the First Year of the Third Five-Year Program," urging the people to dedicate themselves anew to

105

national construction. This appeal reflects Communist China's determination to concentrate on nation building.

Initially, the third five-year plan was to have been undertaken from 1963, but owing to three consecutive years of natural disasters since 1959, the suspension of Soviet economic assistance, and general mismanagement, three years have had to be spent on making necessary preparations. To put it bluntly, it started out as a "plan without a plan." It will be recalled that the National People's Congress which was to meet at least once a year under the provisions of the constitution did not meet in 1965, forcing the plan to be postponed without deliberations. It is also irregular that the third five-year plan was launched without announcing the projects for the first year.

These circumstances undoubtedly are caused by the existence of uncertain factors in Communist China's domestic and foreign policies. The major factor is the confrontation with the United States over the war in Vietnam, or more specifically the prospects of American escalation; another is the course of Communist China's opposition to the Soviet Union.

In preparations for its showdown with the United States, Communist China is vigorously and openly building up and strengthening its defensive power. Despite three years of natural disasters and a general food shortage, Communist China was able to go ahead with its efforts at nuclear tests. It goes without saying that future nuclear power development will impose a heavy burden in formulating the third plan.

According to the *Peking People's Daily,* the underlying policy of the third state plan is to develop agriculture as the basis and industry as a guide, with the ultimate goal of reaching the highest world levels within twenty to thirty years from now. This will transform Communist China into a powerful socialist nation with modern agriculture, industry, and high defensive and scientific technology. However, even in the case of domestic construction, a dangerous element exists

JAPAN'S ASIAN DIPLOMACY **107**

because the objective is not merely for the benefit of the Chinese people and Chinese revolution, but is aimed at American imperialism and world revolution.

While the Chinese communists are in the final analysis desirous of achieving world revolution through their own methods, their current world policy is to oppose by all means the attempt of American imperialism collaborating with Soviet revisionism to control the world. They are particularly vigilant against any moves of the Soviet Union, using its influence over North Vietnam, to compromise in its peace efforts in the Vietnam war.

It can be safely assumed that Communist China, from the point of view of her world policy, feels that the longer the Vietnam war continues the more advantageous it will be for her. In other words, Communist China aims to nail down the American forces in South Vietnam as long as possible, and at the same time strengthen her own military posture. In the meantime she hopes that the struggle of the Viet Cong will develop into an Asian people's struggle. This strategy calls for the formation of a unified front against American imperialism as a fuse to launch an Asian revolution which would ultimately lead to a world revolution.

As long as the Vietnam war is accompanied by a confrontation of Communist China and the United States, no improvement in the relations between Japan and Communist China is possible. Japan's diplomacy is based on cooperation with the United States, and no matter how much Japan may desire to improve relations with Communist China, it is unthinkable that Japan would disregard the realities and move in the direction of closer ties.

Prime Minister Sato's statement that "the problem of Communist China and the problem of Vietnam are inseparable" simply means that until the Sino-American confrontation eases, no progress can be made in attempting to normalize relations with Communist China.

Vietnam Peace Efforts

While the savage war in Vietnam continued, the United States suspended air raids over North Vietnam for thirty-seven days from Christmas Eve in 1965. At the same time, she launched an unprecedented diplomatic drive to achieve peace. This effort was confirmed by President Johnson in his 1966 State of the Union Message in which he declared that "able and experienced spokesmen have visited on behalf of America forty countries, and we have talked to more than a hundred governments."

These spokesmen included not only Averell Harriman, the United States roving Ambassador, but also Hubert Humphrey, Vice President; McGeorge Bundy, Special Assistant to the President; Arthur Goldberg, the American Ambassador to the United Nations, and Mennen Williams, Assistant Secretary of State, carrying the fourteen points outlining the United States Peace Conditions for an end to the Vietnam war. These American peace maneuvers, however, produced no tangible results as they were branded as trickery by Communist North Vietnam and the Viet Cong.

The said "fourteen points" for the restoration of peace in Vietnam was contained in the United States government's memorandum on Vietnam made public by Vice President Humphrey on January 3, 1966. The communists for their part have produced two sets of proposals, the "four points" as enunciated by Premier Pham Van Dong and adopted by the North Vietnam National Assembly on April 13, 1965, and the "five-point" plan of the Viet Cong's central committee of March 22. Since these opposing conditions are regarded as a key to peace in Vietnam, they are being closely studied.

One of the chief questions is whether the United States will agree to the seating of a Viet Cong representative at the conference table to discuss peace in Vietnam. Although the United States regards the Viet Cong as a puppet of North

Vietnam, it does not altogether deny its existence. This flexible stand is evident in the fourteen-point proposal which states that once Hanoi decides to cease aggression the Viet Cong would not find it difficult to join the talks to express their views.

On the other hand, the communist side is demanding that the United States recognize the Viet Cong as the sole representative of the South Vietnamese people. This should present no problem as they would be able to attain the objective which the United States has been trying to forestall.

The second question is the communist conditions as contained in the Viet Cong formula for the settlement of the South Vietnam problem. This formula was drawn up in December, 1960, calling for the overthrow of the American colonial system and a servant of United States imperialism. What is not clear is whether the South Vietnam government which has been "democratized" after the withdrawal of the American forces will be absorbed by the so-called national civil administration or whether its existence will be completely denied.

The United States is taking the view that the government of South Vietnam should be established through free elections by the people of South Vietnam themselves, and that in order to ensure democratic elections free from violence and terrorism they should be carried out under international supervision. Moreover, the will of the majority of the people other than the Viet Cong should be reflected in the elections.

The third question is how the reunification of South and North Vietnam can be realized. The United States merely insists that "it should be decided by the free will of the Vietnamese people themselves." Aside from this condition, there appears to be nothing insurmountable. On the other hand, North Vietnam insists that the "question should be resolved without foreign interference" and the Viet Cong formula stresses the need for gradual unification.

Other than this sharp clash of principles, there is no serious disagreement on minor points. In its fourteen-point declaration, the United States is calling for "unconditional talks," adding that it has no desire to maintain American bases in Southeast Asia or American forces in South Vietnam after the restoration of peace. Moreover, the United States is agreeable to the countries of Southeast Asia taking either a nonaligned or neutral policy.

While the Vietnam peace efforts appear to be floundering as a result of the unacceptable conditions set forth by both sides, it is difficult to see why a compromise cannot be reached for initiating talks if the communist side really has any desire to reach a peaceful settlement.

I should like to say a few words here about the "respect for 1959 Geneva Agreements" which both the United States and the communist side bring up from time to time. In this connection, the United States has called for the holding of an international conference on the basis of this agreement, but the communist side has rejected this suggestion, firmly advocating the strict adherence to the provisions of the Geneva Agreements. However, the two sides do not agree on the interpretation of the agreements. It should not be forgotten that the United States and South Vietnam did not participate in the said agreements on grounds that the adherence to agreements might be construed as tacit recognition of and guarantee for the North Vietnam communist regime.

Despite American efforts to achieve peace, it is reported that bombings of North Vietnam were resumed because of Hanoi's rejection of all American peace feelers and the fact that North Vietnam utilized the pause in the aerial attacks to step up its act of infiltration of South Vietnam.

Simultaneously with the resumption of the bombing of North Vietnam, the United States requested an emergency meeting of the United Nations Security Council to debate the Vietnam question, and urged world public opinion to join in peace efforts. This action was followed by President Johnson himself going to Honolulu to discuss the strengthening of military forces and improvement in the conditions of the civilian population in South Vietnam with the government leaders of the war-torn nation. In this manner, the United States is preparing to wage the struggle in South Vietnam on both the war and peace fronts, while at the same time sparing no efforts to strive for peace.

With the Vietnam situation becoming more and more critical, there has been a notable shift in Japan's attitude toward the question, from mere professions of desiring peace in Vietnam to one of positively engaging in side efforts to assist the United States in achieving a peaceful solution.

Although no hoped-for results came out of the visit of Foreign Minister Etsusaburo Shiina to Moscow in January, 1966, Japan did act independently in lending its weight to the mission of peace, dispatching the Vice President of the Liberal Democratic Party, Kawashima, in February to the United Arab Republic and other Near and Middle East countries, and Ambassador Yokoyama to various countries in Europe, the Near and Middle East, and Asia. At the United Nations, Ambassador Matsui of Japan made similar efforts for peace as chairman of the Security Council and as representative of the Asian bloc of delegates. It is to be hoped that as a nonpermanent member of the Security Council Japanese diplomacy will be able to play a significant role.

The Nuclear Age and Asia

While aggravating still further her policy of confrontation against the United States, Communist China is going ahead with her development of nuclear weapons at a surprisingly rapid tempo. On December 10, 1965, the United States Secretary of Defense Robert McNamara addressing the NATO Council, predicted that Communist China would possess medium range missiles by 1967 and intercontinental ballistic missiles by 1975, but in any event the day is not far off when the countries bordering Communist China will come within the range of her rockets armed with hydrogen bombs. There is a grave danger that this ominous threat will trigger a chain reaction of nuclear proliferation in the Asian region. In the event the nuclear situation in areas bordering Japan changes radically, Japan and her Asian neighbors will face the serious problem of ensuring security in the so-called nuclear age.

Notwithstanding the fact that Japan has hitherto possessed sufficient ability to manufacture nuclear weapons, she has not only been fundamentally opposed to nuclear arms production as a matter of basic policy, but has also opposed the introduction of such weapons into her territory. However, if the nuclear arms race continues unabated, and Asia becomes engaged in nuclear proliferation, the problem of guaranteeing the safety of Japan will take on added complexities. Actually, there has recently been talk of "nuclear security" and "nuclear discussion" in countries neighboring Japan.

Although a resolution was adopted by the 20th General Assembly of the United Nations in the autumn of 1965 calling for the holding of a world disarmament conference before 1967, to which Communist China would be a party, there appears little prospect that such a conference will ever materialize. As long as her right of representation in the United Nations is not restored and the Nationalist government is not ousted from the world body, Communist China is firmly opposed to participating in any conference sponsored by the United Nations or its related organizations.

But that is not all. Communist China is anxious to avoid even the slightest limitation to her program of accelerated development of nuclear missile armaments. There are a number of factors which prompt Communist China's nuclear development. By possessing nuclear arms, she feels that she can improve her position to challenge American imperialism and Soviet revisionism, increase the political and psychological effects of her efforts to assist so-called wars of liberation, and at the same time raise the prestige and voice of Communist China.

On the occasion of her first and second nuclear tests, conducted in October 1964 and May 1965 respectively, Communist China made an appeal to the world to convene a summit conference of all powers to discuss nuclear disarmament, a proposal which she had earlier put forward several times. However, the disarmament theme of Communist China's world summit conference is limited to the ban on the use of all nuclear weapons. Communist China, like France, which belatedly entered the nuclear race, is generally interested only in disarmament measures aimed at paralyzing the overwhelming nuclear power of the United States and the Soviet Union. The Communist Chinese plan clearly has this intention, and France's demand calls for the destruction of the means of delivery. These two countries have turned a cold shoulder to any efforts to achieve a stop to nuclear tests and steps to halt proliferation.

Communist China's nuclear arming has a very profound effect on the countries of Asia and utmost vigilance is necessary in the future. By extending the Japan-United States Security Treaty to cover nuclear protection, Japan will be able to have nuclear security, but there still remains the question of other countries in Asia which do not possess any such assurance of security. In cases of nonaligned countries, such as India, since they cannot request such security arrangements from other nuclear powers, the discussions relating to the United Nations nuclear nonproliferation treaty are beginning to touch upon the problem of protecting countries like India that are without nuclear protection.

In these circumstances, India facing the threat of Communist China has taken the view that the mere shutting out of countries not possessing nuclear weapons by the "nuclear club" of the five nuclear powers offers no solution whatsoever.

It is, therefore, stressing the importance of the nuclear powers giving nuclear protection to countries capable of developing nuclear weapons.

The future course of India, which has the capability of developing such dreaded weapons in a year and a half, is being watched closely. In the meantime, Great Britain, grappling with the problems of defense east of Suez, is reportedly considering the disposition of an international nuclear force in either the Indian or Pacific Ocean as a means of affording nuclear protection to India, Malaysia, and other countries.

When the British Minister of State in charge of Disarmament Lord Chalfont, visited Japan, he discussed this vital issue with the Japanese government, and views were also exchanged on this question between Japan and India at their recent regular series of meetings.

In countering this Communist Chinese nuclear arms development, the United States has taken its own military measures to contain the threat from Peking. In early 1965, the United States dispatched a Polaris submarine to the western Pacific, and with the escalation of the war in Vietnam they have also ordered their B-52 strategic bombers to participate in the aerial bombings, as well as dispatching the nuclear-powered aircraft carrier "Enterprise" to Vietnam waters. At home, they have speeded up the development of the antimissile missile, the Nike X.

The United States has also appealed to allied powers to take similar measures. This was reflected in the speech before the NATO Council by Secretary of Defense McNamara, as earlier pointed out. This American view has also been placed before Japan. Vice President Humphrey and Secretary of State Rusk have both referred to talks on nuclear strategy and nuclear power, and there is every likelihood that the question will eventually be taken up.

Under this heavy cloud of nuclear threat, it is a great relief to learn about the Swedish proposal to establish a "nuclear detection club" composed of six or seven countries, including

Japan. The development of seismology has greatly increased the ability to detect underground tests. It is said that even after the 1963 Partial Nuclear Test Ban Treaty the nuclear powers are conducting underground tests at the rate of one blast every ten days.

The importance of the treaty to prevent the spread of nuclear weapons can never be overemphasized, but it is inadequate as this only limits the present countries not possessing nuclear weapons and leaves the great powers to continue their armament buildup. The purpose of the "nuclear detection club" is naturally aimed at a total ban of nuclear tests, but it is to be hoped that it can also envisage the international control of underground tests which still remain uncontrolled.

Solidarity and Economic Cooperation of the Free Nations

The normalization of relations between Japan and Korea which came into effect on December 18, 1965, as emphasized by Prime Minister Sato, may well be regarded as Japan's first major step in Asian diplomacy. Separated only by a narrow strip of water, Japan and Korea have close historical and geographical ties and are both members of the free nations of East Asia. It is indispensable that these two countries march shoulder to shoulder toward coexistence and coprosperity for the sake of the peace and prosperity of Asia.

Following the normalization of relations between the two countries, it is noteworthy that voices are often heard in high government quarters in Korea for closer ties between Japan, Korea, and the United States. However, Japan feels that as the United States already has such links as the Japan-United States Security Treaty and the United States-Korea Mutual Defense Pact with the two countries concerned, the ties binding the three countries are sufficiently strong. Even without the formal treaties between them, if Japan and Korea make joint efforts and receive American assistance and support, there will be a feeling of unity between them as free nations.

The United States, on the other hand, has taken no fresh military or political steps to meet the "new age of Japanese-Korean relations." There is no appeal for a so-called Northeast Asia treaty organization or a regular tripartite among Japan, Korea, and the United States.

In addition to the question of strengthening the ties among the three nations, we should not overlook the fact that Korea is displaying unusual enthusiasm on the need to tighten the bonds linking the free nations of Asia. Recognizing that it would be difficult to alter the present stand of Japan, Korea has been addressing itself to the other free nations of Asia to form so-called anticommunist nations, such as Nationalist China and South Vietnam, to win the adherence of the Philippines and Thailand.

It must be fully recognized that Thailand and the Philippines regard the threat of Communist China as being very real. Not only geographically, but also economically and politically these countries are very vulnerable to Communist Chinese infiltration tactics. Being surrounded on all sides by sea, and with a booming economy and political freedom, the people of Japan find it difficult to imagine the seriousness of the situation in the aforementioned countries.

The former also regard the war in Vietnam with the same feeling of realism. They are keenly aware that the fate of the countries of Southeast Asia hinges on the type of settlement reached in Vietnam. To them, the domino theory is no myth, but uncomfortably real.

It is within the context of this situation that Australia has recently been very active in the diplomatic field in addition to extending economic aid to both Thailand and Cambodia. The reasons for Australia and New Zealand, which have dispatched military units to South Vietnam, making strenuous efforts to bring the two countries closer together, is based on the realization that the Indo-China peninsula is an important region that can affect their own national security.

Even in the event of Communist China revising its present policy of rejecting the peaceful coexistence line, the free nations of Asia cannot disregard the problem of unity. The principle of peaceful coexistence involves the mutual observance of noninterference in the domestic affairs of other nations, and is a means of demonstrating the superiority of the contending systems through peaceful economic competition. In other words, peaceful coexistence may also be described as competitive coexistence.

It is, therefore, imperative that the free nations of Asia strengthen their solidarity in meeting the economic competition of Communist China and other countries of the Red bloc. Communist China itself is such a vast country that it alone can be said to constitute a regional community. To counteract this competition, the free nations should at least establish a regional economic community.

In uniting the free nations on the basis of this broad viewpoint, it must be said that Japan, the only nation in Asia which is highly industrialized, has a significant role to play. In order to fulfill this role, Japan must consider its economic diplomacy and her policy of assistance to the developing nations.

The Soviet Line and Asia

Lastly, I should like to draw attention to the unusually active Soviet diplomacy directed at Asia since the beginning of 1966, among them the visit of the Soviet Communist Party Secretary Alexander Shelepin to Hanoi, Prime Minister Alexei Kosygin's mediation efforts in which he invited the leaders of India and Pakistan to Tashkent, and the visit of the First Secretary of the Soviet Communist Party Leonid Brezhnev to Mongolia. All these visits were made to countries surrounding Communist China, primarily aimed, it seems, at offsetting Communist China's diplomatic maneuvers and containing her influence. The visit of Japanese Foreign Minister Shiina to Moscow may also be regarded as having been made within the scope of this Soviet policy.

Some hopes were held that Shelepin's visit to Hanoi would result in Soviet pressures on North Vietnam as part of America's peace efforts, but these hopes were summarily dashed. However, it is felt that the Soviet Union knows that it cannot hope for America's complete collapse and unconditional withdrawal from Vietnam. This Moscow view appears to run counter with the view held by Peking, and it would be jumping to conclusions to suppose that the Soviet attitude has suddenly hardened.

Prime Minister Kosygin's efforts to mediate in the Indo-Pakistan conflict and his being able to persuade the two countries at Tashkent to sign a joint communique renouncing the use of force to settle the Kashmir dispute were undoubtedly a great success for Soviet diplomacy. One of the aims of this conference was certainly to show that the Soviet Union is an Asian nation, a point which it has been strongly stressing since its status was questioned at the Second Afro-Asian Conference in 1965.

What is even more significant is that during the mediation, the Soviet line of Marxism-Leninism was not advocated. The Soviet Union, moreover, adopted a neutral stand from beginning to end, showing no signs of intending to get involved in the "racial liberation" issue. Consequently, there is even an opinion voiced that the Tashkent Conference was the first step toward Soviet-American peaceful coexistence on the Asian continent.

Hemmed in by the giant Soviet Union to the north and the equally large Communist China to the south, Mongolia has been relying on the Soviet Union ever since the beginning of the Sino-Soviet differences. Responding to the Mongolian attitude, First Secretary Brezhnev visited Ulanbator to sign a treaty of friendship, cooperation, and mutual assistance between the two countries. This treaty, replacing the twenty-year-old treaty which has lapsed, stipulates that the two countries shall extend mutual assistance in case either is attacked by a third power.

The recent visit of Foreign Minister Shiina to the Soviet Union has been fruitful in fostering Japanese-Soviet diplomacy in the future, but it is reported that the Soviet Union failed to make any positive responses either on the question of peace in Vietnam or on the question of Japan's claim to its northern territories as a precondition for signing the peace treaty.

During the visit, the period of the trade and payment agreement was extended from three to five years, but the hoped-for Siberian development plan was not included in the agreement, indicating that Japanese-Soviet trade is in a state of stagnation.

Under the air agreement, the two countries are expected to allow the flights of their respective aircraft over each other's territories after recognizing the right of joint flights over Siberia. The question of joint flights being a test case, many complicated questions are expected to crop up which must be solved on the basis of international trust.

At any rate, the Sino-Soviet differences have engendered a mood of fostering better relations with Japan. But there has been no change in the Soviet line of stressing the need to remain united within the communist camp, including Communist China. I should like to point out, too, that the party organ of the Soviet Communist Party, *Pravda,* declared on the occasion of the sixteenth anniversary of the conclusion of the Sino-Soviet Treaty of Friendship, Alliance, and Mutual Assistance on February 12, 1966, that unfortunately there has arisen, through no fault of the Soviet Union, difficult relations between the two countries. Although the American imperialists are sticking to the idea that the international communist movement is unable to form an anti-imperialist united front, the Soviet Communist Party and government are endeavoring always to normalize relations with the Chinese Communist Party and government. (February, 1966)

CHAPTER **10**

Ideal Pattern of Japan-United States Relations

What Is Meant by Japan-United States Cooperative Setup

AMERICAN cooperation was absolutely necessary for Japan's rebirth after World War II as a free, democratic country and for attaining today's peace and prosperity. In gaining its independence, Japan was compelled to choose between multilateral peace and an overall peace. The Yoshida Cabinet and the then ruling Liberal Democratic Party chose the former without hesitation. The Peace Treaty was signed in September, 1951, and at the same time the Japan-United States Security Treaty was concluded. In this manner, a firm tie was knotted between Japan and the United States superseding past obligations and hatreds. This marked Japan's entry into Free World ranks led by the United States and Japan's reliance on cooperation of the giant United States for its defense. Herein lies the spirit of the so-called Japan-United States security setup.

I want to emphasize here the fact that the security treaty setup was an inevitable consequence of the balance of power in international politics. In other words, Communist China and the Soviet Union concluded, in February, 1950, a Treaty of Friendship, Alliance, and Mutual Assistance by regarding

121

122 MODERN JAPAN'S FOREIGN POLICY

Japan as their hypothetical enemy. Furthermore in June, 1950, North Korean troops, backed by Communist China and the Soviet Union, stepped across the 38th parallel and started the Korean War. It was only natural for Japan and the United States to join hands and work out countermeasures when the communist forces in the Far East unveiled their true aggressive purposes. The balance of power condition which prevailed in the Far East at the time of the conclusion of the Japan-United States Security Treaty still remains unchanged.

Today when the antagonism between the Free World and the communist camp seems unlikely to thaw in the near future, the problem of security concerns not only military matters but also politics, economy, and even culture. When the security treaty was revised six years ago, the so-called economic clauses were inserted into the text of the revised treaty as a means to consolidate Japan-United States cooperation in the economic field also.

The development of nuclear weapons by Communist China has given rise to the question of peace and security of Asia in the nuclear age. In January last year when Prime Minister Sato visited the United States, it was confirmed once again the United States would protect Japan from nuclear attack under the existing security treaty. Accordingly, the Japan-United States Security Treaty setup satisfies these two major needs more than adequately.

The history of Japan-United States relations is quite old. It was Commodore Perry who knocked at the closed door of isolationist Japan in the middle of the 19th century. The arrival of the Black Ship awakened feudalistic Japan from its comfortable sleep and opened its eyes to the current of modern times. But soon the United States became engrossed in the Civil War and became too busy with the exploration of the West to make overseas advances. Before long, Japan became friendly with Great Britain and concluded the Anglo-Japanese Alliance, which served as a prop helping Japan to attain prosperity from the Meiji era through the Taisho era.

Through repeated renewals, the Anglo-Japanese Alliance remained in effect for twenty years. During these twenty years, the United States extended aid to Japan out of kindness during the Russo-Japanese War and maintained a friendly attitude toward Japan. However, when the United States gained a bigger voice as a Pacific nation after World War I, the Anglo-Japanese Alliance was abrogated to give way to the five-nation agreement among Japan, the United States, Great Britain, France, and Italy concerning the reduction of naval armaments, the four-nation agreement among Japan, the United States, Great Britain, and France concerning the maintenance of the *status quo* of the Pacific islands, and the nine-nation agreement concerning China.

I will not touch on the deterioration of Japan-United States relations following the outbreak of the Manchurian Incident and on the Pacific War because those days constitute a vacuum in the history of Japanese diplomacy. As is evident from the above, Japan-United States relations have a history of more than 110 years. I am filled with deep emotion when I think of the fact that the two countries are united firmly in their liberal and democratic outlook on the world and are determined to share the same fate in the latter half of the 20th century.

Need for Long-Term Security and Extension of the Treaty Until 1980

To begin with, the Japan-United States Security Treaty has a ten-year term, and it can be abrogated anytime on a year's notice after this ten-year term expires.

The existing treaty expires in 1970. However, if nothing is done to scrap the treaty, it can remain effective practically forever. In view of this, the government has taken the stand that it is not necessary to make an issue of the security treaty unless certain points require revision. The ruling Liberal

Democratic Party, too, has tried to avoid making an issue of this treaty in order not to create unnecessary trouble. The reason the government and the ruling party have taken a passive attitude toward the security treaty issue is that the so-called renovationist forces, including the Japan Socialist Party, Sohyo (General Council of Labor Unions), and the Japan Communist Party, have been engrossed in organizing an antisecurity treaty struggle. It is still fresh in our memory that they organized huge antitreaty demonstrations and created a big disturbance at the time of the revision of the old treaty.

In the meantime, the United States Secretary of State Dean Rusk and Assistant Secretary of State for Far Eastern Affairs William Bundy as well as other leaders of the United States government have availed themselves on every occasion to stress the importance of the Japan-United States Security Treaty. However, taking for granted that the treaty will continue to remain effective unless the current international situation changes, the Japanese government has not made an issue of the security treaty yet. However, the renovationist forces of Japan are gradually showing an increased zeal in organizing a struggle to abrogate the treaty with 1970 as the target year. We cannot remain idle spectators indefinitely.

Needless to say, various preparations are now being made by some members of the Liberal Democratic Party to organize a national movement to counter the renovationists' antitreaty struggle. Opinion favoring the extension of the treaty by five or ten years has been gaining ground recently because Liberal Democratic members have come to realize that their usual indifference will not help them tide over the 1970 crisis, now that the expiration of the treaty is only four years away.

The climate surrounding the security treaty being such, Prime Minister Sato's statement before the Upper House Budget Committee on March 8 this year attracted the people's attention. Sato said: "The defense structure must be built on a long-range basis. It is necessary to give longevity to the security treaty when its current term expires." On the following day, March 9, Sato elaborated on this remark and said: "It is possible that Japan and the United States will agree that neither country will give notice of abrogation. It is also possible that a new security treaty exactly the same as the existing one will be signed." Sato thus referred in a concrete way to the steps that might be taken when the ten-year term expires and promised to conduct further studies on the matter.

I find immeasurable joy in the fact that both the Liberal Democratic Party and the government have begun, though belatedly, to tackle this problem vigorously and in earnest, because I have long felt the need for extending the term of the security treaty. I have long believed that the Foreign Affairs Study Council of the Liberal Democratic Party, of which I am chairman, must take the initiative in creating among the members of the government party a climate favoring the extension of the existing security treaty.

Unless something is done to frustrate the renovationists' opposition to the extension of the treaty, there is a possibility that a much greater confusion than in 1960 will be with us as the year 1970 approaches. This confusion, if ever created, is feared to become a routine affair after 1970. If so, there is a fear of the cold war being brought into Japan, with the possible result that the whole of Japan will be involved in a state similar to that of a civil war. In order to avoid the so-called 1970 crisis, some preventive steps must be taken before it becomes too late.

On January 28 last year, I took the floor in a plenary session of the Upper House and expressed my wish that the Japan-United States Security Treaty be extended by another ten years until 1980 and asked the government if it had any intention of doing so. In expressing my wish, I reasoned that the term of the treaty, which was concluded as a counterbalance to the Russo-Chinese alliance, should be extended until 1980 when the Russo-Chinese alliance also expires. Prime Minister Sato said in reply that it was essential for

Japan to maintain the security treaty but that he had no intention of revising the treaty just for the sake of extending its term, because extension is possible even under the existing agreement.

Back in 1960, I advocated that the term of the treaty be extended till 1980. In those days, the late Kichisaburo Nomura, former Japanese Ambassador to the United States, was the only person who supported my suggestion. Some people said that it was too long to extend the treaty till 1970 and they said that a five-year extension would suffice. If the treaty had been extended by another ten years then, there should be no commotion whatever today.

It seems that there has been no U.S. reaction yet to Prime Minister Sato's statement in the Diet. Probably the United States government is too busily occupied with the North Atlantic Treaty Organization (NATO) which expires in 1969, one year ahead of the Japan-United States Security Treaty, as well as with the Vietnam war and the issue of Communist China to think about the Japan-United States Security Treaty.

Difference of Opinion Regarding Vietnam War and Communist China

Next I have to refer to the gap between the United States and Japan in their understanding of the Vietnam war, which is the most important of all problems currently faced by the U.S. as well as the Communist China problem. The United States has never asked Japan to extend military aid for the Vietnam war. However, the United States has been irritated by Japan's attitude toward these problems. The United States apparently is not satisfied with the moral and psychological support being offered by Japan in the Vietnam war. Former United States Ambassador to Japan Edwin O. Reischauer accused the Japanese people of lacking enthusiasm in understanding the United States purpose of fighting the Vietnam war as well as in supporting the United States efforts in Vietnam. He said that the Japanese people were too obsessed by a fear that they might become involved in the Vietnam war to try to understand the United States stand.

He pointed out that "biased or inaccurate reporting" by Japanese newspapers was responsible for the negative attitude assumed by the Japanese people toward the war in Vietnam.

Special Presidential Envoy Henry Cabot Lodge, Assistant Secretary of State Bundy, and a *New York Times* columnist, James Reston, who visited Japan from last year through this year, expressed unanimous dissatisfaction at the lukewarm attitude of the Japanese people. The United States government authorities have a tendency to overestimate the opinions of the Japan Socialist Party, other leftist organizations, and the so-called progressive intellectuals. It is feared that United States authorities are apt to be deluded into thinking that the opinions of these groups represent the majority opinion in Japan.

Former United States Ambassador to Russia George Kennan probably is a typical case. On February 10, Kennan said at a public hearing of the United States Senate Foreign Relations Committee: "The trust and friendly feeling of the Japanese people is the greatest asset the United States has in East Asia. We have betrayed the trust and goodwill of the Japanese by our military actions in Vietnam, especially by our strategic bombing of the North." But we must say that many of the Japanese whom Kennan thought the United States has betrayed by its policy in Vietnam are die-hard anti-Americans who call the United States an imperialist country. In order to regain the trust of such Japanese, the United States will have to pull out not only from South Vietnam but also from Japan. If the United States should ever do this, it will eventually disappoint and betray the majority of the Japanese who believe the keynote of Japan's diplomacy is in its cooperation with the United States.

In the United States, vigorous debates were held on the

Vietnam issue and the Communist China problem at public hearings of the Senate Foreign Relations Committee from February through March this year. Criticisms of the United States government's policy were given larger space in newspapers published in Japan. The fact that even debates denouncing the government's stand could be carried out so actively without restriction provides us with evidence of the soundness of American democracy. But we must not form a view by just swallowing only antigovernment opinions.

The public hearing on the Vietnam issue was conducted in a manner as if Senator William J. Fulbright, chairman of the Foreign Relations Committee, was pressing for a showdown with the government. The public hearing created a big sensation in the United States. However, it became clear in the course of heated debates that there was no wise solution to the Vietnam issue other than Johnson's middle-of-the-road war guidance. The public hearing on the Vietnam issue was of value because it taught the people that the two extremes were not good solutions of the Vietnam war.

The gap in opinion between Japan and the United States regarding the Communist China issue has also been pointed out time and again. During his talks with President Johnson in January last year, Prime Minister Sato explained Japan's basic policy of promoting nongovernmental contacts between Japan and mainland China on the principle of separating economic affairs from political affairs, while Johnson stressed Communist China's militant policy and expansionist attitude. This was recorded in the joint communique issued at the end of the Sato-Johnson meeting. It is said that this shows the gap between the two countries.

People in Japan are trying to attribute this gap between the two countries on the Vietnam and Communist China issues generally to the difference of thinking between Europeans, or especially Americans, and the Orientals. In other words, the American way of thinking follows the pattern of "confrontation between God and Devil," while Orientals think that there are two sides to everything—bright and dark—and that morning comes around because there is night. The majority of Japanese people say they are anticommunists and that they have approaches typical of Asians in countering communism. I think there is some truth in this. However, if there is a gap between Japan and the United States on the Communist China issue at all, I attribute it primarily to geographical and historical factors. Such a difference of opinion is by no means fundamental, I should say. I do not think it would be difficult to make the United States understand this point.

I expect that exchange of professors and students between the two countries will become more and more active in the future as result of the Japan-United States Committee on Education, Cultural Interchange, and other similar meetings. I hope, therefore, that mutual understanding on matters of common interest will be deepened gradually.

Okinawa: Sore Spot in Japan-United States Relations

Twenty years after World War II, the Okinawa issue constitutes a sore spot in Japan-United States relations. When Prime Minister Sato visited Okinawa in the summer of last year, he said: "The postwar period of Japan will not come to an end, unless Okinawa is restored to its fatherland." It seems unlikely that these islands, which serve as important military bases for the United States, will be returned to Japan in the foreseeable future, because it appears almost impossible that the threat of war and tension in the Far East resulting from the confrontation between the United States and Communist China over Vietnam and Taiwan will be alleviated in the near future.

Okinawa forms a strategic pivot in the United States defense of Japan and other free countries of the Far East. It serves as an advanced military base essential for speedy and effective operational actions.

According to the United States High Commissioner Albert Watson, the United States armed forces will lose a great deal of freedom of military action if the United States is deprived of even a portion of its administrative rights over the Ryukyus, and that the value of Okinawa as a U.S. military base will be reduced accordingly. In other words, the United States must reserve the right to transfer troops and equipment to this military base without delay, store on this island equipment necessary for preventing invasion, transport from there troops, equipment, aircraft, and ships to areas which the United States has pledged to defend, and provide from there logistic support to troops at any time as required by operations under mutual defense treaties. Watson says that if the United States loses its administrative power over Okinawa, it will lose such freedom of action, with the result that it will not be able to defend Okinawa, Japan, and other free countries of Asia.

In December last year, the United States consented to the indirect election of the chief executive of the Ryukyus by the legislature. Under the old system, the chief executive was appointed by the United States military high commissioner. This action should be lauded as a courageous decision which has expanded the self-rule of the Okinawan people. The new system under which the person elected by a majority vote of the legislature is appointed chief executive automatically by the United States military high commissioner should be regarded as a United States gesture to respect the opinions of the local residents, although the new system is still far from a direct public election system as desired by the local residents.

It is said that the reason the United States still hesitates to adopt a direct public election system is that it fears that a person who might obstruct the value of Okinawa as a United States military base might be elected. Some others say that the United States fears that political strife over the election of the chief executive might become so intensified as to create political unrest in Okinawa.

The Japanese government has decided to extend ¥5.8 billion ($16.1 million) in aid to Okinawa during the current fiscal year. In increasing its aid, the government is trying to prepare for the day when Okinawa will be returned to Japan by eliminating the gap between the Ryukyuans and the mainland Japanese in social welfare and education.

At the same time, the United States Civil Administration and the Ryukyu government are now jointly working out a long-range plan extending from the 1966 fiscal year to the 1971 fiscal year. This plan primarily aims at raising the per capita annual income of the Ryukyuans from $364 in 1965 to $637 in 1971, so that the living standard of Okinawans will become almost as high as that of the Japanese in Japan proper.

Here I must mention the fact that the defense debate in the Japanese Diet even touched on the defense of Okinawa and created an unexpected stir. On March 8, Prime Minister Sato at the Upper House Budget Committee said in reply to an interpellator: "If Okinawa is attacked, the United States forces will primarily engage in the defense of the islands. But Japan should also take up the defense of Okinawa." This statement was taken up by the opposition Socialist Party as hinting at the dispatch of self-defense forces to Okinawa. Since Japan has no administrative rights over the islands, mutual obligations for the defense of the islands are stipulated in the minutes to the Treaty of Mutual Cooperation and Security exchanged between Japan and the United States.

The minutes stipulate: "If an armed attack occurs or is threatened against these islands, the two countries will of course consult together closely under Article 4 of the Treaty of Mutual Cooperation and Security. In the event of an armed attack, it is the intention of the government of Japan to explore with the United States measures which it might be able to take for the welfare of the islanders.

"In the event of an armed attack against these islands, the United States government will consult at once with the government of Japan and intends to take the necessary measures for the defense of these islands, and to do its utmost to secure the welfare of the islanders." Although the minutes do not prohibit Japan from taking measures in fields other than welfare of the islanders, the dispatch of self-defense forces to Okinawa, over which Japan has no administrative rights, is considered inappropriate in the light of the existing Self-Defense Force Law.

The prime minister's statement was nothing but a straight-forward manifestation of the Japanese people's sentiment that the people of Japan cannot remain indifferent to Okinawans if they are ever exposed to an armed attack, because Okinawans are fellow countrymen. At the end of the above-mentioned statement, Sato added a remark to the effect that considering the military capability of the United States, he was confident that Okinawa would never be involved in a war as long as the United States armed forces are stationed there. In this manner, Sato stressed that an armed attack on Okinawa was a hypothetical matter. After all, Sato supplemented his earlier remark on March 15 by adding: "As long as the United States holds the administrative rights over Okinawa, it is impossible for Japan to invoke the right of self-defense and to dispatch self-defense forces to Okinawa." I am sure that there is no Japanese who dares to think that Okinawans should die miserable deaths in case of an armed attack.

Japan-United States Trade and Asia-Pacific Common Market

The economy of Japan made a wonderful recovery from war devastation, thanks to financial aid from the United States. Even after Japan became independent, it was able to achieve a miraculous recovery by asking the United

States to shoulder responsibilities for Japan's defense. The economic relations between Japan and the United States are firm not only in the foreign trade field but also in the matter of international monetary currency. The trade between Japan and the United States in the 1965 fiscal year reached $4,986 million, Japan's exports amounting to $2,620 million and its imports to $2,366 million. The trade with the United States accounted for nearly 30 per cent of Japan's total U.S. imports of iron and steel, while the United States supplied 30 per cent of Japan's total import of foodstuffs.

Japan's trade with the United States is occupying a greater portion of Japan's total trade year by year. Japanese businessmen are trying to contact U.S. traders by regions or states, while U.S. businessmen are organizing trade missions on the basis of states and sending them to Japan in their efforts to promote trade between the two countries.

Japan-United States trade has become the second largest bilateral trade, next only to United States-Canada trade. The United States is Japan's No. 1 customer, while Japan is the United States' largest customer, next to Canada.

Yet, there are still import restrictions imposed on Japanese goods by the United States. These restrictions are hampering the healthy development of international trade and expansion of world economy. It is hoped, therefore, that these trade barriers will be removed at the earliest possible date. Now that the trade between Japan and the United States involves nearly $5 billion both ways, it may be inevitable that various problems should arise between the two countries. However, I believe that since both countries, which uphold democracy and free economy, have a common ground, any problem can be settled before long in a manner which is fair and advantageous to both on the strength of public opinion and market power.

The two-year cotton trade agreement concluded in Washington on January 15 this year is an unprecedentedly forward-looking one. It took Japan almost ten years to conclude such a favorable agreement with the United States. This agreement can be regarded as the result of the United States government's efforts to place its trade with Japan on a more stabilized basis.

The dollar crisis remains a source of world distrust in the United States mainly because of the continued increase in U.S. military expenditures. Today, many countries are criticizing the current international currency system based on gold. Talks are under way among ten advanced countries to reform the existing international currency system. Since many of the advanced countries hold gold reserves, there is a possibility that any decision on a new currency system will be made to favor those countries which hold gold. Japan's foreign-exchange reserves amount roughly to $2 billion, most of which are in U.S. dollars. Japan's gold reserves amount to only $300 million. Yet, Japan did not ask for the conversion of its dollar holdings into gold at the time of the dollar crisis in the United States although many European countries did so.

If Japan should try to increase its gold reserve now, Japan will eventually meet strong resistance from the United States which is engrossed in reducing the outflow of dollars. It requires, therefore, careful study to determine to what extent Japan should try to increase its gold holdings.

One of the most important future economic problems lying between Japan and the United States is the development of Asia. In April last year, President Johnson proposed to offer $1 billion in aiding the development of Southeast Asia. The United States places great expectations on positive Japanese participation in the development of Southeast Asia, because Japan is closely situated to Southeast Asian countries and has adequate experience in the development of underdeveloped regions.

The United States hopes Japan will take the leading role in carrying out Johnson's $1 billion Asian development plan, although it is willing to furnish necessary funds and engineering techniques. The United States believes it would be more effective to develop Asia under the leadership of Asian countries rather than under the guidance of the United Nations.

At the Fourth Joint Japan-United States Committee on Trade and Economic Affairs held in Washington in July last year, United States Secretary of State Dean Rusk sought Japan's cooperation in the development of Southeast Asia in line with Johnson's economic development plan in connection with the Vietnam situation. He stressed that priority should be given to the problem of Southeast Asia which is suffering from aggression and poverty rather than to the economic problems pending between Japan and the United States.

At this committee meeting, the Japanese delegation was not able to come up with a detailed aid plan, although it revealed a plan to contribute $200 million to the Asian Development Bank. Admitting that United States-Japanese cooperation in international economy was important, the Japanese delegation expressed the hope that the committee would concern itself more with coordinating views over individual problems arising between the two countries. The outcome, however, was that the joint communique issued at the end of the committee meeting noted that both Japan and the United States had agreed to strengthen an economic assistance structure to be built on the initiative of Asian countries in order to promote the economic development of Asia.

It is obvious that the economic development of Asia is very important. What is needed most in Southeast Asia today is a regional economic community which could even pave the way to the organization of an Asia-Pacific common market.

At this joint trade committee, Japan promised to set aside 1 per cent of the national income (about $600 million) for economic assistance to Southeast Asia in one or two years from now. Japan, therefore, will be obliged to meet the United States expectations by mapping out a detailed aid plan to contribute to the economic development of Asia.

As Regards Liberal Peace Diplomacy

Before concluding this thesis, I find it necessary to say a few more words about the relation between Japan's diplomacy toward the United States and the independent peace diplomacy that Japan advocates. Although a gap in opinion between the United States and Japan as regards the Vietnam war has been made an issue, the United States reportedly is satisfied with Japan's recent attitude to extend positive cooperation to the United States.

From the last few days of the old year through the New Year, Vice President Hubert Humphrey and Special Presidential Envoy Averell Harriman came to Japan in close succession and asked Japan to take an active role in promoting United States efforts to bring about peace in Vietnam after the Christmas ceasefire. Accordingly, Foreign Minister Shiina conveyed to the Soviet government the United States intention when he visited Moscow in the middle of January and tried to persuade Russia to work on North Vietnam. However, Shiina was given a cold shoulder by the Russian government. Moreover on February 17, Japan received a written protest from the Soviet government saying that Japan had been cooperating with the United States in the latter's aggression in Vietnam.

On February 26, the Japanese government sent a reply to the Soviet government defending U.S. military efforts in Vietnam. The reply said: "It is appropriate for the U.S. armed forces to procure goods by utilizing Japanese facilities and areas under the provisions of the Japan-United States Security Treaty."

Earlier in late January when the United States resumed

bombing of the north, Japan expressed regret not over the resumption of the bombing itself but over the circumstances which necessitated the United States to resume it. In short, the Japanese government denounced Communist China-backed North Vietnam's stubborn rejection of U.S. peace efforts. At the directors' meeting of the United Nations Security Council in February, Japanese Ambassador to the United Nations Akira Matsui, who was the chairman of the council for February, tried to win support from member countries for his proposal for an early peace in Vietnam and for the convocation of a peace conference in line with the 1945 Geneva Agreement.

Matsui's efforts to make his peace proposal in the form of a declaration by the chairman failed, and it was made in the form of a circular. It was apparent that he tried his utmost to back up the U.S. efforts to bring about peace in Vietnam. Assistant Secretary of State Bundy who came to Japan on February 22 conveyed the United States government's gratitude to the Japanese government for its efforts to back up the U.S. peace moves. Matsui's endeavors in the United Nations won praise from the United States Ambassador to the United Nations Arthur Goldberg at a New York press conference on February 28, while on March 4 United States Ambassador Reischauer conveyed the United States government's gratitude to the Japanese government upon instructions from Washington.

Japan's cooperation with the United States is often criticized by the Socialists and other left-wingers and progressive intellectuals as servitude to the United States. Their way of thinking must be condemned as servile. Diplomacy must be conducted to safeguard national interests. So, it is possible for the government to follow the United States for the sake of national interests, depending on circumstances. Such an attitude, therefore, does not run counter to Japan's autonomy and independence.

I recall the days when Japan concluded an alliance with

Great Britain. The Anglo-Japanese Alliance which remained in force from the Meiji era through the Taisho era was comparable to the Japan-United States Security Treaty of today.

The Japan-United States Security Treaty aims at mutual defense of Japan, under which Japan is obligated to offer land, facilities, and service, while the United States is obligated to dispatch armed forces. It is wrong for us to argue about "autonomy" or "equality" in the case of an agreement like the Japan-United States Security Treaty which pledges cooperation between countries sharing the same interests in international politics.

I have heard that some people in the United States denounce the treaty as a one-sided obligation in that it is aimed at defending the territory of Japan. People are said to be demanding that Japan's obligations be increased and its military defense power strengthened. At any rate, Japan-United States relations firmly united under the existing security treaty will remain unchanged as long as the present international situation continues. It should not be changed, either. Since this treaty is purely defensive in nature, it does not hamper the promotion of friendship between Japan and the Soviet Union or Japan's efforts to remove stumbling blocks in relations with Communist China.

I am dreaming about the day when a collective security setup involving Japan, the United States, Communist China, and the Soviet Union will be established in the Asia-Pacific area to replace the Japan-United States Security Treaty. I should like to stress that the Japan-United States Security Treaty setup is essential so that Japan can pursue an independent diplomacy toward realization of such a collective security system. (March, 1966)

CHAPTER 11

Russo-Japanese Relations

Friendly Mood and Confrontation

THE RECENT heightening of the friendly mood between Japan and the Soviet Union is a pleasing phenomenon. A similar mood prevailed ten years ago when the two countries resumed normal diplomatic relations, but it did not last long. Therefore, it should be recognized beforehand that the present friendly mood will have its limitations too.

This is because a settlement of the cold war between the Free World and the communist bloc is still far off and because Japan and the Soviet Union actually are in confrontation with respect to the balance of power in the Far East where the Japan-United States Security Treaty and the Soviet-Communist China Treaty of Friendship, Alliance, and Mutual Assistance are in operation.

Upon her unconditional surrender at the end of World War II, Japan became a vacuum in international politics and, inevitably, the United States and the Soviet Union raced against each other to fill the vacuum. Fortunately, respective disposition of American and Russian troops at that time made it possible for the United States alone to occupy the whole country. Japan was saved from being split into two, thanks primarily to General Douglas MacArthur's summary rejection of the Soviet proposal to send its troops into Hokkaido.

The clashes over occupation policy between the Russians,

139

the Americans, and other Western Allies in the Far East Commission in Washington and the Allied Council for Japan in Tokyo, and the Soviet attempts to Bolshevize Japan are still fresh in our memories.

When the communist regime was established in mainland China, the Soviet Union concluded the above mentioned military alliance with it and, at the same time, instigated North Korea to start the Korean War. Soon afterward, the United States took the initiative in concluding the Peace Treaty with Japan, but the Soviet Union refused to sign the treaty, being dissatisfied with the territorial provisions concerning Southern Sakhalin and the Kurile Islands.

When Japan, thus, concluded the peace treaty with the majority of the Allied powers, the United States concluded the security treaty with Japan. When a truce was realized in the Korean War, the cold war in the Far East also temporarily came to a state of lull. It was at this time that the Hatoyama Cabinet keenly felt the need of terminating the state of war prevailing between Japan and the Soviet Union.

With many important problems pending between the two countries, such as the issue concerning Japanese detainees in the Soviet Union and fisheries issues, there was a need for Japan to open a way for direct discussions with the Soviet government for early solution of these urgent problems. Furthermore, the Soviet Union was exercising its veto power to block Japan's entry into the United Nations, and Japan needed an avenue of direct approach to the Soviet government in order to make it abstain from using the veto so that Japan could join the international society.

The two countries shortly afterward began negotiations for re-establishing normal relations. Japan succeeded in obtaining Soviet agreement that the talks should be conducted without reference to the Japan-United States Security Treaty and that the Soviet Union would not only refrain from opposing Japan's admission into the United Nations but also would support Japan's entry.

However, the Soviet Union did not make any concessions on the so-called northern territorial dispute concerning Southern Sakhalin and the Kuriles. The two countries shelved the territorial issue lest they delay the resumption of normal relations for a long period of time. In October, 1956, an agreement was reached and the two countries signed the Joint Declaration, under which they resumed normal diplomatic relations.

In the declaration, the two countries confirmed they would refrain from the threat of use of force in any manner, a principle contained in the United Nations Charter. The two countries also confirmed the principle of nonintervention in each other's domestic affairs. They agreed that they would continue negotiations for a peace treaty and the Soviet Union promised to return to Japan Habomai and Shikotan islands after such a treaty has been concluded.

This relationship between Japan and the Soviet Union, however, was aggravated in 1960 when Japan and the United States revised the security treaty. The Soviet Union, together with Communist China, actively called on Japan to take a neutral policy. When the revised Japan-United States Security Treaty was signed, the Soviet Union, completely in disregard of the Joint Declaration, made a unilateral declaration that it would not return Habomai and Shikotan islands until after foreign troops have withdrawn from Japan, even if a peace treaty were signed between Japan and the Soviet Union.

It was at this time that the Soviet Union threatened Japan on several occasions saying that Japan might be in danger of atomic bombings just like Hiroshima and Nagasaki as long as Japan continued to allow foreign troops to use bases in Japan.

It is needless to say that such threats served to encourage the movements to oppose the revision of the Japan-United States security pact which threw the country into confusion. It is obvious that such threats constitute a violation of the nonintervention principle of the Joint Declaration.

The relations between Japan and the Soviet Union improved again later because of the progress toward United States-Soviet peaceful coexistence and the intensification of the confrontation between Moscow and Peking. However, it should be noted, that no moves have been made to hold negotiations for a peace treaty, which was agreed upon in the Joint Declaration. This is because Japan takes the stand that the northern territorial issue, as a matter of course, should be taken up at such talks, while the Soviet Union stubbornly insists that the issue has already been settled.

Northern Territorial Issue

Item C, Article 2 of the San Francisco Peace Treaty provides merely that Japan renounces all rights, title, and claim to the Kuriles and part of Sakhalin and its surrounding islands over which it obtained sovereignty under the 1905 Portsmouth Peace Treaty. The item does not stipulate to which country such areas belong, because the Allied Powers including the Soviet Union had failed to reach agreement on the extent of the territories to be renounced by Japan.

The Soviet Union refused to sign the San Francisco Peace Treaty because it was dissatisfied with the decision to carry over the territorial issue. At the San Francisco negotiations, the Soviet delegation bitterly denounced Japan as an aggressor and demanded that the peace treaty plainly define that Southern Sakhalin and the Kuriles belong to the Soviet Union, contending that Japan had taken possession of such areas through aggression.

The Japanese delegation refuted that the Soviet accusation was completely unfounded. The Japanese delegation pointed out that even Tsarist Russia had raised no objections to the Japanese claim that Kunashiri and Etorofu islands were, at the time Japan was opened to foreign intercourse, Japanese territories. The Japanese delegation emphasized that Habomai and Shikotan islands were part of Hokkaido but that the islands were occupied by the Soviet Union only because there were Japanese military facilities on the islands at the time of Japan's surrender.

Even before the San Francisco negotiations, the Soviet Union was making one-sided attacks against what it termed Japanese aggression. This selfish attitude on the part of the Russians may in a way be attributable to the fact that the Japanese government neither raised any objections nor protested against the unilateral ruling of the International Military Tribunal for the Far East that Japan was responsible for the war.

The military tribunal, presumably having a regard for the feelings of the Soviet judge, ruled that Japan had invaded the Soviet Union, completely in disregard of the fact that it was the Soviet Union which unilaterally abrogated the Soviet-Japanese Treaty of Neutrality during the latter part of the war and launched attacks against Japanese troops.

The military tribunal also ignored the fact that the Japan-Germany-Italy tripartite alliance contained an article which excluded the Soviet Union from the area to which the treaty was applicable and that Japan stubbornly rejected repeated requests by Germany that it should attack the Soviet Union. Such being the situation, the Soviet accusation that Japan was guilty of aggression against the Russians cannot be recognized. It should be noted in passing that Nikolai Lenin highly evaluated the significance of the Russo-Japanese War (1904–5) as having dealt a severe blow to Tsarist Russia.

However, the late Joseph Stalin during World War II appealed to the Russians to take revenge on the Japanese for the Russo-Japanese War and tried to revive the situation which prevailed before the 1904–5 war by abrogating the Portsmouth Peace Treaty. As these instances show, Russia has always kept its hands off a strong country, but if it considered a country to be weak it would immediately push forward.

As far as this expansionism is concerned, there is no difference between the Tsarist regime and the present regime. Therefore, even if a country concludes a neutrality treaty or a nonaggression treaty with Russia, it could not rest easy because Russia does not observe such a treaty faithfully as do the United States and Great Britain.

The dispute over the northern territories revolves around the ownership of the Kuriles. Japan takes the stand that the Kurile Islands extend as far south as Urup Island but no farther. As mentioned earlier, the Russo-Japanese Treaty of Amity, concluded in 1855 when Japan was opened to foreign intercourse, stipulated that the border between Japan and Russia lies between Urup Island (Russian territory) and Etorofu Island (Japanese territory). The treaty stated that the islands lying north of Urup Island belonged to Russia.

The 1874 treaty providing for the exchange of the Kuriles and Sakhalin stipulated that the eighteen islands extending as far south as Urup Island and as far north as Shumshu Island are called the Kurile Islands. These treaties plainly prove that the Kunashiri and Etorofu islands were not part of the Kuriles, not to speak of the Habomai and Shikotan islands.

During the negotiations for normalizing relations, the Japanese delegation pointed out that the Kunashiri and Etorofu islands were historically Japanese territory and that these islands should not be handed over to the Soviet Union. Soviet attention was called to the principle of nonexpansion contained in the Atlantic Charter and the Cairo Declaration. The United States during the San Francisco Peace Treaty talks assumed the same stand as Japan concerning the Habomai and Shikotan islands.

As for the Kunashiri and Etorofu islands, the United States in the so-called John Foster Dulles memorandum of 1956 said that the islands should be placed under Japanese sovereignty. On the other hand, the Soviet Union contends that the northern territorial issue had already been settled under the Yalta

Agreement. However, there is no reason why Japan, which was not a signatory nation, should be bound by the agreement.

The Dulles memorandum plainly explained that the Yalta Agreement concluded by the United States, the Soviet Union, and Great Britain, is simply a statement of common purposes by the heads of the three participating powers and is not in itself an instrument with legal effect.

It seems that the northern territorial issue will require a long period of time to solve and that there is no alternative for Japan but to continue its efforts patiently. It is to be noted that when Foreign Minister Shiina visited the Soviet Union in January, 1966, there was no change in Moscow's stand on the matter.

It is said that there is a possibility that the Soviet Union will retain the Kunashiri and Etorofu islands as well as the Habomai and Shikotan islands for strategic considerations so long as the cold war between the West and the East continues, relating this issue to the occupation by the United States of Okinawa and Bonin (Ogasawara) islands.

The Soviet Union is saddled with a far bigger territorial problem which concerns Germany. If the Soviet Union yields even an inch in its territorial disputes with Japan, it will be placed in a disadvantageous position concerning the German territorial problem. This is another reason why the Soviet Union has been showing no signs of making concessions and sticking firmly to its established policy as far as the northern territorial issue is concerned.

Russo-Japanese Trade and Development of Siberia

With respect to the economic exchange, which should be an important factor in the friendly relations between Japan and the Soviet Union, there has been no appreciable increase shown recently. Under a new five-year agreement signed in

Moscow in January, 1966, the two countries set a conservative trade target of slightly more than $400 million a year both ways.

Most of the Japanese exports are industrial goods, while most of the Soviet exports are raw materials. One of the major obstacles in Russo-Japanese trade is the fact that the Soviet Union can offer only a few items which Japan wants to import. Of the four major Soviet export items—lumber, petroleum, coal, and pig iron—Japan plans to increase imports of petroleum particularly. But there is a limit to the amount that can be shipped from ports along the Black Sea.

And so long as Japan cannot increase its imports, it cannot expect an increase in its exports because Russo-Japanese trade is carried out under the principle of balanced imports and exports. A promising factor which can break the stagnation is the Soviet Union's Siberian development plan, which is part of the Soviet Union's new five-year economic program, begun in 1966. At the first meeting of the Japan-Soviet Joint Economic Committee held in Tokyo from March 14 to 23, 1966, both delegations held concrete discussions on the program. The joint committee was established in line with the Japanese government's policy of holding periodical consultations with business leaders of countries trading with Japan with a view to solving pending problems and promoting economic relations.

Similar committees had been established between Japan and the United States, Great Britain, France, Italy, Canada, India, and the Republic of Korea. These joint committees aim at discussing from a free position any problems which cannot be taken up at government meetings. Another advantage of the committees is that delegations made up of business leaders will be able to discuss problems from the point of view of national interests without being bound by the interests of specific industries.

However, before proposing the Japan-Soviet Joint Committee, the Japanese government had doubts whether this formula would bring about any practical results because the political and social systems of the Soviet Union differ completely from those of Japan.

After having the Foreign Office and other government agencies concerned look into the possibilities, the Japanese government reached the conclusion that such a joint committee would be helpful not only in developing Japan's trade markets, but also in promoting further the diplomatic relations between the two countries.

Thus, the first meeting of the Japan-Soviet Joint Committee was held. The Soviet delegation was headed by Mikhail V. Nesterov, president of the All-Soviet Chamber of Commerce, and made up of leading officials of government offices and agencies concerned with economic affairs. The Japanese delegation was headed by Tadashi Adachi, president of the Chamber of Commerce and Industry, and was composed of leaders of industrial and financial circles.

With both delegations exchanging candid views, the meeting was said to have been helpful in deepening mutual understanding on how Russo-Japanese trade should be carried out in the future. Among the main points disclosed at the meeting were that the Soviet Union assumes a very positive attitude toward development of western Siberia and the Far East, and that it pins great hopes on Japanese economic cooperation.

The Soviet Union proposed adoption of the so-called PS (Production Sharing) method, through which Japanese exports would be paid for with products to be developed under the Siberian program under a deferred payment system. The Soviet Union revealed that it is prepared to export machinery under a deferred payment system.

Thus the Tokyo meeting provided a footing for the future expansion of Russo-Japanese trade.

However, many doubtful points remain in connection with detailed problems and the views of the two countries are still wide apart on many points. For example, the Soviet Union revealed at the meeting that its Siberian development pro-

gram covers western Siberia east of the Ural Mountains, eastern Siberia, and the Far East. This scope was far wider than
expected by the Japanese. Japanese business circles expected
Japanese cooperation to cover only the Far East and Sakhalin.

In fact, the Soviet Union hitherto had exerted considerable
efforts in the development of Siberia, but they had not brought
about the desired results. Therefore, it may be said that it
will be impossible for Japan to extend cooperation until after
the Soviet Union has laid down closely woven plans explaining in detail how it intends to carry out the Siberian development project.

Siberia is blessed with almost inexhaustible resources of
iron, nonferrous metals, coal, water, and lumber. Recently
resources of petroleum and natural gas were discovered in
western Siberia. However, there is a serious shortage of manpower in Siberia east of the Ural Mountains with the population in the vast area totaling only twenty million. Transportation facilities are inadequate in the area and the climate is
severe with the mercury dropping to fifty degrees centigrade
below zero on many days during the long winter season.

As for the development-and-import system, there is nothing
wrong with the PS formula itself. However, it is not in accordance with international custom for the Soviet Union to
propose that it be allowed to pay for Japanese steel tubes for
use in pipelines, with petroleum products to be developed
under the project under a twenty-year deferred payment
system. Such a formula is disadvantageous to Japan whose
financial ability is limited.

If the Soviet Union intention is to construct metal and
chemical factories as part of its development project, it should
realize that there is not much possibility of Japan importing
aluminum or fertilizers.

On the other hand, Japan earnestly hopes that the Soviet
Union will develop copper mines, but the Soviet Union is not
very enthusiastic.

The Tokyo meeting issued a joint communique in which

Japan and the Soviet Union expressed their views about development of oil wells, copper resources in Siberia, and natural gas in Sakhalin. Japan strongly proposed that the communique should note that the development of the natural gas in Sakhalin would be the touchstone of Japan-Soviet economic cooperation, and that Japan is deeply interested in the development of copper resources in the Udokan area. The Soviet side raised no objection to the former proposal because the Russo-Japanese Trade Agreement contained an article to that effect. The Soviet side, however, hesitated to accept the latter proposal maintaining that it was planning to develop copper resources under the five-year program only for domestic use. But it finally accepted Japan's proposal.

The joint communique briefly mentioned the development of oil wells in Siberia and establishment of pipelines because both sides agreed that they should discuss the matter after the Soviet Union has worked out concrete plans.

Anyway, Japan should not be overly optimistic regarding Siberian development. Japan should keep in mind that the Soviet Union's basic principle is to carry out the Siberian development project independently as far as possible. Although it hopes for Japanese cooperation, it intends to accept such cooperation as a supplement to the Russian efforts.

Now that the Soviet Union has only one negotiation window in dealing with the vast development program, the Japanese side should also establish a negotiation setup which conforms to such a situation so that Japanese enterprises would not engage in self-competition. The consequence of unwarranted competition will be that they will be compelled to agree to disadvantageous terms in concluding contracts.

Japan and the Soviet Union are now conducting negotiations of fishing operations in the North Pacific, which experienced rough sailing. They were concluded recently and Soviet Fishery Minister Alexander A. Ishkov will visit Japan during the middle part of June to sign the treaty.

On the other hand, the negotiations in Moscow between

Japan and the Soviet Union for a consular treaty are expected to be concluded shortly. The Soviet Foreign Minister Andrei A. Gromyko is scheduled to visit Japan during the latter part of July to sign the treaty.

Under a civil aviation treaty signed in January, a plane carrying the mark of Japan Air Lines and Aeroflot, the Soviet state-operated air carrier, is expected to fly over Siberia on the Moscow-Tokyo route in June. After that, planes operated jointly by the two flag carriers will serve the direct Tokyo-Moscow route once a week.

In November, a Soviet trade fair will be held in Osaka and a large-scale mission headed by the chairman of Gosplan, Soviet State Planning Committee, or a person equivalent to deputy premier, is expected to visit Japan.

With such economic exchange as a shaft, the relations between Japan and the Soviet Union are about to enter into a new stage. However, the Russo-Japanese economic relations should not cause Japan to neglect economic exchange with countries in the Free World. Japan should recognize its position as a member of the Free World, fully taking into consideration today's international situation.

The 23rd Communist Party Congress and Profit-Allowing Formula

The Soviet Communist Party held its 23rd congress for 11 days beginning March 29. The congress attracted the attention of the whole world because of various factors: it was the first to be held under the regime of Leonid I. Brezhnev, First Secretary of the Party, and Alexei N. Kosygin, Premier, who came into power after the downfall of Nikita Khrushchev; the international situation was strained because of the Vietnam war, and Communist China boycotted the congress with the communist parties of Albania, New Zealand, and Japan.

According to the rules of the Soviet Communist Party, the

party is to hold a congress once or more than once every four years. This means that the 23rd congress was held belatedly because the 22nd congress was held in October, 1961.

Pravda said that the 23rd congress would mark a new step in Soviet economic development aimed at constructing a communist society. Domestic problems such as a five-year people's economic plan beginning this year and a reshuffle in the central organs of the party were taken up as main subjects for discussion. It is needless to say, however, that the international situation, including the Vietnam war, United States-Soviet relations, Communist China-Soviet relations, and German problems, were taken up as important subjects.

With fifty years having elapsed since the revolution, various contradictions have appeared in many phases of planned socialist economy. Bureaucratic red tape has brought to a standstill the centralized production management structure. The backwardness of agriculture necessitated the import of nearly 10 million tons of wheat to tide over a poor harvest. The people are no longer satisfied with a consumer economy which forces them to share poverty. There are no bright prospects for a favorable turn in the confrontation between the Soviet Union and Communist China, and the Soviet Union finds itself in a dilemma which compels it to compete against the United States in defense and space development projects.

In contrast to the showy policies of former Premier Khrushchev, the Brezhnev-Kosygin regime has been assuming a modest posture and exerting efforts to revise the Khrushchev policies. For example, the new five-year plan adopted at the congress estimates a relatively modest increase rate in industrial production. The increase had been set at more than 8 per cent a year under the old seven-year plan which ended last year. However, the rate for the first year of the new five-year plan was set at 6.7 per cent.

The decrease in the estimated increase rate in the industrial production also is attributable to the fact that the Brezhnev-Kosygin regime adopted new business management systems, including the idea of allowing profit-taking, by rectifying the old policy of placing emphasis only on increasing the quantity of industrial production. The adoption of the new systems is aimed at improving the quality of industrial products.

The idea of allowing profit-taking indeed is an epochal change in the Soviet business management policy. With the number of industrial enterprises having increased to 200 thousand producing 20 million different kinds of goods, it has become extremely difficult to organize production, distribution, and consumption in a planned manner.

As a result, targets for plans have been set recklessly and this has made it all the more difficult to control the economy. As a means of overcoming the difficulty, the authorities have begun to recognize the need to allow enterprises to have independence or autonomy so that they can exercise their initiative. The need to give material impetus to workers in order to raise their will for production was also recognized. Before then, a group of "reformist" scholars, headed by Professor Lieberman at Kharkov Technical College, had advocated a new system under which the profit rate would be the only index showing the business records of enterprises.

The Central Committee of the Soviet Communist Party at a meeting in September, 1965, decided to adopt the system as a means of invigorating Soviet enterprises.

Under the formula advocated by the group, business records of enterprises will be evaluated with the profit rate instead of the gross production as in the past. Under the system, enterprises will be given greater independence and autonomy and urged to place importance on profits, while indexes for plans will be set only for key projects. When enterprises produce commodities, which are highly demanded by the consumers, and raise their profit rate, distribution of profits to such companies will be increased. In other words, the system is aimed at giving an impetus to workers' will for production and, thereby, raising the efficiency of the national economy as a whole.

According to a report by Premier Kosygin to the party congress, the new system is proving a success in many enterprises. It is said that the new system will be applied to one-third of the total industrial workers by early next year.

The agricultural industry has been an "Achilles' tendon" in the Soviet economy since the Khrushchev era. Stagnation of the industry was one of the major factors which caused the downfall of Khrushchev.

In the new five-year plan, the target for agricultural production is set at a level which is 25 per cent higher than the average annual production during the preceding five years. During the seven-year plan which ended last year, the agricultural production remained almost on the same level, and the production in the fiscal year 1964, the year of the best harvest during the seven-year period, was an increase of only 12 per cent over the fiscal year 1963, which had the worst harvest. This indicates how serious the agricultural problem is in the Soviet Union.

In order to raise the farmers' will for production, the Soviet government previously had taken various measures, such as raising the government purchase price of agricultural products and easing of restrictions on the utilization of privately owned fields. Under the new five-year plan, state investment in the agricultural industry has been doubled. One of the major targets of the plan is rationalization of agricultural work by mechanization in order to relieve farmers of hard manual labor.

Some quarters attach importance to these economic reforms including the adoption of the system of allowing profit-taking and regard the reforms as being just as epochal as the introduction of new economic policies by Nikolai Lenin or as a turning point in the history of communism. Of course, the idea of allowing profit-taking is different from the idea of profit-taking under capitalism. And it is extremely difficult for the Soviet Union to consolidate price structures needed for allowing profit-taking. Therefore, it is not proper to interpret the profit-taking system as an indication that Soviet economy is creeping toward capitalism.

However, once the Soviet government has allowed profit-taking, there is the possibility of the government recognizing or allowing individuals to use their initiative and ingenuity as a second step, and, thus, virtually drawing near to the systems of countries in the Free World. And if such changes in policies prove to be a wonder-working medicine for a high growth rate in the Soviet economy, the changes might possibly have effect in some way or other on the Soviet political system.

Anyway, the new policy of the Soviet Union is expected to greatly encourage Czechoslovakia and other countries in Eastern Europe which have been conducting similar experiments on a larger scale. But, on the other hand, Communist China, which follows a dogmatic line, is expected to launch intensified attacks against the Soviet Union, denouncing the adoption of the new policy as the decadence of socialism.

At the party congress, the presidium of the Central Committee was renamed the Politburo and the position of the first secretary of the party was renamed general secretary with First Secretary Brezhnev being appointed general secretary. The change in the title attracted wide attention because it represents a return to the title used during the Stalin regime and because new General Secretary Brezhnev seems to have solidified further his position as the man with the highest authority.

However, the new party leadership under Brezhnev is expected to continue entrusting Premier Kosygin with the task of controlling the government and to retain the collective leadership system supported by Kosygin, Nikolai V. Podgorny, chairman of the Supreme Soviet, and Mikhail A. Suslov and Alexander N. Shelepin, both members of the Politburo and the Politburo-Secretariat.

Peaceful Coexistence

It seems necessary to examine the peaceful coexistence policy of the Soviet Union which was discussed at the 23rd party congress.

The peaceful coexistence policy, which is the basic political line, at first was laid down by Khrushchev and was continued by the Brezhnev-Kosygin regime. Noteworthy is that Brezhnev in his report to the congress said that the Soviet Union will stick firmly to the policy of peaceful coexistence with countries whose political systems differ from that of the Soviet Union. However, he emphasized that there is no room for peaceful coexistence in national liberation struggles.

The Soviet Union follows this line with great confidence despite its confrontation with Communist China. This confidence was strengthened further by the fact that communist and socialist parties of eighty-six countries sent delegations to the congress—especially by the fact that North Vietnam, the Viet Cong, and North Korea sent delegations.

It is beyond doubt that North Vietnam and the Viet Cong are grateful to the Soviet Union for its military and economic assistance to fight through the Vietnam war. North Korea also had received a large amount of aid from the Soviet Union and moreover it borders on the Soviet Union. In other words, the leaders of Asian communist countries do not have an ill-feeling toward Moscow.

Forming the core of the Soviet-Communist China antagonism is the confrontation between the Soviet world policy of peaceful coexistence and the Communist Chinese world policy of emphasizing wars of national liberation. The Moscow-Peking confrontation during the past two or three years passed beyond the stage of an ideological dispute between the communist parties of the two countries and developed into an issue involving practical policies. The confrontation has intensified further over the Vietnam war, as recognized even by the two communist parties themselves.

Therefore, it is not accidental that Communist China recently attacked the growing contacts between the Soviet Union and Japan, relating it to the Vietnam war.

Communist China bitterly criticized the Japan-Soviet joint communique, which was issued when Japanese Foreign Minister Etsusaburo Shiina visited the Soviet Union in January, 1966, because the communique did not attack the United States in connection with the Vietnam war but said briefly that the Vietnam war was a threat to peace.

The *Peking People's Daily* in its February 2 issue charged that the Japan-Soviet approach had been made in compliance with the scheme of American imperialism to encircle Communist China. The paper also charged that the fact that the Soviet leaders had been strengthening their collusion with the reactionary elements in Japan is an important link in the Soviet plot to control the world through the concord with the United States.

However, it is beyond doubt that the Soviet Union hopes that Japan will abrogate the Japan-United State Security Treaty, extricate itself from the United States influence, and follow a neutral line. On the other hand, it also is beyond doubt that the Japan-United States Security Treaty is an eyesore on the part of Communist China which is immerced in its confrontation with American imperialism.

Such being the situation, it is not inconceivable that the Soviet Union is taking at face value Communist Chinese criticism of Moscow. The Communist Chinese charge that the Soviet Union is taking part in the United States policy of encircling Communist China must sound nonsensical to Moscow. It is to be pointed out that the Soviet Union, taking every occasion possible, has emphasized the existence and significance of the Soviet-Red China Treaty of Friendship, Alliance, and Mutual Assistance, which some quarters say had already been invalidated because of intensifying Moscow-Peking antagonism.

On February 24, which was the 16th anniversary of the conclusion of the treaty, *Pravda* and other newspapers in chorus carried commemorative articles about the treaty. At the latest party congress, Brezhnev said in his report that the Soviet Communist Party is always mindful of strengthening its defense capability and military alliances with other socialist countries.

According to Brezhnev, the United States-Soviet peaceful coexistence of today is in a "frozen state" because of American "acts of aggression" in Vietnam. Concerning the Vietnam war, the Soviet Union assumes a considerably rigid stand that it would not respond to United States appeal for discussion of the Vietnam problems until after the four conditions including withdrawal of United States troops from Vietnam, which were laid down by North Vietnam, have been fulfilled.

The fundamental reason for the Soviet Union daring to switch to the peaceful coexistence policy during the Khrushchev regime was nothing but a recognition of the absolute need of evading total nuclear war. Therefore, it may be said that the Soviet Union still wants to retain the coexistence policy. It is to be pointed out that, despite the Vietnam problem, the Soviet Union recently has concluded the fourth cultural exchange agreement with the United States, and at the Geneva Disarmament Conference it is continuing its effort toward prevention of proliferation of nuclear weapons and an overall nuclear test ban.

However, if the Soviet peaceful coexistence policy is based on the so-called balance of terror stemming from the threat of total nuclear war, there is the possibility that the *raison d'être* of the peaceful coexistence policy will end at the very moment when and if by chance the West loses its determination of nuclear defense or its defense capability.

This possibility should be pointed out as a warning to those shortsighted persons who do not pay attention to the "balance of power" and the "balance of terror" factors which are both decisive in international politics today and to the so-called pacifists who shut their eyes to such decisive factors. (April, 1966)

CHAPTER **12**

Free Asia and Japan (I)

World Peace and Regional Collective Organization

To WITNESS my long-cherished vision of a regional collective organization among the free nations in Asia and the Pacific area taking a concrete shape is a source of deep personal satisfaction. Such an organization is necessary not only to strengthen the security and prosperity of the nations but is also a contributing factor in consolidating the foundations of world peace.

Although, as is generally known, the United Nations exists as an international peace organization, it must solve a large number of important problems before it will be able to fully carry out its great mission. In these circumstances, I believe that the formation of a regional collective organization to serve as an intermediate body between such a world organization as the United Nations and various racial groupings among the member nations is a dictate of history.

Chapter 8 of the Charter of the United Nations stipulates that "nothing in the present chapter precludes the existence of regional arrangements or agencies for dealing with such matters relating to the maintenance of international peace and security as are appropriate for regional action. . . ." The chapter also states that it encourages the development of such regional arrangements or agencies, provided that they are consistent with the purposes and principles of the United Nations.

The world today is precariously maintaining peace by the balance of power between the free nations and the communist bloc, or by the so-called nuclear stalemate between the United States and the Soviet Union. In Europe there is a more relaxed mood in the relations between Western and Eastern Europe, giving rise to hopes that the cold war is finally thawing.

In Asia, on the other hand, the Vietnam war and the Mao Tse-tung-Lin Piao line of policy in Communist China have sharply aggravated the relations between the United States and Communist China, sending dark clouds hovering over the entire expanse of Asia. By continuing to explode one nuclear device after another, Communist China is outstripping Great Britain and France in the field of nuclear weaponry in an effort to become the world's third nuclear power. Thus, the path to peace remains precipitous and even appears to be fading away.

The differences between Europe and Asia can ultimately be attributed to the degree of security in the power balance of the two contending sides. In Europe, the balance of power over the entire continent is being maintained by NATO (North Atlantic Treaty Organization), comprising the free nations, and the Warsaw Treaty Organization, comprising the communist bloc. This idea of a regional collective organization has respectively developed into the Atlantic community and the Socialist community.

These regional collective organizations are, of course, discharging their functions as collective security organizations but are backed by such economic regional collective organizations as the EEC (European Economic Community) and COMECON (Council for Mutual Economic Assistance).

In the case of the EEC, it is now directing its efforts from economic unification to political integration, as well as toward its amalgamation with EFTA (European Free Trade Association), including Great Britain, and there is no doubt that this movement constitutes the fundamental basis for present-day European stability.

On the contrary, the situation is very fluid in Asia where the balance of power between the contending Free World and communist bloc powers is not as solidified as in Europe. In Asia there exist collective security organizations concluded on a bilateral basis between the United States on the one hand, and Japan, Korea, Taiwan, and the Philippines, on the other, as well as the broader based treaties of SEATO and ANZUS (mutual defense treaty among Australia, New Zealand, and the United States).

Within the communist bloc, there are the treaties between Communist China and the Soviet Union, Communist China and North Korea, and the Soviet Union and North Korea. However, with the exception of Japan the countries of Asia are in the developing stage, characterized by political and economic frictions and unrest. To overcome these difficulties, there is a pressing need to form a regional collective organization, but its formation is seriously hampered by the existence of these frictions and disturbances.

The situation has been undergoing a drastic change since the September 30 abortive *coup d'état* in Indonesia which completely ousted the procommunist elements from power and injected a favorable factor for the rapid formation of a regional collective organization in Asia. This reversal of Indonesia's attitude struck a decisive blow at the growing strength of Communist China in Southeast Asia, leading to a peaceful settlement of the three-year old Indonesia-Malaysia dispute and producing an epoch-making transformation in the entire political picture of Asia. Consequently, there has been a significant and spontaneous move toward friendlier ties between the noncommunist nations in the Asian and Pacific regions.

One tangible example of this change of mood was the resurrection of ASA (Association of Southeast Asia), which had been in a state of lapse for three years, at the Third Foreign Ministers Conference held in Bangkok in August, 1966, attended by Thailand, the Philippines, and Malaysia. Although ASA is primarily a regional collective organization for promoting economic activities, the three nations issued an appeal to other Asian nations for the establishment of an Asian peace committee aimed at settling the war in Vietnam.

Earlier, in April of the same year, Japan hosted in Tokyo the Southeast Asian Ministerial Conference for Economic Development, the largest postwar international conference ever sponsored by Japan, attended by ministers of Japan, the Philippines, Thailand, Malaysia, Singapore, South Vietnam, and Laos, and observers from Indonesia and Cambodia. This conference was followed in June by the Asian and Pacific Ministerial Conference on Economic and Cultural Cooperation, sponsored by South Korea in Seoul, and attended by South Korea, Japan, Nationalist China, the Philippines, Thailand, Malaysia, South Vietnam, Australia, and New Zealand, with Laos as an observer.

The Tokyo conference of ministers was imbued with an unprecedented spirit of regional cooperation with Prime Minister Phouma of Laos suggesting the formation of an "Asian Federation" and other delegates proposing concrete measures for economic and technical cooperation, such as the convening of the Agricultural Development Conference, the establishment of the Economic Development Center, Economic Development Promotion Center, the Marine Product and Fishery Development Center, and the Southeast Asia University. The participants also agreed to hold the second conference in Manila in 1967.

The Asian and Pacific Ministerial Conference in Seoul, on the other hand, stressing the joint objective of achieving peace, freedom, and prosperity among the peoples of Asia and the Pacific region, decided to hold the next conference in Bangkok in 1967 and to call on the other noncommunist countries in the region to participate in the collective endeavor.

In the case of ASA, which had been the subject of discussion before and after the Bangkok conference, proposals were advanced by President Marcos and Foreign Minister Ramos of the Philippines, Prime Minister Thanom and Foreign Minister Thanat of Thailand, and Prime Minister Rahman and Deputy Prime Minister Razak of Malaysia for the formation of a "New Southeast Asian Federation," or "Asian Federation."

Meanwhile, the idea of "Maphilindo," comprising Malaysia, the Philippines, and Indonesia, is again seeing the light of day, but Foreign Minister Adam Malik of Indonesia has already made it clear that he desires a concept of unity covering a much broader area.

Formation of Free Asia and Japan

For the United States, imbedded in the morass of the Vietnam war, the changing situation in Asia must have offered hope and promise. After attending a series of important conferences in June and July of last year in the Asian and Pacific regions, such as the SEATO and ANZUS councils and the Joint Japan-United States Committee on Trade and Economic Affairs, United States Secretary of State Dean Rusk declared that behind the shield of the Vietnam war waged by the United States, the countries of Free Asia have been rapidly advancing toward economic and political stability.

On the basis of his report to President Johnson, the President and Secretary of State Rusk on July 12, 1966, announced a new concept of American policy applicable to the whole of Asia rather than being limited to the Vietnam issue. This announcement aroused widespread interest not only in the United States but also in other parts of the world.

In a television speech delivered to the American Alumni Council at White Sulphur Springs, West Virginia, on July 12, 1966, President Johnson laid great stress on United States policy toward Asia and appealed for public support. While declaring that the United States is a Pacific power, the President was firm in his determination to honor America's commitments to defend the freedom and security of free nations in Asia. He also emphasized the significance of the formation of a new Asia behind his nation's efforts in South Vietnam, and warmly praised this new Asian development.

In his message to the nations of the Pacific region, President Johnson proclaimed: "They claim that we have no business but business interests in Asia; that Europe, not the Far East, is our proper 'sphere of interest.' These arguments have been tested, and found wanting. They do not stand the test of geography: we are bounded not by one but two oceans—and whether by aircraft or ship, satellite or missile, the Pacific is as crossable as the Atlantic. They do not stand the test of human concern: the people of Asia matter—we share with them a common humanity. Asia is no longer sitting outside the door of the 20th century. She is here, in the same world with us, to be either our partner or our problem."

Referring to the formation of new Asia, the President said: "In the last year, Communist China's policy of aggression by proxy has begun to show signs of failing. One country after another has achieved rates of economic growth beyond the most optimistic hopes of a few years ago. Japan and Korea have settled their long-standing disputes and established normal relations with promise of closer cooperation. Japan has become a dramatic example of economic progress through political and social freedom and has begun to help others. Throughout free Asia you can hear the echo of progress."

Similarly, Secretary of State Dean Rusk, at a news conference on July 12, 1966, stated that from Australia in the south to Japan and Korea in the north, he felt that new winds were blowing. He made special reference to the rising unity of the free nations and the mounting interest in regional cooperation by the nations of the entire region.

Secretary Rusk cited three fundamental factors contributing to the new winds in Asia, the first being the fact that the nations of the western Pacific are showing deeper concern about their security and peace. Second, they are making rapid strides economically as well as socially, and third, these nations are moving rapidly toward regional cooperation.

Concerning Japan, Rusk said that the country, on the threshold of becoming the world's third largest industrial power, was playing an increasingly constructive role in the affairs of the western Pacific and the Free World generally.

As borne out by the statements of these two American leaders, it is an undeniable source of satisfaction to recognize that the accent of the domestic and foreign policy of the Asian nations is now on steady economic construction and cooperation.

At the same time, although she may feel dissatisfied with the Japanese government's attitude toward the issues of Vietnam and Communist China, the fact cannot be overlooked that the United States is gradually recognizing that Japan's foreign policy is contributing to the political and economic stability of Free Asia.

For reasons of economic difficulties or political uncertainty, Japan has at times shown reluctance to face up to the question of Asia. While showing its displeasure at such an attitude, the United States has, at the same time, deplored Japan's wishful thinking regarding the communist-controlled countries. However, this hitherto immutable image of Japanese-American relations is gradually beginning to dissolve.

In any event, it is in the field of economic cooperation that Japan can play a most effective role in Asia, and this diplomatic policy of economic development and raising the standard of living of the peoples should be carried out with energy and confidence. It may be assumed that the United States will respect and encourage this course of Japan's foreign policy. Thus, the time is ripe for Japan to pursue a truly independent foreign policy.

Later, on October 24 and 25, 1966, the leaders of seven

nations engaged in the war in Vietnam gathered in Manila to review the conflict in South Vietnam. President Johnson who attended this conference also took the opportunity to visit the five allied powers, Australia, New Zealand, the Philippines, Thailand, and Korea, as well as Malaysia.

The Manila Conference was sponsored by three nations—the Philippines, Thailand, and Korea—and the United States policy responded to the initiative taken by the Asian nations, a response to the "new winds blowing in Asia." The purpose of President Johnson's visit to the various nations was to hear at first hand the views of the Asian leaders regarding concrete measures for bringing about peace and prosperity in the Asian region, stressing in particular the political, economic, and social aspects of the problems involved.

During the course of his visits to the various countries in Asia, President Johnson sent a special message to Prime Minister Sato, expressing regret that Japan was excluded from the Presidential itinerary. It was reported that, since the Manila Conference was being sponsored by nations directly involved in the war in Vietnam, it would not have been appropriate for President Johnson to visit Japan either immediately before or after such a conference. Appreciating the discretion on the part of the President, Prime Minister Sato replied that, although Japan could not render any military assistance, she would strive in other ways for the restoration of peace in Vietnam.

President Johnson's act attracted wide attention as an official recognition of Japan's peculiar stand regarding the Vietnam problem. Hitherto, the United States had expressed desire to see Japan play a more positive role in Vietnam, with some Americans even suggesting military involvement. In view of these circumstances, it must be frankly admitted that American understanding of Japan's foreign policy had taken a new step forward.

At the Manila Conference, the participating nations agreed

that the conference should not develop into a regional military organization, and at its conclusion adopted three documents: "Joint Communique," "Goals of Freedom," and "Principles for Future Peace and Progress in the Asian and Pacific Region."

It was noted in the Joint Communique that the allies in Vietnam would withdraw their military forces after close consultation when the opposing side withdraws its forces to the North, ceases infiltration, and significantly reduces its acts of violence. When the above conditions are fulfilled, the warring allies would agree to evacuate their forces as quickly as possible, and not later than six months.

Shortly thereafter, William Bundy, United States Assistant Secretary of State, explained that the aim of the declaration was to assure the communist bloc that the United States really intended to withdraw its forces from Vietnam.

While the participating nations in the conference agreed that no positive move should be made to threaten the sovereignty or the territory integrity of neighbor states, not to speak of requesting regional cooperation of a military nature, they did stress the need to declare the fundamental principles which the free nations in Asia should observe. It was at the strong insistence of President Ferdinand Marcos of the Philippines that the declarations on the "Goals of Freedom" and "Peace and Progress in the Asian and Pacific Region" were adopted.

Among the freedom goals, the seven nations gathered in Manila proclaimed the following four points to be relevant in Vietnam and in the Asia and Pacific areas:

1. Freedom from aggression.

2. Conquest of hunger, illiteracy, and disease.

3. Construction of a region of security, order, and progress.

4. Seeking of reconciliation and peace throughout Asia and the Pacific region.

The above is known as the Manila Declaration, explaining the four principles clarified in the goals of freedom, among which the third was as follows:

"We must strengthen economic, social, and cultural cooperation within the Asian and Pacific region." It went on: "Together with our other partners of Asia and the Pacific, we will develop the institutions and practice of regional cooperation . . . economic and cultural cooperation for regional development should be open to all countries in the region, irrespective of creed or ideology."

It is said that the Manila Conference highly evaluated Japan's efforts in the nonmilitary fields as outlined in (2) and (3) of the goals of freedom, and strongly desired that Japan should increase her efforts for Asian development in the future.

The participants emphasized that they should continue their individual efforts within the cooperative organizations in which they were members, and disclaimed any idea of forming an exclusive group among the seven nations. The visits of William Bundy, Assistant Secretary of State, to Taiwan and Japan, and Averell Harriman, Ambassador at Large, to Indonesia and India after the conference were aimed at briefing these nations on the results of the Manila Conference which was not inspired by a spirit of exclusiveness.

Earlier, the speeches on the formation of Free Asia by U. Alexis Johnson, delivered prior to his assumption of the post of United States Ambassador to Japan, had attracted public attention. In this connection, I should like to cite certain portions of his address on regional community as it affects nationalism in Asia, a subject which was part of the ambassador's speech entitled "A Look at the Free Countries of Asia Today" made before the Far East-America Council of Commerce and Industry in New York on October 4, 1966.

"The developing nations in Asia increasingly realize that their aims of nationalism and independence are not compatible with communism. This is because the very nature of the system requires central direction and control. . . . Our basic interest in Asia is served, as it is elsewhere in the world, by a community of independent states freely cooperating together and with us for common purposes. . . .

"However, the word 'community' is of equal importance with the word 'independent' in the phrase 'community of independent nations.' This means a recognition of wider common interests and cooperating together to achieve those interests rather than the anarchy of egocentric nationalisms. It is to be expected that the vigorous nationalistic assertion of independence will come first, as it did with our own country, and only following that will there be the growth of a sense of community. . . .

"We have recognized that, to have any viability, the thrust must come from within the Asian countries themselves. Engaged in their own internal problems, wracked by their historical animosities, separated by their deep religious, racial, and cultural difference, and with competitive economics heavily tied to Western countries, it is not surprising that regional consciousness has been slow to develop. However, there have been a series of notable developments occurring particularly during the past year that are worth noting, and which mark important first steps." (June, 1967)

CHAPTER 13

Free Asia and Japan (II)

Japan's Role as a "New Wind" Leader

WHILE threatening clouds still hang ominously over the vast expanse of Asia because of the prolongation of the war in Vietnam and the chaos and confusion stemming from the Cultural Revolution in Communist China, the "new winds" whipped up by the upsurge in joint consciousness and promotion of regional cooperation among the free nations in Asia are dispelling these dark clouds.

Meanwhile, Japan which has assumed her role as the leader of the "new winds" is being highly appraised by the United States and other Asian countries, all of whom entertain great hopes for Japan. This rising confidence in Japan is attributable to the fact that her influence has been a stabilizing force for peace and prosperity in Asia, and her reputation has been elevated internationally.

In other words, Japan's ability to attain political stability under a democratic system, without swinging either to the extreme right or to the extreme left, as well as her miraculous economic growth have engendered a feeling of trust and confidence in Japan, befitting an advanced country of Asia, on the part of the nations in the region. Another factor which reinforced this feeling of reliability and confidence was the overwhelming victory of the Liberal Democratic Party in the

January, 1967, general elections of the Lower House of the Japanese Diet.

That Japan has been able to exist as a stabilizing force in Asia and enjoy security and prosperity are due in great measure to the Japan-United States Security Treaty. Expressed in a different way, Japan, which owes her present stability and prosperity to the existence of this security treaty, can continue to enjoy its benefits in the future as well.

Through a series of international conferences in Asia and the Pacific region during 1966, Japan was able to bring her role as a leader of the "new winds" into sharp relief. The country played an important role in adjusting the views among the various nations participating in the Southeast Asian Ministerial Conference for Economic Development in April, the General Meeting for the Establishment of the Asian Development Bank in November, and, in December, the Southeast Asian Agricultural Development Conference, all of which Japan sponsored in Tokyo, as well as the Asian and Pacific Ministerial Conference on Economic and Cultural Cooperation in June in Seoul.

In the United States, Japan's activities in fanning the "new winds" have been properly assessed not only by government circles, but also by Congress and mass communication media which have been full of praise for Japan's attitude. For example, whenever Secretary of State Dean Rusk, Assistant Secretary of State William Bundy, or Special Assistant to the President Walt Rostow speak of the "new winds" in Asia, there is always specific reference to Japan's political stability and economic growth as well as her contributions to the economic development of Southeast Asia.

However, the fact should not be overlooked that the United States has not encouraged the "new winds" of Asia as an instrument to be used by the Free World to confront the communist bloc, particularly Communist China. While pursuing the so-called containment, rather than isolationist, policy toward Communist China, the United States is hoping to change Communist China's present position of confrontation to one of flexibility and peaceful coexistence. Prior to the upheavals sparked by the Great Cultural Revolution in mainland China, the United States had been striving to build up an atmosphere of "consultation" and not "confrontation."

As a stabilizing force in Asia, although it is natural that Japan should not adopt a policy of confrontation against Communist China, it is worthwhile to recall her position at the ASPAC (Asian and Pacific) Ministerial Conference in Seoul in 1966, where her attitude was observed with keen interest.

Hosted by the Republic of Korea, participants of the ASPAC Conference included Japan, Nationalist China, Malaysia, the Philippines, South Vietnam, Thailand, Australia, New Zealand, and Laos, though the latter attended as an observer. In the joint communique, the conferees agreed to strengthen the solidarity among the nations in Asia and the Pacific region, aimed at achieving peace, freedom, and prosperity; to disapprove nuclear testing (while avoiding any denunciation of Communist China by name); to reaffirm the United Nations decision for the unification of South and North Korea, and to hold the second conference in Bangkok in 1967.

At the first ministerial conference of ASPAC in Seoul, both Japan and Malaysia were regarded as being lukewarm in their stand on communism by South Korea, Nationalist China, South Vietnam, Thailand, and the Philippines who were imbued with anticommunism. But Japan's aim was to prevent the Soviet Union, Communist China, or North Korea from branding the Seoul conference as a conspiracy to form an anticommunist Asian military alliance.

Stressing the complicated situation in Asia and the need to avoid further aggravating the tension and divisions between opposing forces in the region, Japan was able to appeal to the good sense of the participants who agreed to accept Japan's basic policy of abstaining from expressing rabid anticommunism and from overemphasizing the military aspects of the conference in the joint communique.

As a result, the Seoul conference, attended for the first time by the nations of Asia and the Pacific region, was of great significance in reaffirming growing cooperation for unity and prosperity of the regional community. Under these circumstances, Japan's middle-of-the-road foreign policy, leaning neither to the right nor to the left, took a giant stride forward in the direction of forming the so-called Free Asia.

Foreshadowing the Asian and Pacific Era

Later in November, 1966, the General Meeting for the Establishment of the Asian Development Bank was held in Tokyo, marking a significant step forward in the foundation of an organ infused with the spirit of regional cooperation. Attending the conference were mainly finance ministers of thirty-one member nations in Europe and America, together with representatives from such international organizations as the International Monetary Fund and the World Bank.

During the conference it was agreed that the headquarters of the Asian Development Bank would be located in Manila and that its first president would be Takeshi Watanabe, Councilor of the Japanese Ministry of Finance. Another major conference held in Tokyo in December was the Southeast Asian Agricultural Development Conference. Since the spirit of this conference was far removed from the hostilities in Vietnam, the attending nations pinned high hopes on Japan's accelerating initiative.

The convening of this agricultural conference was one of the resolutions of the Southeast Asian ministerial conference held in April. The participants of the conference agreed on two points, namely: (1) to request the Asian Development Bank to establish an agricultural development fund as part of the bank's special fund, and (2) to create an operations department for the establishment of a Fishery Development Center.

It will require some time before these steps can be finalized, but the conference marked an important beginning in fostering regional cooperation in the field of agricultural development and in delivering the agricultural community in this region from the debilitating effects of stagnation and isolation.

The Japanese Ministry of Foreign Affairs meanwhile has worked out a new concept of "Asia and the Pacific Region" as part of Japan's development of a wider Asian diplomacy, taking into account the interests shown in the Pacific Basin Community by the United States, Canada, Australia, New Zealand, and other nations bordering the Pacific Ocean. This concept was strongly supported by Foreign Minister Takeo Miki at his inaugural press conference soon after assuming his cabinet post. This concept was evolved on the basis that, politically and economically, countries other than the United States, including Canada, Australia, and New Zealand, were not only increasing their relations with the countries of Asia, but the cooperation of these industrially advanced countries were also essential in furthering the development of Asia.

As a concrete step toward materializing this new concept, the Japanese Foreign Ministry dispatched a special delegation to Australia and New Zealand in the middle of January to hold a series of conferences at the administrative level. As a result of these visits, both Australia and New Zealand acquired a deeper understanding of the intentions underlying Japan's new concept of an Asian-Pacific Community as expounded by Foreign Minister Miki as part of the concrete proposals and in principle agreed to the convening of regular meetings at ministerial level.

Two months later in March, Australia's Foreign Minister Paul Hasluck visited Japan, and agreed to hold the ministerial conferences and to make every effort to promote the realization of Japan's concept of a wider Pacific cooperation.

Japanese financial circles, on the other hand, have already

prepared the ground for intensifying economic cooperation in the Pacific region by establishing Japan-United States, Japan-Canada, and Japan-Australia joint economic committees. The Japan-Australia Joint Economic Committee since its second conference in 1964 has taken up the question of economic unification in the Pacific region. This objective was pushed a step further after the Fifth Meeting of the Japan-Australia Joint Economic Committee in April with the convening of a conference attended by delegates from financial circles of Japan, Australia, and New Zealand as well as an observer of the United States.

Consequently, five nations, including Canada, representing the advanced countries of the region, set up the Pacific Economic Committee under the first presidency of Shigeo Nagano, Vice President of the Tokyo Chamber of Commerce.

In connection with the problem of regional cooperation in the Pacific area, differences of opinions have existed between the Japanese financial circles and the Foreign Ministry, the former believing that economic cooperation among the advanced nations should first be consolidated before embarking on full-scale assistance to the underdeveloped countries in Southeast Asia, and the latter advocating that the economic development of Southeast Asia should take precedence and the advanced nations should consider how best to cooperate in this cooperative endeavor. The two parties have now agreed to shelve their differences and to concentrate on getting the project started.

It is relevant to note here that President Johnson in his State of the Union message in January, 1967, revealed that Congress would be asked to provide him with authority to disburse $200 million for the promotion of the Southeast Asia regional development project. Official American sources have pointed out that this move by President Johnson is the first concrete indication that the President's original proposal made in Baltimore in April, 1965, to spend $1 billion toward Southeast Asian development was finally assuming a definite shape. They also expected that the administration would launch a vigorous campaign to persuade Congress, which had lately been showing signs of indifference, to adopt a more positive attitude toward overseas assistance.

If this proposal gains congressional approval, it is believed that a part of this allotment will be invested in the special fund of the Asian Development Bank and in the development fund set up by the Southeast Asia Agricultural Development Conference in December, 1966. Funds may also be appropriated on a preferential basis for other purposes, such as the Mekong River Valley Development Project, improvement of educational standards in Asia, and the expansion of transportation and communication facilities, including the use of artificial satellites.

The development of Japan's concept of an "Asian and Pacific Community" is being encouraged, as previously stated, by the United States government which would welcome the creation in the Pacific area of collective organizations such as the Atlantic Community's NATO or OECD. At the same time, the United States does not expect that a regional organization comparable to the organizations of the Atlantic Community can be formed overnight. Among the obstacles in the Pacific region, they point to the lack of political and economic stability in Southeast Asia and the absence of any concrete proposal for the formation of a Pacific collective organization.

In promoting the establishment of such an organization, the United States view is that cooperation among the industrialized countries for the economic development of the developing countries should take precedence over the economic cooperation or economic exchange among these countries. Based on the fact that there already exists bilateral cooperative organizations among the industrially advanced nations, and that these countries face very few problems that require urgent solution by a multilateral cooperative organization, the United States is laying stress on economic development of the developing countries while continuing to promote economic cooperation among the industrialized countries.

In any event, until the idea of an Asian-Pacific regional economic cooperation organization takes positive shape, official United States circles hope to continue the present system of cooperation and to deepen mutual understanding with Japan. At the same time, they look expectantly to Japan to clarify her new project at the coming meeting of the Japan-United States Trade and Economic Joint Committee.

In conclusion, I would like to mention that Foreign Minister Miki in his speech to the 55th special session of the National Diet on March 25, 1967, referred hopefully to the "new winds" blowing in Asia—the "new winds" of growing cooperation and solidarity among the nations in Asia and the Pacific which will eventually lead to the formation of a Free Asia.

The Foreign Minister's reference is also a happy augury that conditions are now ripening for the realization of an Asian and Pacific collective organization which I have long advocated. Just as the United States is geographically an Atlantic nation as well as a Pacific nation, Japan, too, is an Asian nation and at the same time a Pacific nation. Accordingly, it can be said that it is Japan's inherent mission to strive for the development of an Asian-Pacific diplomacy. (June, 1967)

CHAPTER 14

Extension of the Japan-United States Security Treaty— "1970 Crisis"

Problems Facing Automatic Renewal of the Treaty

THE EXISTENCE of the Japan-United States Security Treaty has doubtlessly been the primary factor ensuring the security of Japan and her continued growth as a liberal and democratic nation since the termination of the Pacific War. When this treaty was revised in 1960, a clause was inserted to the effect that after the treaty has been in force for ten years, either party may give notice of its intention to terminate the treaty, whereupon the said treaty would become inoperative a year later.

In view of this situation, the so-called 1970 crisis, the year notice can be served to abrogate the treaty, has become a topic of heated debates. Public interest in the debates heightened when Prime Minister Sato stated in the National Diet on March 8, 1966, that "since permanency is essential in the nations' defense system, it would be necessary to appropriately deal with the question of permanency upon the expiry of the Japan-United States Security Treaty. On the following day, he hinted that there is a possibility that Japan and the United States might reach a prior understanding not to terminate the treaty, or the two countries might conclude a new agreement embodying the same provisions as the present treaty.

Not only the Japanese government and the Liberal Demo-

178

cratic Party, but the Socialist and Democratic Socialist parties as well as others have been seriously grappling with the question of Japan's defense treaty. But it is truly regrettable that instead of standing on a common platform with the people, the stand taken by the governing and opposition parties has been one of confrontation. Japan's journalistic circles must also shoulder a great responsibility for this state of affairs.

Notwithstanding, the majority of the Japanese people now recognize that the Japan-United States Security Treaty is indispensable for the country's liberal and democratic progress. Despite this recognition, the Socialist Party, the largest opposition party, mustering the forces of Sohyo and leftist elements, have, together with the Communist Party, been advocating immediate abrogation of the security treaty and denouncing what they call American imperialism.

In this connection, the central executive committee of the Socialist Party on August 31, 1966, published an official pamphlet entitled *For Japan's Peace and Security* in which the party states that "with the broad backing of the people's movement, diplomatic procedures will be taken to abrogate the security treaty." This posture does not indicate any change in the Socialist Party's policy.

By advocating Japan's demilitarization and neutralization, conclusion of nonaggression treaties with the Soviet Union and Communist China, abrogation of the Japan-Korea Treaty, and establishment of diplomatic relations with a unified Korea, the Socialist Party has cast serious doubts as to where its true interest lies.

While recognizing the indispensability of the Japan-United States Security Treaty, there are people who feel and those who do not feel that it is necessary to have a fixed period of validity for the treaty after 1970 as earlier alluded to by Prime Minister Sato in the National Diet. If no action is taken the treaty will no doubt be allowed to run indefinitely until such time as when the United Nations is able to take effective measures to maintain peace. Most people in the former group favor a fixed period of ten years, while the latter group favors automatic extension, arguing that an attempt to fix such a period for the treaty would only cause unnecessary friction.

They contend that to raise the question of extending the treaty for ten years at the present juncture would only result in pouring oil on the fire of opposition stirred up by the Socialist Party and others and play into their hands. They maintain that there would be no crisis in 1970 as the treaty would be automatically continued. Moreover, they believe that it is problematical whether the United States would easily accept Japan's proposition to renew the treaty for a further ten years in its present form when the ten-year initial period expires.

On the other hand, as long as the Socialist Party continues to adhere to its position as a Marxist party, a clash between the government and opposition parties is inevitable over the question of the security treaty. Thus, unless there is a long-term period affixed to the treaty, there are bound to be disorders on a scale far greater than the turmoil erupting over the revision of the security treaty. The antisecurity treaty campaign will become such a daily and chronic affair that the nation's security will be seriously jeopardized.

It is a generally accepted fact that the Socialist Party, not to speak of the Communist Party, and other forces opposing the security pact, are making every effort to mobilize their strength to meet the so-called 1970 crisis. It is further reported that, if the situation is favorable, they are even scheming to move into the stage of revolution by resorting to forceful methods, such as the calling of a general strike.

At the same time, with 1970 in mind, Communist China's Premier Chou En-lai and Foreign Minister Chen Yi have been incessantly calling on the procommunist elements in Japan to repudiate the Japan-United States Security Treaty, and the North Korean plan to complete the mobilization of all major industrial plants by the year 1970 is causing concern in South Korea. In the light of these circumstances,

Japan must be fully vigilant to the dangers posed by any large-scale offensive which international communism in Asia might precipitate, taking advantage of the widespread unrest which the latter foresees in Japan in 1970.

In case Japan proposes giving the treaty a period of permanency, the official United States attitude whether to attach a fixed period or to automatically extend the treaty remains unclarified. However, it need hardly be said that the maintenance of the Japan-United States Security Treaty is essential in the national interests of the United States. From the point of view of her own security and prosperity, the United States is convinced of the importance of solidifying the free nations of Asia, including Japan, and the nations of Southeast Asia in particular.

Hence, there is absolutely no divergence of views on whether to continue or to abrogate the treaty as in the case of Japan. The American Assembly, an influential American international affairs institute, completed in July, 1966, a series of forums held in various cities of the United States on the subject of "The United States and Japan" which the Assembly had begun in October, 1965.

A report on these forums reveal that there is no reason for the United States to positively propose a revision of the treaty when it expires in 1970. There was a minority opinion which felt that it was desirable to revise the treaty so as to strengthen the mutual obligations under the treaty. The proponents of this opinion felt that since the United States had the one-sided responsibility of defending Japan, the country should, together with the United States, be obliged to cooperate with the United States for the security of Asia as soon as she had built up her defense capabilities.

There is realization, however, that such a request should not be made under pressure, and the United States has made it plain that adverse political complications would accompany such a compulsive step leading to a possible crisis in Japanese-American relations.

Hitherto, even without disregarding the so-called peace constitution, the United States has occasionally intimated its dissatisfaction at Japan's inadequate defense efforts and its lack of understanding and support for America's Asian policy. The present Japan-United States Security Treaty stipulates in Article 5 that the obligations of mutual assistance in case of an armed attack against either party is confined to the territories under the jurisdiction of Japan. In Article 6, Japan grants the United States the use of its facilities and territories by the United States armed forces not only for Japan's own security but as a contribution toward the maintenance of international peace and security in the Far East.

Even if certain dissatisfaction felt by the United States were to be removed by revising the present treaty, it is not anticipated that the United States would make unreasonable demands that would be embarrassing to Japan. The world has entered into an era of collective security, and Japan is also a nonnuclear power. Thus, in any effort aimed at seriously consolidating her defensive strength, Japan must do so within the limitations of her constitution.

The general observation is that the United States has no strong objections to the present treaty being continued beyond 1970. This opinion is also reflected in the statement made to the press by Edwin O. Reischauer, the former American Ambassador to Japan, on the eve of his departure from Japan that the question of the form which the Japan-United States Security Treaty will take after 1970 is a problem for Japan, not the United States.

Security and Balance of Power
Ten-Year Extension of Treaty Desirable

What I wish to emphasize at this time is that the Japan-United States Security Treaty was an inevitable outcome of the Sino-Soviet Treaty of Friendship, Alliance, and Mutual

Assistance. In other words, the treaty was a logical consequence of the basic principle of international politics: the balance of power.

Owing to the antagonism between the Free World and the communist bloc, the world today is precariously maintaining peace on the balance of power between the two contending forces, or more truthfully, relying on the preponderance of power of the free nations. While it is regrettable and undesirable for each to be dependent on the balance of power, no one can turn his eyes away from this cold reality of our times.

As for the background to the Japan-United States Security Treaty, it is well to remember that in September, 1949, two years prior to the conclusion of the treaty, a communist Chinese regime was established on the Chinese Mainland. This regime in February, 1950, signed a Treaty of Friendship, Alliance, and Mutual Assistance with the Soviet Union, in which Japan and countries allied to her were regarded as hypothetical enemies.

Then in June of the same year, North Korea, with the backing of Communist China and the Soviet Union, crossed the 38th parallel and brought on the Korean War. It was under these circumstances that Japan signed the security treaty simultaneously with the peace treaty with the United States. Both Japan and the United States took these countermeasures because the communist bloc exposed its aggressive nature. Even today, the basic principle of the balance of power in the Far Eastern situation still applies.

As mentioned earlier, the Japan-United States Security Treaty can be terminated on and after June 23, 1970, by giving a year's advance notice. In comparison, the Sino-Soviet pact of alliance runs for thirty years. If a year's advance notice is not given by either party after 1980, the treaty automatically remains in effect for another five years. The treaty is actually perpetual until notice of termination is delivered, being automatically extendible on a continuing basis for additional periods of five years. From the balance of power point of view, the Japan-United States Security Treaty offers a serious handicap.

During my interpellations in the plenary session of the Upper House of the National Diet on January 28, 1965, I reiterated my firm view that it would be most desirable for Japan to extend the validity of the Japan-United States Security Treaty to 1980, rather than wait for 1970, so as to bring the period of the treaty into line with that of the Sino-Soviet pact of alliance.

There are, of course, some observers who believe that with the intensification of the Sino-Soviet split and confusion in the wake of the Cultural Revolution in Communist China the Sino-Soviet pact of alliance has become a "scrap of paper."

But it would be difficult to predict the future outcome of the struggle between the rival political groups in China, those representing the "main current" and those who actually wield power. In case of a prolonged struggle, Sino-Soviet relations can easily take a different turn, depending on the nature of the settlement.

The Soviet Union appears to take the position that as long as the "main current" in China acts in a manner detrimental to the unity of international communism, there can be no victory for the "main current" and that Communist China will eventually return to normalcy by restoring the same line of policy originally followed by the Chinese Communist Party.

In the wake of the riotous demonstration involving the encirclement of the Soviet Embassy in Peking, the Soviet Union on February 2, 1967, lodged an unusually vehement protest, in which it referred to the spirit of the Sino-Soviet pact of alliance and expressed the strong hope that a situation will not be created by the "main current" group whereby the treaty becomes a dead letter.

It is worth noting in this connection that U Thant, Secretary General of the United Nations, had referred to the existence of the Sino-Soviet pact of alliance in his warning about the possibility of the war in Vietnam escalating into World War III, at a luncheon given by the United Nations Press Association in New York on May 11, 1967.

Despite her policy of peaceful coexistence and insistence that a people's liberation war runs counter to that principle, the Soviet Union is not discouraging the institution and assistance of such aggression. Needless to say, it is together with Communist China calling on Japan to adopt a policy of neutrality and continuously endeavoring to drag Japan into the communist bloc.

Under these circumstances, as long as the Soviet Union and Communist China clearly fail to give up their ambition for world communization based on the principles of Marxism-Leninism and cease to agitate for confrontation against the so-called American imperialism, the Sino-Soviet pact of alliance must be regarded as valid and very much alive.

My plea for an extension of the Japan-United States Security Treaty to the year 1980, based on the preservation of the balance of power, received a great impetus with the publication of "The Interim Report on Japan's Security" by the Security Problem Study Committee of the Liberal Democratic Party in June, 1966, in which the fixing of the treaty's validity for ten years received almost unanimous support from members of the committee.

Since there are arguments within the Liberal Democratic Party in favor of automatic extension, the party's Foreign Relation's Committee, of which I had been chairman, has yet to reach a conclusion on this issue, an issue on which I hold definite views, as expressed on a number of previous occasions.

Examples of the principle of the balance of power playing a role in the diplomatic relations between states are seen in the days of ancient Greece and later in relations between cities during the period of the Italian Renaissance. It appeared in a more classical form in international politics around the 16th century, a period which saw the beginnings of the rise of modern states. This fact is patently revealed in the preambles of the Treaty of Westphalia (1648), the Treaty of Utrecht (1713), and the Treaty of Vienna (1815) which declare: ". . . for the restoration of the balance of power in Europe . . ." From that time, international peace has mainly been maintained on the principle of balance of power.

Outstanding examples in more modern times have been the Triple Alliance of Germany, Austria, and Italy against the Triple Entente of Great Britain, France, and Russia prior to World War I, and later the tripartite accord of the Axis powers, Germany, Italy, and Japan, arrayed against the Allied powers of Great Britain, France, the United States, and the Soviet Union before World War II. This balance is now seen in Europe in the case of NATO (North Atlantic Treaty Organization) and the Warsaw Treaty Organization.

A look at the situation around Japan reveals that besides being linked in the Sino-Russian pact of alliance, the Soviet Union and Communist China have signed a treaty of mutual assistance with North Korea. Therefore, as long as the Sino-Soviet pact of alliance remains in force, it would be a mistake and a danger for Japan's own security to ignore the principle of the balance of power by abrogating the Japan-United States Security Treaty.

I believe that it would be relevant here to recall the Anglo-Japanese Alliance which formed the pillar on which Japan, an island nation, was able to emerge as a world power in the years spanning the Meiji and Taisho eras. The First Anglo-Japanese Alliance was concluded in January, 1902, to counteract the Russo-Chinese Secret Convention of 1896 and Russia's subsequent advances in the Far East. The term of validity stipulated by the treaty was five years, at the end of which it could be terminated with a year's prior notification.

After the Russo-Japanese War, Japan and Great Britain concluded the Second Anglo-Japanese Alliance in August, 1905, and the Third Anglo-Japanese Alliance in July, 1911, both of which ran for ten years with one year's advance notice for invalidation. It is noteworthy that in the third year of the First Anglo-Japanese Alliance, the two countries found it fitting to conclude the Second Alliance, and the Second Alliance was renewed by the Third Alliance during the sixth year of its ten-year term of validity.

The primary aim of the Second Alliance was to discourage Russia's ambitions in India and East Asia and to divert its attention toward Europe, with the hope that Russia would eventually cooperate with the alliance powers. In the case of the Third Alliance, Great Britain felt that the treaty would assist her in dealing with Germany, the latter's rising naval power, as well as in tackling Eastern and colonial problems. For Japan, the treaty was an instrument for maintaining peace in Asia and for expanding her commercial interests on the Asian mainland.

Taking advantage of the expiry of the Third Anglo-Japanese Alliance in 1921, the United States took the initiative to summon a historic conference in Washington D.C. to be attended by nations with interests in Asia and the Pacific region. Although prior to this conference, both the Japanese and British governments evinced a desire to renew the alliance, the treaty was terminated due to Canadian opposition and at the United States' request. In its place, Japan, the United States, Great Britain, and France concluded the Four Power Treaty for the maintenance of security and the *status quo* in the Pacific area.

At the same time, a Naval Limitation Treaty placing a ceiling on capital ship tonnages of the United States, Great Britain, Japan, France, and Italy was signed, and an agreement was reached on a Nine Power Treaty by Japan, Great Britain, the United States, France, China, Italy, Belgium, the Netherlands, and Portugal to respect China's sovereignty and to observe the principles of open door and equal opportunity in matters affecting China.

In the case of the termination of the Anglo-Japanese Alliance, new agreements were concluded to govern developments in the Far East and the Pacific region. However, in the event of abandoning the Japan-United States Security Treaty there would be no similar arrangement to fill in the vacuum. If, as the Socialist Party proposes, a collective security system for Asia and the Pacific area among Japan, the United States, Communist China, and the Soviet Union can be concluded, this could be considered one of the alternatives.

Should the Japan-United States Security Treaty be extended for a further ten years, it will reach the end of its validity at the same time as the Sino-Soviet pact of alliance. In that event, provided the international situation has substantially changed for the better by that time, the four-power proposal may not be a fantasy.

In reviewing the question of automatic extension, it should be pointed out that there is a section of public opinion which holds that the treaty, with a validity of ten or twenty years, can be abrogated with a year's advance notice after it has run its full course. However, such an opinion lacks proper understanding and consideration of all the manifold factors involved. As was earlier pointed out, the Anglo-Japanese treaty was renewed on two separate occasions even before the expiration of the treaty's validity.

The North Atlantic Treaty Organization, for instance, expires after twenty years in 1969 and may be terminated with a year's notice, but members of the Western European Union (Great Britain, France, Belgium, Holland, Luxembourg, West Germany, and Italy) which rely on the NATO military organization signed a treaty earlier in 1948 which runs for a period of fifty years and promises mutual assistance in military and other fields. On the other hand, the Warsaw Treaty which has a twenty-year period of validity is renewable for a further period of ten years in the absence of a year's notification to terminate the treaty. Likewise the Soviet-East Germany Treaty of Friendship, Cooperation, and Mutual Assistance concluded in 1964 is valid for twenty years, after which it will be valid for a further ten years in 1984, in case no notification for termination is served by either party.

Supporters of automatic extension also point to the fact that mutual defense treaties signed by the United States with the Philippines, Nationalist China, and South Korea respectively, are of indefinite duration and can be terminated with one year's notice. But it should be pointed out that in the case of these treaties, the Philippines has outlawed the Communist Party, and Nationalist China and South Korea are in direct confrontation against Communist China and North Korea.

In view of the fundamental difference in the nature of the relations between Japan and the United States in concluding the security treaty, it is out of the question for advocates of automatic extension to attempt to quote these treaties to support their contention. (June, 1967)

CHAPTER 15

United States Policy Toward Communist China and Japan's Position

As A CONSEQUENCE of the stalemate in the war in Vietnam, the question of Communist China has loomed larger and larger in heated debates in the United States from 1965 through 1966. Most notable of these debates have been the public hearings in the Foreign Relations committees of both houses of congress, in which prominent scholars and experts on Communist China have given testimonies admitting that the country is today a very hard member to get along with in the international community of nations. As a matter of fact, every outcry from Peking is a denunciation of American imperialism, unduly provocative, militant, and uncompromising.

During the public hearings, the government was urged to adopt certain attitudes and policies, but the general consensus of opinion appeared to favor continuing a policy of "containment without isolation." Although the phrase "containment without isolation" was coined by Professor Barnet of Columbia University, it has become associated with United States policy toward Communist China ever since Vice President Hubert Humphrey declared on the heels of Professor Barnet's statement that the United States policy in dealing with Communist China was not aimed at isolation, but only containment.

These series of congressional hearings on the question of

190

United States policy toward Communist China, from the standpoint of how to apply pressure and how to associate with the latter, did not fundamentally change the policy hitherto pursued by the United States government. At these hearings Secretary of State Dean Rusk revealed that the efforts made by the United States to establish contacts with Communist China had consistently been spurned by the latter. It is a matter of record that during the past several years of Sino-American talks, Communist China has always refused to entertain American proposals for broader contacts, such as the exchange of newspapermen and scholars.

I believe that it would be pertinent at this stage to examine the United States government's basic policy toward Communist China as enunciated by Secretary of State Dean Rusk before the closed session of the Foreign Relations Committee of the House of Representatives on March 15, 1966, and made public on April 16. The main elements of this policy consist of the following ten points:

1. We must remain firm in our determination to help those allied nations which seek our help to resist the direct or indirect use of threat of force against their territory by Peking.

2. We must continue to assist the countries of Asia in building broadly based effective governments.

3. We must honor our commitments to the Republic of China and to the people of Taiwan who do not want to live under communism, and will continue to assist in their defense.

4. We will continue our efforts to prevent the expulsion of the Republic of China from the United Nations or its agencies. So long as Peking follows its present course, the United States opposes its membership.

5. We should continue our efforts to reassure Peking that the United States does not intend to attack mainland China.

6. We must avoid assuming the existence of an unending and inevitable state of hostility between ourselves and the rulers of mainland China.

7. We should continue to enlarge the possibilities for unofficial contacts between Communist China and ourselves.

8. We should keep open our direct diplomatic contacts with Peking in Warsaw.

9. We are prepared to sit down with Peking and other countries to discuss the critical problems of disarmament and nonproliferation of nuclear weapons.

10. We must continue to explore and analyze all available information on Communist China and keep our own policies up to date.

Concerning the Sino-American ambassadorial talks in Warsaw, it should be noted that these talks have been continuing for more than ten years. The 130th meeting took place on May 23, 1966. Never before in history have two nations, who have not recognized each other internationally, held such a prolonged series of talks.

Referring to these talks, Secretary of State Rusk said that the direct Sino-American contacts in Warsaw are helping the two nations to exchange information and convey the respective stands in an emergency.

A concrete example of this usefulness was provided during the Kinmen crisis in 1958 and 1962 when the United States was able to allay the fears of Communist China by assuring the latter that the United States did not intend to assist the Nationalist government to launch a counterattack against mainland China.

In any case, the representatives of the two countries have been officially appointed by their respective governments. While it is unlikely that their contacts will develop into actual diplomatic recognition, it is hardly possible to deny the existence of such a possibility in the future. Added significance was given to these talks by Secretary of State Rusk when he said that "they provide an opening through which, hopefully, light might one day penetrate."

Furthermore, on May 18, Secretary of Defense Robert S.

McNamara, in an address before the American Society of Newspaper Editors in Montreal, Canada, called for the erection of a bridge to Communist China as a step toward averting a war with Communist China arising out of misunderstanding.

Mr. McNamara continued: "There are many ways in which we can build a bridge toward nations who would cut themselves off from meaningful contact with us. We can do so with properly balanced trade relations, diplomatic contacts, and in some cases even by exchanges of military observers."

This proposal envisaged the two countries conducting balanced trade, maintaining diplomatic contacts, and exchanging military observers. Although the phrase "building a bridge" has appeared frequently in speeches made by President Johnson and Secretary of State Rusk with reference to relations with countries of East Europe, Mr. McNamara was the first member of the Cabinet to apply this expression to relations with Communist China. Similarly, the proposals of "balanced trade relations and exchange of military observers" had not earlier been mentioned by Rusk. However, these expressions reflected the sincere desire of the United States government to come to a friendly understanding with Communist China once it gave up the policy of the use of force in its relations with countries of the noncommunist world.

On July 12, President Johnson revived public interest in United States policy toward Asia when he spoke before the American Alumni Council, emphasizing that "the United States is determined to meet its obligations in Asia as a Pacific power. The peace we seek in Asia," he said, "is a peace of conciliation." He added: "Lasting peace can never come to Asia as long as the 700 million people of mainland China are isolated by their rulers from the outside world."

Evoking special attention was his statement that "a misguided China must be encouraged toward understanding of

the outside world and toward policies of peaceful cooperation
. . . the greatest force for opening closed minds and closed
societies is the free flow of ideas and people and goods."

It is regrettable that, whereas the United States has been
endeavoring to create an atmosphere of conciliation rather
than confrontation, Communist China has been thrown into
the paroxysm of the Cultural Revolution in which the uncompromising line of Mao Tse-tung is adding fuel to the
raging fire.

In Warsaw, where the American and Chinese envoys were
meeting for their usual round of talks on September 7, 1966,
the 131st of the series, the Chinese envoy Wang Kuo-chuan
held an unexpected press interview after the conference. He
bluntly charged the United States of repeatedly violating the
arrangement for these talks by unilaterally divulging details.
Touching on such questions as Sino-American relations,
Taiwan and Vietnam, the Chinese envoy made it clear that
Communist China would not budge an inch from its original
position.

Reacting calmly to these invectives, the United States
State Department declared that there was nothing new to
the assertions made by Wang Kuo-chuan, and attended the
132nd meeting which took place on January 25, 1967.

Compared to the United States, Japan has closer historical
and geographical relations with Communist China. This
fact should make Japan all the more conscious of any new
development in the area and of the need to constantly keep
her policy abreast with the changing circumstances.

The so-called principle of separating politics and economics is aimed at promoting economic and cultural exchanges while fully taking into account the existence of the
Communist Chinese regime which effectively administers the
Chinese Mainland. At the present time, the step-by-step
method must be followed in finding a just solution for the
question of Communist China without digressing from the
policy of separating politics and economics.

Insofar as political issues do not conflict with the basic policy of separation, Prime Minister Sato has stated that Japan is prepared to discuss any proposal that would be helpful in resolving the present situation. While it is one thing to come up with a concrete plan to deal with the present situation, it is quite another for Japan to consider the need to further strengthen her contacts with Communist China.

Convinced that Japan should deal with the problem of recognition of Communist China from her own special position, I emphasized in my interpellations in the Budget Committee of the Upper House of the National Diet on March 6, 1964, that, providing the following four preconditions are satisfied by Communist China, Japan should move toward its recognition:

1. Communist China recognize the Japan-United States Security Treaty.

2. The Japan-Republic of China Peace Treaty be respected.

3. Communist China renounce the right to claim reparations from Japan.

4. Adhering to the principles of nonintervention in internal affairs, Communist China to promise not to engage in communist subversive propaganda or undertake indirect aggression against Japan.

My opinions were generally affirmed by the then Prime Minister Ikeda, as well as by the majority of public opinion.

Since a new cabinet assumed office, I again directed the same question to Prime Minister Sato in my position as representative of the Liberal Democratic Party in the Upper House plenary session on January 28, 1965. In response to the request for a reaffirmation of these principles, Prime Minister Sato declared that he believed all the points mentioned in the four preconditions deserve serious consideration, but as to what concrete steps should be taken on these points would have to be left as problems for future action.

In view of the fact that no objections were voiced by members of the ruling Liberal Democratic Party, I believe that Japan should consolidate her policy toward Communist China on the basis of the four preconditions for the recognition of the latter.

As for the question of Chinese representation in the United Nations, there appears to be no prospect of Communist Chinese admission into the United Nations this year following a series of setbacks in her Afro-Asian policy since 1965. However, like the United States, Japan should maintain a consistent policy of including the question of the representation of China on the agenda as an important item.

Moreover, in the eventuality that Communist China is welcomed as a member of the United Nations, Japan should at the same time adopt all necessary measures to prevent Nationalist China from being ousted from the world organization. (June, 1967)

CHAPTER **16**

Establishment of Japan-Korea Relations

IN HIS policy speech before the National Diet on November 21, Prime Minister Eisaku Sato, whose cabinet was newly installed on November 9, 1964, stressed the importance of successfully concluding the Japan-Korea negotiation as quickly as possible. With the concurrence of the Korean side, the seventh conference to normalize Japan-Korea relations entered the final stage on December 3.

Appointing Kim Dongjo, the Chief of the Republic of Korea (ROK) Mission in Tokyo, as head of its delegation, Korea appeared just as determined as Japan to carry the negotiations to a satisfactory conclusion. Although the negotiations were marred by the sudden death of Japan's chief delegate, Michisuke Sugi, on December 14, the newly appointed chief delegate, Shiinichi Takasugi, who assumed his post on January 6, 1965, led the talks to the committee stage. The two sides set up three committees to deal with the questions of fisheries, the legal status of Korean residents in Japan, and the basic relations between the two countries.

The negotiations gained further prominence and hope with the visit of Japanese Foreign Minister Shiina to Korea for four days from February 17. As a result of the talks with his Korean counterpart, Lee Dong Won, the two countries initialed the Japan-Korea Basic Treaty on February 20.

The basic treaty stipulated the conditions under which the relations between the two countries would be normalized.

The contents of this treaty had hitherto been the source of heated debates between the two parties from the very beginning of the negotiations.

Since Japan had already accorded diplomatic recognition to Korea, it felt that it was unnecessary to conclude a new agreement and that an exchange of ambassadors between the two countries would be sufficient to establish diplomatic relations.

Korea, on the other hand, insisted that the conclusion of a basic treaty which would contribute toward friendly relations between the two countries should be the first step in that direction.

The results of the sixth conference gave added impetus to the Japan-Korea negotiations. As an alternative to a treaty, Japan proposed that the two countries sign a joint statement similar to the Japan-Soviet joint statement, but this proposal was rejected. Accordingly, energetic efforts were made at the seventh conference to draft the provisions of the treaty.

In drafting the accord, the negotiators had to overcome a number of difficulties, such as the questions of confirming the scope of the administrative jurisdiction of the ROK government and the invalidity of the old treaties signed between Japan and Korea. With regard to the former, Japan's position was that the jurisdiction was limited to the region south of the 38th parallel, but Korea insisted that it extended north beyond the said demarcation line.

Basing its policy on the resolution of the United Nations on the Korean issue, affirming recognition of the government of the Republic of Korea as the only legal government of Korea without acknowledging its jurisdictional control over the entire Korean peninsula, Japan found it difficult to accede to the ROK interpretation from a realistic point of view.

Consequently, in the basic treaty Japan did not go beyond reaffirming the resolution of the United Nations that the Republic of Korea is the only legal government of Korea.

On the issue of invalidated treaties, Korea took the stand

that the Protectorate Convention and the Treaty of Annexation were both invalid as they had been illegally imposed on Korea by Japan. On the contrary, Japan pointed out that the San Francisco Peace Treaty had nullified these conventions and that it would be historically incorrect to claim that they were null and void from the start. The two countries finally agreed to delete the exact date of invalidation, merely acknowledging that the old Japan-Korea treaties were no longer in effect.

It is undeniable that the visit of Foreign Minister Shiina to Korea and the initialing of the Japan-Korea Basic Treaty greatly contributed toward the mood for a peaceful settlement of outstanding questions between Japan and Korea. By acquiescing to Korea's policy of first settling the comparatively easier problems in order to create such a mood of conciliation, the Japanese government found itself under public attack for having deviated from its original principle of seeking an overall rather than a piecemeal settlement.

The Japanese government, denying that the initialing of the basic agreement was inconsistent with its original purpose, declared its intention of submitting the treaty and the separate agreements at the same time to the National Diet for approval. The only major obstacles still awaiting solution were the questions of fisheries and the so-called Rhee Line to which Japan attached particular importance.

Among the pending questions, the one concerning compensation had already been agreed upon in the Ohira-Kim Memorandum, and on the question of the legal status of Koreans residing in Japan negotiations were proceeding on the basis of allowing a limited number of Koreans to permanently reside in Japan and receive treatment equal to that of the nationals of Japan. Despite Japan's concessions on both of these issues, there still remained a wide difference of opinion between the parties regarding Japan's demand for the abolition of the Rhee Line and for a guarantee of safe fishing by fishermen of western Japan.

Meanwhile, with the arrival of the ROK Minister of Agriculture and Forestry, Cha Kyu Hi, in Tokyo on March 2, 1965, the long-awaited fisheries negotiations got underway between Cha Kyu Hi and his Japanese counterpart, Munemori Akagi, from March 4 in an effort to reach an agreement on a preliminary draft. The main points taken up in the ministerial meetings were:

1. How to draw the basic line in order to determine the scope of exclusive fishing grounds in which South Korea could operate exclusively.

2. The extent of Japan's recognition of the direct basic line, especially around Cheju Island which is regarded as a rich fishing ground.

3. Determination of the number of Japanese fishing vessels to be permitted to operate in the joint fishing areas in order to conserve marine resources and the amount of annual hauls.

4. Penalization of fishing vessels which violate the agreement governing the joint fishing areas and the agreement on judicial rights.

After a number of deadlocks, the controversial fishery talks in Tokyo between Japan and South Korea reached an agreement on March 24.

Earlier, ROK Foreign Minister Lee Dong Won who arrived in Tokyo on March 10, en route to the United States, had met with Foreign Minister Etsusaburo Shiina and Agriculture and Forestry Minister Munemori Akagi for a final round of talks on the pending issues. Nine formal conversations took place between the Japanese and Korean foreign ministers.

During the hard-fought negotiations between the two countries, the question of the Rhee Line was not placed on the agenda since its existence had not been formally recognized by the Japanese government. By accepting Japan's stand, the Rhee Line had, for all practical purposes, been removed.

Salient points of the agreement were as follows:

1. The confirmation of the principle of the freedom of the open sea.

2. Recognition, in principle, that the outer border beyond twelve nautical miles of the exclusive fishing grounds shall be regarded as open sea.

3. From the standpoint of protecting marine resources, the establishment of a joint restricted area along the outer fringe of the exclusive fishing grounds.

4. Acceptance of the principle that the supervision and juridical jurisdiction within a joint restricted area of any fishing vessel shall belong to the country in which the vessel has been registered.

5. Agreement to establish temporarily a prohibited zone of fishing for Japanese fishing boats around Cheju Island.

6. Fixing of the total annual haul at 1.5 million tons, with a 10 per cent flexibility—either more or less—in the fixed tonnage.

With the abolition of the Rhee Line, in fact if not in name, and the confirmation of the principle of the freedom of the open sea as well as the acceptance of control of ships by the country of registration, the agreement offered safeguards not only against unlawful inspection by Korean patrol boats and detention of Japanese fishermen, but also ensured peaceful fishing operations.

Behind the establishment of the Rhee Line, there lurked the problem of the great difference between Japanese and Korean fisheries standards. Accordingly, during the Japan-ROK negotiations on fisheries, their talks also touched upon the possibility of Japan extending a private loan to assist Korea to elevate its fisheries standard to that of Japan within a few years. As a result, it was agreed that Japan would extend a private loan of $90 million with interest on part of the capital offered at a low rate of 5 per cent annually to assist South Korean fishermen.

The documents setting out agreements on fisheries, property claims, economic cooperation and the legal status of Koreans living in Japan were finally initialed on April 3, 1965. While the formal drafting of the provisions of the treaty was in progress, the only outstanding major issue perplexing the two countries concerned the question of sovereignty over Takeshima Island situated in the middle of the Japan Sea.

In a last minute bid to remove this hurdle, Foreign Minister Lee Dong Won of the Republic of Korea, who had hurriedly arrived in Tokyo on June 21, and Foreign Minister Etsu-saburo Shiina of Japan decided on June 22 on a formula for the settlement of the disputed island, just four hours before the formal signing of the Japan-Korea treaty was to take place.

In the light of anti-Japanese feeling in Korea, it was agreed that the question of sovereignty over Takeshima Island would be treated as a general dispute between the two countries to be settled through diplomatic negotiations. Should these diplomatic endeavors fail, the two parties expressed their willingness to refer the issue for mediation in accordance with agreed procedures as a means of reaching a settlement.

The treaty, agreement, and related documents for the normalization of relations between Japan and Korea were signed at 5 P.M. on June 22, 1965, at the Japanese Prime Minister's official residence in Tokyo. At the signing ceremony witnessed by Prime Minister Sato, the plenipotentiaries for Japan were Foreign Minister Shiina and Chief Delegate Taka-sugi and for Korea Foreign Minister Lee Dong Won and the Chief of the ROK Mission in Tokyo, Kim Dongjo.

The signing of the first Japan-Korea treaty was an epoch-making event, preceded by fourteen years of protracted nego-tiations since the first preliminary conference was held on October 20, 1951, through the good offices of the General Headquarters of the Allied Occupation Forces.

The diplomatic documents signed by the Japanese and Korean delegates included "The Treaty on the Basic Rela-tions between Japan and the Republic of Korea," four agree-ments relating to fishery restrictions, the legal status of Koreans living in Japan, South Korea's property claims against Japan, and economic and cultural cooperation, protocols, exchanged official documents, and mutually agreed minutes of the proceedings.

Later on July 12, the special session of the Korean National Assembly was convened to ratify the Japan-Korea treaty. The ratification of the treaty on August 14, however, was unilaterally pushed through the Assembly by the governing Democratic Republican Party which had no other alternative in the face of violent opposition by the opposition People's Party, students, and a group of intellectuals in the capital city of Seoul.

In Japan, at about the same time, the 49th special session of the National Diet was convened on July 22, following the elections for the Upper House, at which the Japan-Korea question figured prominently in the debates. The movement against ratification in Japan was led by the Socialist Party and a group of leftists.

Elements opposing the Japan-Korea treaty and agreements can be roughly divided into two broad categories. The first group included those who were hostile to any formal relationship between Japan and South Korea while the second group were dissatisfied with the terms of the treaty and the related agreements. In other words, the former were unconditional opponents and the latter were conditional opponents. Whereas the opposition in Korea were mainly of the conditional type, the preponderance of opposition strength in Japan lay with the irreconcilables.

But the opposition to the treaty in Korea continued even after its ratification with students taking to street demonstrations and clashing with army troops. The failure of the opposition to thwart the government's efforts is due in large measure to the firm position adopted by President Park Chung Hee who boldly declared that he would shoulder the entire responsibility for the ratification, while awaiting the impartial judgment of history.

The position of the opposition was also rather tenuous. Opposition parties and intellectuals spoke in abstract terms about the dangers of a revival of Japanese aggression, but offered no alternative policy in keeping with the actual conditions in Korea. It was reported also that the people generally were unresponsive to the student demonstrations. Having tasted the bitterness of the Korean War, the vast majority of the people were strongly antagonistic toward communism, gave precedence to the issue of reunification over Japan-Korea reconciliation, and were unsympathetic to any appeal for neutralism.

In short, when the verbiage of the opposition in Korea was shorn of its superfluity, it was discovered that the opposition was due only to discontent over the contents of the treaty. One of their main dissatisfactions was over the fisheries agreement which they regarded to be disadvantageous to Korea.

First, they charged that if the signing of the treaty removed the Rhee Line as an actual defensive line, it was tantamount to a surrender of Korea's sovereignty. Second, they claimed that the outright grant of $300 million and the long-term loan of $200 million at low interest were too small a price to compensate Korea for Japan's colonial control of thirty-six years.

In reply to the protests of the opposition, the government and the ruling party counseled for moderation, pointing out that two parties were involved in the negotiations. The proponents bluntly asked the opposition if they had the confidence to reach a more favorable settlement if they had been the negotiators.

During the debate on the treaty in the Korean Assembly, there were certain instances when the government's interpretations of the provisions of the treaty differed substantially from those of Japan, but the discrepancies were overlooked as being attributable to the complexities of the internal situation in Korea.

Although under Article 3 of the Japan-Korea Basic Treaty, the Republic of Korea is the only legal government of Korea, in the light of the actual existence of a separate government of the Korean People's Democratic Republic, the administrative power of the South Korean government extends only to the area south of the armistice line (38 degrees north latitude).

Concerning the Rhee Line, with the coming into effect of the Japan-Korea fisheries agreement and the acceptance of the principle of the freedom of the open sea, the fishery operations of the two countries would be regulated by the agreement. Regardless of the nature of the national laws of the Republic of Korea, the Rhee Line would not, insofar as Japan is concerned, be a factor in endangering the safety of Japanese fishing operations.

Insofar as Takeshima Island is concerned, the dispute remains unsettled in view of the refusal of the Republic of Korea to recognize Japan's oft-stated claim to the island. Its existence as a "dispute between the two countries," mentioned in the documents exchanged between Japan and Korea, is a matter of fact.

On jurisdictional rights and the Rhee Line, according to Foreign Minister Shiina, Japan would unquestionably protest to the government of Korea if its interests were infringed upon, but to take up the issues unsubstantially would be meddling in Korea's domestic affairs.

On the issue of Takeshima Island, as the two countries agreed in an exchange of documents to try to find a solution to this dispute through diplomatic channels, turning to mediation in case of failure, Mr. Shiina felt that Korea would respond to Japan's approach.

As far as the Japanese government was concerned, since the treaty and agreements had been mutually agreed to by the two governments, with each word carefully scrutinized, it could hardly admit of two different official interpretations.

However, the chairman of the Socialist Party Mr. Sasaki and others voiced their resolute opposition to the Japan-ROK agreements in their attacks on the government's policy. They contended that the normalization of Japan-Korea relations would perpetuate the division of North and South Korea and would, in fact, link Japan to the Northeast Asian military alliance. In addition, the economic assistance amounting to $800 million could be interpreted as economic aggression by Japanese monopolistic capital.

In reply to Chairman Sasaki's questions, Prime Minister Sato outlined the views of the government and the ruling party as follows:

1. A great many members of the United Nations have extended recognition to the government of South Korea, and Japan concluded the Japan-Korea treaty solely out of a desire to establish friendly relations with a neighboring country. This step had nothing to do with the questions of either Vietnam or military alliances.

2. Admittedly there is a regime in North Korea, but Japan has not yet arrived at a stage where it felt that it could engage in concrete talks with that regime. The question of the right to make claims has not been touched upon, and the holding of tripartite talks between North and South Korea and Japan cannot be contemplated.

The reasons for the inability to unify North and South Korea is traceable to objective conditions, and there is no hope that such conditions will be dissolved in the foreseeable future. Japan naturally hopes this unfortunate division will be ended as soon as possible, but if this is impossible it is only natural for Japan to enter into relations with the Republic of Korea, Japan's nearest neighbor and a country with which it has such close interests.

Furthermore, for the stability of Japan, it is indispensable that there should at least be a stable and friendly government in existence in South Korea. Geographical proximity as well as historical relations between the two countries prove that this is true.

Only the communists and fellow travelers refute the importance of South Korea being stable and prosperous at the time the two divided states are united. If it is true, as the opponents declare, that the extension of recognition to only South Korea would perpetuate the division of Korea, why is not the same charge made against the countries of the communist bloc which recognize only North Korea?

Communist China and the Japan Socialist Party, which share the same views, have denounced the restoration of Japan-Korea relations as being the first step toward a Northeast Asian military alliance and a plot to make Asians fight Asians.

The posture of Communist China which had acted provocatively in both the Korean War and the Sino-Indian border conflict, its flouting of the principle of peaceful coexistence, its opposition to the Vietnam talks, its refusal to listen to the views of other countries, and its avowal that it alone is infallible amount to nothing more than hopeless doctrinairism.

Needless to say, Japan's economic assistance and private loans amounting to $800 million were directed toward the economic rehabilitation and stabilization of the political and social life of the people of South Korea. To accuse Japan of economic aggression falls wide of the mark. A country with a paucity of local capital requires foreign assistance and cooperation for industrial expansion. Even Communist China which proclaims a policy of self-reliance had had the basis of its industrial power laid by Soviet cooperation. Nevertheless, it is important that Japan should not engage in unfair competition in capital investments and commercial rights, avoiding at all costs even the slightest suspicion on the part of the Korean people that Japan was guilty of economic aggression.

The 50th special session of the National Diet, known later as the Japan-Korea Treaty Ratification Diet, was convened on October 5. In his policy speech delivered on October 13, Prime Minister Sato, in stressing the necessity of ratifying the treaty, declared that if peace cannot be established with South Korea, the nearest neighbor of Japan, then Japan was not qualified to talk about peace. He also clarified the following points:

1. The Japan-Korea treaty—the result of fourteen years of tireless efforts—by dissolving past differences between the two countries in order to establish permanent, neighborly and friendly relations would form the basis of a new era of cooperation and prosperity.

2. Through the exchange of official documents, the path toward the peaceful settlement of the Takeshima problem had been opened. Needless to say, the island of Takeshima has been Japan's territory since time immemorial, and the government intended to adhere strongly to this stand in the future also.

3. The argument of a section of the people that this treaty would develop into a military alliance has no substance whatever. From the spirit of our constitution, this claim is incredulous.

In a diplomatic policy speech, Foreign Minister Shiina alluded to the failure of North Korea to agree to free elections under the supervision of the United Nations as being the direct cause of obstructing the unification of Korea and stressed that the argument that the conclusion of the Japan-Korea treaty hampered the unification of North and South Korea was totally at variance with the objective facts.

The Lower House, after establishing a Japan-Korea special committee, deliberated on the issue for ten days from October 26. With the Democratic Socialist Party showing signs of approving the Japan-Korea bill on November 5 during the general meeting of its parliamentary members, the ruling party forced the passage of the bill on November 6, simultaneously with the meeting of the special committee.

As soon as the plenary session of the Lower House began deliberations on November 8, the Socialist Party, the unions affiliated with the General Confederation of Trade Unions and the Communist Party staged opposition struggles for many days outside the National Diet. Inside the Diet, the opposition parties made every effort to prevent the ratification. In view of the failure to get proceedings going and the deadlock among the contending parties, Mr. Naka Funada, the Speaker of the Lower House, used his powers to summon the plenary session on November 9. The Socialist Party countered this move by tabling a series of no confidence motions against the Foreign Minister and other cabinet members. They employed such tactics as the so-called cow's-pace during the balloting to slow down proceedings and forced the deliberations to continue throughout the night.

Declaring that such tactics obstructed normal procedures, the speaker rammed the Japan-Korea bill through the Lower House and sent the bill to the Upper House.

In the Upper House, the speaker also used his powers to open the plenary session to pass the resolution to establish the Japan-Korea special committee presented by the Liberal Democratic Party. Under these circumstances, the Diet proceedings were in a state of suspension.

Speaker Shigemune finally succeeded on November 19 in calling a plenary session, at which it was decided to refer the Japan-Korea bill to the special committee of the Upper House. Although deliberations began on November 22, the Socialist Party and its supporters were determined to hold up the bill concerning the Japan-Korea domestic laws and to turn the treaty itself into a dead letter. Actions similar to those taken in the Lower House were adopted in the Upper House to delay the passage of the bill.

On December 4, a motion by the Liberal Democratic Party was submitted during the questionings by a Socialist member in the Japan-Korea special committee to curtail the deliberations. Shortly thereafter, the Japan-Korea treaty bill and related domestic laws were passed. The opposition parties charged that the move was invalid, but on December 8 the plenary session of the Upper House was summoned by the speaker to deal with the bill.

At this plenary session, the Socialist Party presented a number of motions and held back the proceedings by resorting to "dragging the feet" tactics. Ultimately, however, on December 11, all bills relating to the Japan-Korea problem were approved in the absence of the Socialist Party, the Communist Party, the Komeito (political party of Soka Gakkai, a powerful new religion), and members of the Niin Club (a political group in the Upper House).

The employment of extraordinary measures by the government and the Liberal Democratic Party to get the two houses of parliament to approve the bill highlighted the grave dangers facing parliamentary procedures. It was deeply regrettable that the ruling and opposition parties had to clash so violently over such an important diplomatic question as the Japan-Korea bill.

The exchange of ratification of the Japan-Korea treaty, promising a new era in the history of Japanese-Korean relations took place at the Central Government Building in Seoul on December 18. The instruments of ratification were exchanged between Foreign Ministers Etsusaburo Shiina and Lee Dong Won in the presence of Prime Minister Chung Il Kwon.

In a special message on the occasion, President Park Chung Hee declared that the feeling of enmity, which had blemished the past thirty-six years of Japan-Korea relations, was now a thing of the past. He stressed that the people of Korea had overcome countless difficulties in normalizing Japan-Korea relations for the sake of Free World unity and for the strengthening of anticommunism in Asia. The Republic of Korea and Japan had embarked on the first step of creating a new landmark in the history of Asia, a history that was not one of aggression or one-sided cooperation, but one of trust and help for the furtherance of their mutual interests.

After fourteen long years and many difficulties, Japan and Korea succeeded in normalizing their relations. Their future path promises to be one of mutual respect, equality, friendship, and neighborliness. Welcomed by all sections of the Japanese people, the treaty foreshadowed a new age for Japan and Korea in which the unfortunate past would no longer mar their newly established friendship. (July, 1967)

CHAPTER 17

Vietnam Policy

WITH THE escalation of the air attacks over North Vietnam by the United States Air Force and the widening military operations in the Mekong Delta by the American and South Vietnamese forces, the tempo of the Vietnam war, the focus of world tensions, has increased in intensity.

The American military escalation has continued because neither side is prepared to shift its oft-stated position. As a condition for a halt in the aerial bombing, the United States is demanding that North Vietnam cease sending military supplies and personnel into South Vietnam, while North Vietnam is demanding an unconditional and permanent cessation of the American air attacks.

As long as North Vietnam refuses to compromise, the United States will continue its present policy of applying military pressure, of which the aerial attack against the North is an important element, and at the same time bolster the position of South Vietnam. On the other hand, it is seeking every avenue to reach a peaceful settlement with North Vietnam, exercising great patience in the hope that Hanoi will eventually become conciliatory.

What should be the attitude of Japan in these circumstances? As a stabilizing force in Asia, it should use all available diplomatic channels to contact every conceivable quarter for the sake of a settlement in Vietnam.

In connection with this effort, it is desirable that Japan

212

should be prepared to participate in the international armistice or peace observation team to be established after the restoration of peace.

However, the past record of the Japanese attitude toward the Vietnam problem, as outlined in a speech delivered by Prime Minister Sato before the 49th extraordinary session of the National Diet in August, 1965, may be summarized as follows:

1. To achieve peace in Vietnam, it is a prerequisite for the parties involved in the conflict to agree to unconditional talks. Since the parties involved refer to the present belligerents, they also include the Viet Cong.

2. Though the continuance of the bombing of the North is regrettable, emphasis should be placed on the fact that the United States is fighting against communist aggression. At the same time, it is recognized that the United States is endeavoring to reach a settlement at the conference table.

3. In connection with the statement made by the then Ambassador Reischauer on his return to the United States that America was unpopular in Japan, it should be pointed out that, while Japan desires the nonescalation of the conflict and an early settlement, it does not believe that the mere withdrawal by the United States will provide the solution.

4. Japan has no intention of according immediate recognition to North Vietnam, and has reservations regarding the practicability of the Vietnam problem being satisfactorily solved at this stage by the Vietnamese themselves. The fact that the Eastern blocs and the Western world are actively supporting one or the other of the regimes belonging to the same race is not only dangerous but unfortunate.

5. Japan is often accused of doing nothing, but the fact should not be overlooked that neither side is prepared to seriously heed its advice. This situation may, of course, change with the lapse of time. The government would welcome any contribution which the Socialist Party can possibly make toward a peaceful solution.

In the debate on the United States military operations in Vietnam during the 49th extraordinary session of the National Diet, attention was focused on the clause concerning prior consultation in the Japan-United States Security Treaty. The issue arose from the incident involving a fleet of B-52 bombers which had taken off on a bombing mission from Okinawa after having allegedly sought refuge from a typhoon. The government took the following stand during the interpellations:

1. In the case of the B-52 bombers, although legality is not questioned in view of American administrative rights in Okinawa, the government will strongly urge the United States against any such repetition in view of the national feelings in Japan.

2. Should United States military aircraft from bases in Guam land in Japan after a bombing mission over Vietnam, such visits will not be regarded as requiring prior consultation as these aircraft did not take part directly in hostilities from bases in Japan and had already completed their military operations prior to landing at Japanese bases. However, if the use of Japanese bases should become a general practice in these aerial operations, the government may be compelled to take up the issue.

3. Whereas the entry of any atomic warhead into Japan will require prior consultation, a carrier without this weapon is excluded from such requirements. The B-52 is regarded as a missile launcher, but in case it is not equipped with an atomic warhead it is not an object of prior consultation. The same may be said of the nuclear-powered submarine.

Needless to say, on these delicate questions the government and the Liberal Democratic Party made every effort to respect national opinion in formulating its policy regarding Vietnam.

Later, on December 2, 1965, British Foreign Secretary Michael Stewart, while on a visit to the Soviet Union, attracted widespread interest when he declared over Moscow Television that both Great Britain and the Soviet Union appealed for an end to the Vietnam war. In this broadcast he called for a conference of all the governments connected with the Vietnam war to work out an agreement for an early end to the fighting.

Giving United States approval to the Stewart proposal, Secretary of State Dean Rusk replied that he would be happy to attend such a conference. The Japanese Foreign Ministry, for its part, simply stated informally that Japan hoped that the efforts of Great Britain and the Soviet Union, the cochairmen of the Geneva Conference, would lead toward a quick solution of the Vietnam situation.

After thoroughly discussing the issue, the government came up with the following conclusions:

1. Irrespective of whether or not they are signatories of the Geneva Conference, all nations which are either involved or have strong interest in the peace of Southeast Asia should take part in the deliberations to find a settlement to the Vietnam problem.

2. Japan should positively support the proposal by British Foreign Secretary Stewart and call on all nations concerned to promptly summon such a conference.

At a dinner of the Japan-British Society on December 7, 1965, Prime Minister Sato, referring to Great Britain's role as the leader of the British Commonwealth of Nations, praised the British government for its role in establishing the Commonwealth peace mission and for its efforts toward a Vietnam settlement. The Prime Minister highly evaluated the proposal made in Moscow by Foreign Secretary Stewart for a conference as another manifestation of that government's continuing traditional efforts for peace. Declaring that Japan had as much interest, if not more so than Great Britain in the peaceful settlement of the Vietnam problem, Prime Minister Sato welcomed the Stewart proposal and promised his full support in promoting a conference of the interested parties. From an expression of a desire for peace in Vietnam, the Japanese government had adopted a more positive stance in seeking a settlement.

Hoping to extricate itself from the quagmire of the Vietnam war, the United States halted its bombings of the North for thirty-seven days, from Christmas Eve of 1965 to the end of January of the following year. During this interval, the United States spared no efforts to explore the possibilities of peace.

Reporting on these efforts, President Johnson in his State of the Union speech revealed that a number of distinguished United States spokesmen, such as roving Ambassador Averell Harriman, Vice President Hubert Humphrey, Special Presidential Assistant McGeorge Bundy, United Nations Ambassador Arthur Goldberg, and Assistant Secretary of State G. Mennen Williams, had visited forty countries of the world and had spoken to the leaders of more than a hundred governments in an effort to explain the fourteen points of America's peace plan for Vietnam. However, no fruitful results were obtained as North Vietnam, the Viet Cong, and the communist bloc branded these efforts as a hoax.

America reported that efforts for peace have not been abandoned, but in view of North Vietnam's refusal to respond to the peace offer and its increased infiltration into South Vietnam during the lull in the bombings, it had resumed its aerial attacks.

On resuming its bombings of the North, the United States requested an emergency session of the United Nations Security Council on January 31, 1966, to discuss the Vietnam issue, and appealed for world-wide efforts for peace. On February 8, President Johnson flew to Honolulu to meet the leaders of the South Vietnam government in order to discuss the augmentation of military strength and the improvement of the people's livelihood. Thus, the United States continued its efforts in South Vietnam on the military as well as civil fronts, seizing every available opportunity to achieve a peaceful settlement.

During this period, Japan supported America's attempts to find peace, and although the visit of Foreign Minister Etsusaburo Shiina to the Soviet Union in January, 1966, did not yield the desirable results, Japan continued to press ahead by dispatching Special Envoy Shojiro Kawashima to the United Arab Republic and other countries in the Near and Middle East, and Ambassador Yokoyama on a three-month tour of Europe, the Near and Middle East, and Asia. As the time was not yet ripe for such endeavors, nothing positive resulted.

The emergency session of the United Nations Security Council met on February 1 to consider the United States request to discuss the Vietnam issue, under the presidency of Ambassador Akira Matsui of Japan. To reconcile the views of the United States, the Soviet Union, and other nations, the Security Council recessed for two days, during which the delegates carried out behind-the-scene parleys.

Obstructed by the firm opposition of the Soviet Union to the discussion of the issue by the Security Council, Ambassador Matsui attempted to resolve the situation by issuing a president's statement, summing up the maximum commitments of the member countries. With the Soviet Union and France, on the one hand, intimating that they were not in favor of such a step, and the United States, on the other, feeling that it would serve no useful purpose to press the issue further in the Security Council at this time, plans to resummon the United Nations Security Council were abandoned.

On February 26, Matsui ended his efforts by sending letters to the Secretary General of the United Nations and member countries of the United Nations, informing them that there existed a strong desire for a peaceful settlement.

The United States issued a statement welcoming Matsui's effort, but the Soviet Union refused to accept the communication, France sent a counter note, and Mali reacted with a note of protest.

Later the same year, the three-nation conference of ASA (Association of Southeast Asia) comprising Thailand, Malaysia, and the Philippines, which met in Bangkok on August 3, issued a call for a conference of seventeen nations of Asia, in the place of the Geneva signatories, to discuss the Vietnam war. The proposal for an Asian peace conference pointed out that the Vietnam war was an Asian problem and that the Asian peoples themselves should attempt to find a solution through mutual discussion. Japan agreed to become a party to the appeal, but the proposal was rejected by Communist China and North Vietnam.

Then on October 24 and 25, in response to the proposal of President Marcos of the Philippines, the seven nations participating in the Vietnam war held a conference in Manila. Japan naturally did not participate in this conference. President Johnson, who attended this conference, took the opportunity to visit the allied countries in the Vietnam war as well as Malaysia, but did not visit Japan.

With Communist China thrown into chaos by the Great Cultural Revolution, it appeared for a time that the increased influence of the Soviet Union in North Vietnam might present a slight chance of a move toward peace. But the Soviet Union, like North Vietnam, merely called for a unilateral halt in the American bombing of the North and took no initiative for a peaceful settlement.

However, during the temporary truce over the New Year holiday of 1967 and the Tet festival (February 8 to 12), the United States Embassy in Moscow sent an appeal for peace talks to the North Vietnamese Embassy. This move was brought to light by the State Department on March 21 when it published President Johnson's letter of February 8 to President Ho Chi Minh of North Vietnam. In his communication, President Johnson stressed the following points:

1. In order to avoid mutual misunderstanding caused by indirect contact, the United States proposes direct talks between the United States and North Vietnam with a view to reaching a peaceful settlement of the Vietnam war.

2. Rejection of the Hanoi demand for an unconditional and permanent halt in the bombing of the North.

3. If North Vietnam ceases its military infiltration into the South, the United States is prepared to cease its bombing of the North and discontinue reinforcing its troops in South Vietnam.

According to the State Department spokesman, four similar approaches were made from January by the American Embassy in Moscow to North Vietnam, restating the position outlined by President Johnson. On January 27, North Vietnam sent a reply which violently denounced the bombing of the North. With this communication pipeline established, President Johnson sent his letter on February 8. The reply from President Ho Chi Minh delivered to the American Embassy in Moscow demanded an immediate and unconditional halt in the bombing.

On March 21, on his return from a conference with South Vietnam government leaders on Guam, President Johnson revealed to pressmen that there had been an exchange of notes with President Ho Chi Minh. He regretted the refusal of North Vietnam to enter into direct talks, but promised that efforts would be continued to find an honorable peace in Vietnam.

In the meantime, Japan adopted a positive stand toward realizing peace in Vietnam, which the Foreign Ministry described in an article entitled: "Ways of Settling the Vietnam Conflict and the Role of Our Country." Foreign Minister Takeo Miki based his policy on the three pillars of (1) Japan continuing its efforts until peace was achieved, (2) a positive plan for peace, and (3) the role of Japan after the establishment of peace.

These three basic points may be separately clarified as follows:

1. Japan should play the role of an honest broker by accommodating the opinions of the two sides. In other words, it should grasp the true will of the United States and South Vietnam and relay this to North Vietnam. Japan should also keep in continuous touch with the views of North Vietnam, and transmit these views to the other side. It is essential that misunderstanding should not be caused by misinformation.

Although the absence of diplomatic relations with North Vietnam is a major handicap, Japan should seize every opportunity to indirectly contact North Vietnam through a third party. Our policy should be to persist in making informal soundings and in relaying America's views.

2. Fundamentally, the 1954 Geneva Agreements will be respected, but the main objective is to re-establish an immediate armistice along the 17th parallel which divides North and South Vietnam. At the same time, international guarantee by an international peace preservation force sponsored by the United Nations shall neutralize both the North and South. On this occasion, all foreign military forces will be withdrawn from North and South Vietnam. The future course of the two zones of Vietnam shall be decided by the Vietnamese themselves, and the problem of the Viet Cong in the South shall be dealt with as an internal problem of South Vietnam.

3. After the restoration of peace, Tokyo is offered as a venue for discussing the concrete conditions of peace by North and South Vietnam and other interested parties. Should the site be in a neutral country such as Burma, Japan is still willing to do its utmost to facilitate the holding of the conference. Moreover, in case of an international guarantee for the neutralization of North and South Vietnam, Japan shall not only participate as a third party, but in the event of the establishment of an international observers' team to oversee the implementation of the peace conditions, it shall dispatch members for the team. The dispatch of members of the self-defense forces is, however, not contemplated.

For postwar rehabilitation in North and South Vietnam, Japan shall increase its aid to promote the stabilization of the people's livelihood.

Despite constant failures, Vietnam peace efforts are still being made, with Secretary General of the United Nations U Thant playing the leading role. Canada and Ceylon have also been making individual proposals. The peace plan of the Japanese Foreign Office takes these international moves into consideration.

While these peace maneuvers are being made, it is imperative that Japan also cooperate in improving the people's livelihood and in accelerating economic construction in the war-weary nation of South Vietnam. In 1964 and in 1966, Japan contributed $1.5 million and $200 thousand respectively, in emergency relief funds for the refugees.

Furthermore, in June, 1967, in an agreement signed between the two countries, Japan offered an additional sum of $1.1 million for medical supplies. This was the first time since 1959, when the reparations agreement was signed, that the two countries entered into a formal agreement.

According to the list of countries sending material aid to South Vietnam announced on March 11, 1967 by the United States State Department, there are thirty-eight donor countries. Japan is credited with having provided medical supplies and transistor radios, and with the construction of electric power plants. The report stresses the need to extend foreign technical assistance in the future—a field in which the equipment and technology of Japan's small and medium industries are playing a helpful role in South Vietnam, whose industry is still relatively undeveloped technologically. It is, therefore, desirable that the Japanese government and business circles should take effective steps to increase the export of industrial technology for peaceful purposes. (July, 1967)

CHAPTER 18

Communist China's
Nuclear Bomb Tests

WITHOUT paying the slightest heed to world public opinion, Communist China created a sensation by carrying out its first nuclear bomb test explosion on October 18, 1964. Since the bomb was considered to be a uranium 235 type, and not a plutonium bomb, the test could not be lightly dismissed, not only from political and psychological points of view, but also from a military standpoint. The atomic blast had grave implications not only for Japan and the countries neighboring Communist China, but for Asia and the rest of the world as well.

In the case of Japan, although the country's security was safeguarded by the Japan-United States Security Treaty, the Communist Chinese nuclear threat made it desirable to clarify the extent of the protective shield. Fortunately, this objective was achieved during the visit of Prime Minister Eisaku Sato to the United States in January, 1965.

Following the two days of talks between Prime Minister Sato and United States President Lyndon B. Johnson on January 12 and 13, a joint communique was issued, in which the two leaders reaffirmed their view that the elimination of any doubt about the maintenance of Japan's security was indispensable for the stability and peace of Asia. The American President went on to reassure Japan that the United States would defend it against any external attack in strict conformance with the terms of the security treaty. The communique served to underline the United States determination to offer Japan a protective nuclear umbrella.

On May 15, 1965, Communist China exploded its second nuclear device. Being an atmospheric test, it showed that Communist China was well on the way toward becoming a nuclear-weapon state. Although the military effects of the tests have been minimized, it is felt that they are bound to have an important bearing on the future military situation in Asia.

Commenting on the effects of Communist China equipping itself with nuclear weapons, the well-known French military affairs expert General Pierre Gallois has emphasized that what is of paramount importance is not the size and effectiveness of the bomb itself, but the very fact that Peking is now a nuclear-weapon state whose influence will radically change the power relationships in Asia.

General Gallois warned that when the vast mainland of China and its huge population are harnessed by the doctrinal Chinese leadership to the power of the nuclear weapon, it will signal the "great transformation of the Far East." He further believes that Asia will pass through a period of tensions similar to that which Europe experienced after the Soviet Union exploded its first nuclear bomb in 1949. In order to counter the possible Soviet nuclear threat, the United States made its military presence felt throughout the length and breadth of Europe, from Norway to Turkey. In Asia, too, the United States may be compelled to fill an even greater military power vacuum extending from Kamchatka to the Persian Gulf.

Whereas—unlike Japan which is directly protected against the Communist Chinese nuclear threat by the Japan-United States Security Treaty—the nations of Asia do not have an equal assurance, the problem of providing security for the nonnuclear-weapon states of Asia is becoming increasingly acute.

British Prime Minister Harold Wilson has been quick to realize the far-reaching implications of this problem. When

Foreign Secretary Michael Stewart visited Japan in October, Prime Minister Sato attracted widespread attention when he joined the British Foreign Secretary in declaring that some measures will have to be taken to remove the feeling of uncertainty against the threat of nuclear weapons among the nonnuclear-weapon states in Southeast Asia. Referring to this problem, the British newspaper, *The Times,* commented that although Europe has NATO, it is a matter of serious concern that in Asia there is a nuclear vacuum.

Of interest, too, is the fact that both Vice President Hubert Humphrey and Secretary of State Dean Rusk of the United States have suggested that Japan should participate in the nuclear discussions. In an interview with Japanese newsmen in November, Vice President Humphrey stated that the time has come for the United States to confer with friendly countries in framing its nuclear weapon strategy and nuclear policy. This suggestion did not imply the transfer of nuclear weapons to these countries, but an awakening that Japan as a major power should join in the deliberations.

Shortly after Humphrey's statement, Secretary of State Rusk told newsmen that in talks on nuclear problems, the United States government policy favors Japan's participation. Mr. Rusk also revealed that the United States is already consulting its allies, including Japan, on this problem, encompassing also the question of nuclear strategy.

In December, United States Secretary of Defense Robert S. McNamara, speaking before the NATO Council of Ministers, attracted unusual interest by declaring that Communist China would by 1967 be armed with an intermediate-range missile capped with a nuclear warhead. He predicted that by 1968 or 1969, Communist China would also develop a number of intermediate-range missile launching pads, increasing that number manyfold by 1976.

In February and March, 1966, McNamara had stressed in Congressional hearings Communist China's capabilities of developing the intermediate-range ballistic missile, and sounded ominous warnings against the dangers of Peking's nuclear arms development.

It should be noted, however, that on the first two occasions of its nuclear bomb tests, Communist China had called for a conference of world leaders to discuss nuclear disarmament. Although this call was made even prior to the tests, the theme of the disarmament conference of world leaders was limited to preventing the use of all types of nuclear weapons.

The main aim of both Communist China and France, which entered the atomic arena belatedly, seems to be directed toward checking the overpowering strength of the United States and the Soviet Union. The Communist Chinese proposal has the same objective, as does the French proposal demanding the destruction of all means of delivery. The two countries have turned their backs on the questions of banning nuclear tests and nuclear nonproliferation.

In other words, Communist China does not desire to have even the slightest limitation placed on her current crash program of developing nuclear missiles. By developing its nuclear arsenal, Communist China hopes to be in a favorable position to challenge so-called American imperialism and Soviet revisionism, give political and moral support to so-called wars of national liberation, and enhance its prestige and influence in Asia.

Later on July 5, 1966, in a speech before the fifth meeting of the Joint Japan-United States Committee on Trade and Economic Affairs, American Secretary of State Rusk declared that, if necessary, the United States would employ all available weapons and all means to honor its treaty commitments. This statement was regarded as the first indication of America's firm resolve to extend its nuclear defense to Asia.

In the meantime, Communist China exploded a rapid series of nuclear bombs, the third on May 14, the fourth on October 27, and the fifth on December 28. These tests were carried out in the midst of great uneasiness caused by the storm of the Great Cultural Revolution. On the occasion of its third nuclear test, Communist China announced what was considered to be a preliminary test of a hydrogen bomb by declaring that the nuclear blast carried out in the atmosphere contained thermonuclear material. To the anxious world, Communist China announced that in the fourth series of tests it had developed a guided missile with a nuclear warhead. There appeared little reason to doubt that Communist China was determined to overtake Great Britain and France to become the world's third most powerful nuclear-weapon state, following the United States and the Soviet Union.

Although no official statement was issued by Peking about the size or nature of the fifth test, American government sources estimated the strength to be in the neighborhood of 200 to 300 kilotons of TNT, somewhere in the range of the hydrogen bomb. In any case, Communist China is sparing nothing to build up its own nuclear strength. The time is obviously not far off when Communist China will be able to graduate from the stage of elementary nuclear missiles to the more advanced stage of having intermediate-range ballistic missiles operational for actual warfare.

Lately, however, views have been expressed that the tempo of development of Communist China's nuclear weapons may slow down as a result of the uncertainties caused by the future course of the Great Cultural Revolution. In this connection, American Secretary of Defense McNamara stated in his Annual Defense Report published on January 26, 1967, that Communist China may not have an effective quantity of tactical missiles by the mid-1970's but, owing to the priority given to nuclear missile development, the country may—according to recent information—launch a space rocket or long-range ballistic missile before the end of the year.

Should it be impossible to halt the progress of nuclearization of Communist China, the United States, not to speak of the neighboring states, will have to adopt measures to deal with the nuclear weapons being developed by Communist China. The latest development on the Chinese Mainland has also placed the Geneva Disarmament Conference in a dilemma, accompanied as it is by the need to provide security for the nonnuclear weapon states especially in the Asian region.

Within this context, Japan is in a unique position because of the protective nuclear umbrella provided by the United States under its security treaty with the latter. A similar situation prevails in the case of South Korea, Nationalist China, and the Philippines, which are allied with the United States in military alliances. There are also multilateral alliances, such as SEATO and ANZUS, but in the case of the former there appears to be a split in the ranks. A problem which must be faced in the near future is whether the present arrangements are satisfactory for these various countries. Will not Asia also require a collective nuclear force? Of course, owing to the difference in nuclear power of the United States and Communist China, the situation in Asia is different from that of Europe. Consequently, for the time being it will not be necessary for the United States to store strategical nuclear weapons in the Far East, including Japan. In view of Communist China's limited nuclear threat, the United States at present has sufficient means of delivering the nuclear weapons by naval vessels.

However, when the idea of nuclear weaponry for Asia, proposed by British Prime Minister Harold Wilson and the the Minister of State in charge of disarmament Lord Chalfont, becomes a subject of serious discussion, there is the possibility of these countries participating in discussions on nuclear strategy and the transferring of nuclear weapons.

A situation similar to that of West Germany in NATO may arise. For instance, although West Germany has abandoned the idea of directly participating in sharing NATO's nuclear strength, it is participating in the discussions and planning of NATO's nuclear defense as a member of the so-called McNamara Committee.

In connection with the nuclear nonproliferation treaty, West German Chancellor Kiesinger does not believe that the path should be closed to participation in the nuclear war potential of the European Union when the European countries, including France, establish the organization in the future.

The position of the nonaligned countries, such as India, also poses a question. India is against relying on alliances and protective nuclear cover by third powers for its own security. Moreover, India, like Japan, has developed nuclear energy for peaceful purposes to a stage where it has a high degree of capability of manufacturing nuclear weapons. Consequently, on the heels of each nuclear test conducted in Communist China, public insistence has been growing in India to manufacture nuclear arms.

Should India take such a step, it is hardly conceivable that Pakistan will remain passive. The danger of chain reaction exists. To avoid such a development, it becomes urgent to provide India with some form of nuclear guarantee.

On the question of the nuclear nonproliferation treaty, India has made it plain that it cannot allow its hands to be tied in the face of the threat posed by Communist China, and has pointed to the necessity of nuclear protection being provided by the nuclear-weapon states.

However, it seems rather shortsighted of India to have welcomed Soviet Prime Minister Kosygin's proposal of February, 1966, to prohibit the use of nuclear weapons against a nonnuclear-weapon state which does not allow stationing of nuclear-weapons within its territory. Should this formula be accepted by the countries of Asia, including Japan, it would mean that the noncommunist countries alone would become a denuclearized zone.

This nuclearized zone, proposed earlier by the Soviet Union, is also advocated by the Japanese Socialist Party. The aim is to neutralize the nuclear deterrent of the United States so that the conventional military power of the Soviet Union and Communist China, especially the massive human wave assaults of the latter, can play a decisive role.

The fact must not be overlooked that the real danger posed

by Communist China is not so much the threat of direct nuclear attack, but interference by conventional armed forces backed by nuclear power, as well as by indirect penetration.

Then, on June 17, Communist China conducted its sixth nuclear test, exploding its first hydrogen device. According to the *Liberation Daily,* the Communist Chinese Army organ, the test was held a month earlier than originally planned. Coinciding with the emergency meeting of the United Nations General Assembly to deal with the Middle East hostilities, it is perhaps safe to assume that the move had political designs.

Whatever the motivation, it must be admitted that the tempo of development of Communist China's nuclear weapons gives cause for alarm. Though circumstances may differ, it took the United States seven years, the Soviet Union four years, and Great Britain five years to advance from the first nuclear device to the hydrogen bomb. France has not yet exploded a hydrogen bomb despite its seven-year history of nuclear-weapon development.

In its announcement, Communist China merely stated that it had successfully exploded a hydrogen bomb in the western area of China. It was probably dropped by aircraft and not a missile-type bomb. However, as a guided missile was utilized in launching the nuclear bomb during the fourth test in October, 1966, it can be expected that the aim is to miniaturize the hydrogen warhead for missile delivery. It is, therefore, only a matter of time before a test using the missile with a hydrogen bomb warhead is conducted.

The well-known American physicist, Professor Ralph Lapp, who has accurately predicted Communist China's nuclear development in the past, said on June 20 that Communist China will probably possess 100 hydrogen bombs or hydrogen bomb warheads by 1970. He also expects that Communist China will by then have developed long-range ballistic missiles capable of attacking strategic targets. Although it may not be the most modern missile in the world, it will serve Communist China's military and political objectives. If they can develop a missile capable of landing within eight kilo-meters of the center of the target, they can destroy such large American cities as Los Angeles and San Francisco.

In the midst of the Middle East crisis, the specter of the 700 million people of Communist China, caught in the throes of the Great Cultural Revolution, the thoughts of Mao Tse-tung, and the development of nuclear weapons, is causing grave concern throughout the world. (July, 1967)

CHAPTER 19

Nonproliferation of Nuclear Weapons

THE FULFILLMENT of mankind's most cherished goal—the still complete elimination of all types of nuclear weapons—is confronted by many obstacles. Following the signing of the partial test ban treaty, the two giant nuclear powers, the United States and the Soviet Union, have been narrowing their differences over the nonproliferation treaty. Although prospects are brighter that the eighteen-nation disarmament conference in Geneva may possibly arrive at an agreement, many twists and turns must still be expected.

Nuclear nonproliferation means, of course, that a nuclear-weapon state shall not transfer to a nonnuclear-weapon state any nuclear weapon, including material and information related thereto, and that the nonnuclear-weapon state shall neither manufacture nuclear weapons nor seek or receive nuclear weapons, nuclear material, or related information.

In reality, since there is scarcely any likelihood that a nuclear-weapon state will either export or transfer nuclear explosives to a nonnuclear-weapon state, the principal effect of the nonproliferation treaty is to prevent a nonnuclear-weapon state from manufacturing nuclear devices. In other words, it would limit the nuclear club to its present membership, the United States, the Soviet Union, Great Britain, France, and Communist China.

A number of years have elapsed since the need for a treaty

was proposed, and the General Assembly of the United Nations has, since 1960, been annually passing a resolution urging the early conclusion of such a treaty.

The nuclear issue assumed ominous proportions when Communist China carried out its first nuclear test explosion in October, 1964, proving that even countries without a high standard of industrialization in the Afro-Asian region could, provided there was a will and a determination, become a nuclear power. It was gravely feared that China's action might set off a chain reaction.

Alive to the dangers, the eighteen-nation Geneva Disarmament Committee urgently took up the nonproliferation issue at its 8th, 9th, and 10th sessions, from 1965 to 1966, but these sessions failed to make any progress due to the Soviet Union's opposition to NATO's plan to establish a Multilateral Force (MLF), and the escalation of the Vietnam war.

However, there is no reason to doubt that the Soviet Union, whose policy is based on maintaining the nuclear monopoly with the United States, regards the early achievement of nonproliferation with a sense of urgency. Besides raising the question of the Vietnam war, the Soviet Union also focused its attention on the nonproliferation treaty as a means of nipping in the bud any likelihood of West Germany acquiring nuclear status. But so long as the United States insisted on keeping alive its plan of a Multilateral Force, in which West Germany might lay hands on nuclear weapons, the Soviet Union refused to countenance any serious negotiations.

With the subsequent lessening of tensions in Europe, the United States shelved the MLF plan as a measure of appeasement to the Soviet Union, substituting in its place the establishment of the so-called McNamara Committee. This cleared the way to renewed negotiations.

West Germany's voice in nuclear matters was, therefore, limited to participation in deliberations regarding NATO's nuclear policy. During the meeting which President Johnson and Secretary of State Rusk held with Soviet Foreign Minister Gromyko in October, 1966, the Soviet Union indicated that it was willing to soften its stand.

At the same time, West Germany which had been strongly insisting on playing a part in the NATO nuclear force agreed to give up the idea. It could no longer ignore the easing of tensions in Europe and the improved American-Soviet relations.

Notwithstanding the earlier agreement by former West German Chancellor Erhard to participate in the McNamara Committee, Bonn was reluctant to accept the nonproliferation treaty unconditionally. This posture has been maintained by the coalition cabinet which came into power in December, 1966, under Chancellor Kiesinger.

During the first high-level United States-West German meeting, since Chancellor Kiesinger came into office, held in Washington between President Johnson, Secretary of State Rusk, and West German Foreign Minister Brandt on February 8, 1967, the latter clearly stated Bonn's position on the nuclear nonproliferation treaty and appealed to the United States to reconsider its position. The views, generally shared by nonnuclear powers, may be classified into the following four points :

1. Since the nonnuclear-weapon state is permanently renouncing any intention to possess nuclear weapons for the sake of world peace and security, the nuclear-weapon state should, in return, reduce its nuclear armaments. In response to the call to make nuclear disarmament a part of the treaty, the United States is reported to have agreed to include this provision in the preamble of the treaty.

2. On the question of ensuring the security of nonnuclear-weapon states, it appears that the United States—as indicated in the message delivered by President Johnson on January 27, 1966, to the Geneva Disarmament Conference that the countries which did not pursue the path toward nuclear weapons can rely on America's full support against the dangers of nuclear attack—was prepared to give a separate general assurance, should the treaty be accepted, of the kind offered by the President.

3. The use of atomic energy for peaceful purposes should be widely available to all nonnuclear-weapon states. Accordingly, the development of nuclear explosion devices should be permitted. In reply to this request, the United States expressed its willingness to endeavor to have nuclear explosion devices for peaceful purposes available to nonnuclear-weapon states under proper international controls.

4. Regarding peaceful purposes, it was unfair that the International Atomic Energy Agency should strictly inspect only the activities of nonnuclear-weapon states. Although the countries of EURATOM (European Community of Atomic Energy) were subject to inspection by the organization, an inspection by the IAEA was detrimental to the independent status of EURATOM.

Soon after the announcement of Foreign Minister Brandt's demands to the United States, the Japanese Vice Minister of Foreign Affairs Shimoda on February 9, 1966, in speaking to newsmen, declared that "if the nuclear nonproliferation treaty includes the prohibition of nuclear explosion for peaceful purposes, the government of Japan may have to seriously review its attitude. This statement from an official Japanese government spokesman, the first clarification of Japan's attitude toward the right of nuclear development, attracted a great deal of attention as an indicator of Japan's future nuclear policy.

Behind the Shimoda statement there was the growing realization that the peaceful uses of atomic explosion, hitherto regarded as purely theoretical, was gradually becoming a practical reality. For Japan, which had the capacity to develop nuclear potentials, it was a matter of principle to reserve the right to utilize nuclear power for peaceful purposes.

On the following day, February 10, Foreign Minister Miki

declared that "while I agree to the nuclear nonproliferation treaty, it is only natural for a nonnuclear-weapon state to reserve its rights. Within this context, the Shimoda statement offered no more than a sidelight to the nuclear issue. A report will be made to the cabinet at an appropriate time for a judgment on the problem in its entirety."

About a week later, Prime Minister Sato told a press conference that "although it is a fact that there is the problem of the peaceful uses of nuclear explosion, the Shimoda statement related to only one aspect of the peaceful uses of the atom. In case a second Panama Canal is to be constructed, it is said that only a relatively short time would be required with the use of atomic explosion. However, the basic policy of our country remains unchanged. That is to say, we shall neither permit the entry nor the development of nuclear weapons."

The 11th session of the Geneva Disarmament Conference which met on February 21, took up the final phases of the drafting of the nonproliferation treaty with the United States and the Soviet Union largely in agreement on its terms. However, because of growing dissatisfaction among the nonnuclear-weapon states, the conference went into a six-week recess from March 23 to May 8.

During this period, the United States ascertained the views of the countries concerned, attempting to persuade them to support the treaty. As the United States accelerated efforts to put the finishing touches to its draft of the treaty to be presented to the disarmament conference, various countries, including West Germany, India, and Japan, sent delegations to Washington to put forward their respective demands. Foreign Minister Miki dispatched Foreign Minister Adviser Ono as a special envoy on April 16 to the United States, and Nishimura, a member of the International Atomic Energy Agency, to West Germany, Italy, Sweden, and India.

Prior to the dispatch of the special emissaries, Foreign Minister Miki met with leaders of the Socialist Party, the Democratic Socialist Party, and the Komeito on April 15.

Through these meetings, he hoped to strengthen Japan's position in the international community regarding the nuclear issue with supraparty participation.

Outlining the government's views to the party leaders, the foreign minister requested their cooperation on the following main points, the nature of which he also intended to convey to other governments through the dispatch of special envoys:

1. To spell out in the treaty itself the obligation of the nuclear-weapon states to work for the realization of nuclear-weapons disarmament.

2. To give full consideration to the security of the non-nuclear-weapon states.

3. To guarantee equal opportunity for utilizing the benefits of nuclear explosion for peaceful purposes—in case this becomes practical—under the supervision of an appropriate international organization.

4. To convene a conference of signatory powers every five years to review the treaty.

Whereas the Socialist Party demanded the complete abolition of nuclear weapons, prohibition of underground nuclear tests, and a ban on the entry of nuclear weapons into Japan, as well as the participation of Communist China and France in the said treaty, the Komeito desired that special efforts should be made to outlaw underground nuclear tests and to gain the adherence of Communist China and France. The Democratic Socialist Party suggested that the nonnuclear-weapon states should form a club of their own in order to apply pressure on the United States and the Soviet Union.

All parties agreed that powerful efforts should be made to gain equal opportunity for the peaceful uses of atomic energy. At the insistence of the Socialist Party, Foreign Minister Miki promised to hold a similar meeting with the three party leaders prior to signing the nuclear nonproliferation treaty. It was also agreed that the views of the opposition parties would be transmitted, together with the government's basic attitude, to the countries to be visited by special envoys Ono and Nishimura.

Despite the fact that Japan is not a member of the eighteen-nation Geneva Disarmament Committee, proper evaluation should be given to the positive attitude of the government as shown by the dispatch of the special envoys. Japan should take advantage of her unique position since she is the only country in the world to have experienced nuclear bomb attacks and possesses the potentialities of becoming a nuclear power.

As a country agreeing to the spirit of the treaty and deeply desiring to see its conclusion, there is nothing contradictory in Japan's efforts to point out the flaws and inequities in the draft treaty, particularly the egoism apparent in the attitude of the nuclear-weapon states, and its efforts to correct the discriminatory treatment with regard to the peaceful uses of atomic energy.

The aim of the nonproliferation treaty is to prevent non-nuclear-weapon states from getting their hands on nuclear weapons. Consequently, it is necessary to have such states with nuclear capability as Japan and West Germany adhere to the treaty. Before affixing their signatures, the nonnuclear-weapon states should fully express their views and reflect them in the treaty.

In pursuance of this policy, Foreign Minister Miki invited the American delegate to the disarmament conference, William Foster, to Tokyo and held talks with the latter on May 8. Simultaneously, Japan's views were relayed to the Soviet Union by the Japanese Ambassador in Moscow.

Owing to the differences between the United States and the Soviet Union, the reconvening of the crucial Geneva disarmament conference was further delayed by ten days. When the conference finally met on May 18, no progress was discernible. The tabling of the joint draft of the United States and the Soviet Union was held up in the face of strong dissatisfaction on the part of the nonnuclear-weapon states, such as West Germany, Italy, and India. This discontent also sharpened the differences between the United States and the Soviet Union, making it extremely doubtful that the nuclear nonproliferation treaty would be finalized by the end of 1967.

The major point of controversy concerned the question of inspection raised by West Germany, Italy, and other member countries of EURATOM. Although the United States agreed to permit EURATOM to conduct an "independent inspection" for a certain period of time after the treaty takes effect, the Soviet Union insisted on a single control system by the International Atomic Energy Agency (IAEA).

Whereas in the revision of the draft agreement the United States was willing to compromise on the right of veto by the nuclear-weapon state for a simple majority of the member nations, the Soviet Union appeared to be adamantly opposed to such a move.

A point of particular interest to Japan is the question of the peaceful uses of nuclear explosion, which is closely related to the peaceful uses of atomic energy. This question is of more than ordinary interest to Japan and the countries of Asia in the light of future developments. According to the joint American-Soviet draft of the treaty, "the nonnuclear-weapon state undertakes not to receive nuclear weapons or other nuclear explosive devices, nor to acquire information concerning such weapons and devices." The same principle that applies to nuclear weapons is applied to nuclear explosive devices, for peaceful purposes, making any increase in the proliferation of the latter a greater threat to nuclear war.

While the peaceful uses of nuclear explosives have not yet reached the stage of practicality, the United States has from 1957 been conducting a research program known as the Plowshare Plan, consisting of natural resources development, mining, and scientific research. It is further reported that the use of nuclear explosives in opening up a second Panama

Canal and in constructing harbors in Alaska are under serious consideration.

At a time when nuclear power is coming into general use, there are a number of countries in the world capable of manufacturing nuclear weapons, principal among them being Japan, India, West Germany, Canada, Sweden, and Italy. If other potential states are included, such as Switzerland, Israel, Czechoslovakia, East Germany, Brazil, Spain, Yugoslavia, the United Arab Republic, Hungary, and Poland, they form a merry crowd.

In addition, the peaceful uses of atomic energy have now reached a stage where a nation's technological standards and national power are directly affected. With the progress of the American Plowshare Plan, the peaceful uses of nuclear explosives are fast approaching the role of the nuclear reactors.

Moreover, since the use of nuclear explosives for peaceful purposes is cheaper, safer, and quicker, the devices can be of practical utilization in the undeveloped areas of Asia, Africa, Central and South America. For example, the devices can be used in constructing a canal across the Malay Peninsula, or in developing the water resources of the Mekong Delta. They may also be used for the Asian highway, the Asian trunk railway, and Asian seaway projects.

In the case of Japan, however, national sentiments of the only people to have directly felt the effects of "atomic terror" would regard any widespread use of nuclear devices as taboo. Besides, the country is heavily populated with a limited land area. Although the nuclear explosion would have to be limited to an underground explosion under the partial nuclear test ban treaty, there is hardly any engineering projects in which nuclear or thermonuclear explosives would be of practical value, even with the assurance that there would be no fear of radioactive contamination.

However, there are fields in which underground nuclear explosives for peaceful purposes could be applied, for instance, in developing sources of natural gas and oil, as well as in mineral mining for copper, iron, etc. Substantial production of various types of radioactive isotopes can also be widely applied in nuclear research.

The problem of differentiating between military and peaceful purposes of the atom may be solved by international inspection, but at the present level of development of the nuclear explosive devices it would be difficult to make a clear-cut decision. It is also uncertain when it will be possible to make any clear differentiation. Not only is it unfair to impose international inspection only on nonnuclear-weapon states, but there is the added disadvantage that the inspection by the International Atomic Energy Agency in Vienna might result in leakage of technological and industrial secrets.

There is strong opposition in West Germany to this part of the treaty which will place the West German nuclear energy industry at a disadvantage. West Germany, notably its scientists and technicians, is strongly reluctant to accept the unilateral inspection of the nonnuclear-weapon states, in accordance with the treaty, as this would make technological secrets readily available to other industrial competitors, particularly the United States, Great Britain, and even the Soviet Union.

In spite of everything, Japan, which has dismissed any thought of possessing nuclear weapons, is in favor of the spirit and objective of the nuclear nonproliferation treaty. Aside from opposing the development and entry of nuclear weapons, Japan is said to be unwilling for the time being even to utilize nuclear explosives for peaceful purposes. But it would be premature to give up all ideas of utilizing the nuclear explosives for peaceful purposes in the future.

Japan must be aware of the expectation with which the other countries of Asia look to her as a leader of the new winds blowing through this part of the world, considering also the possibilities which the peaceful uses of the atom can open up in developing the continent on a multinational scale.

It is difficult to predict the immense potentialities of the atom in promoting the future development of the Asian-Pacific Regional Community, but it may be desirable to establish an Asian-Pacific community of atomic energy, patterned after EURATOM, for the purpose of coordinating regional cooperation in nuclear energy development.

In the light of these circumstances, Japan is opposed to any limitations being placed on the research and development of the peaceful uses of atomic energy in the nuclear nonproliferation treaty, and views with disfavor any discrimination in the system of inspection of the peaceful uses of nuclear energy between nuclear-weapon states and nonnuclear-weapon states.

Furthermore, Japan adheres to the stand that when the peaceful uses of the energy of nuclear explosives become practical, the right of equal opportunity for nonnuclear-weapon states to share in the benefits should be guaranteed. It believes that if the validity of the treaty is limited to five or ten years, it would facilitate the participation of nonnuclear-weapon states.

While the American-Soviet draft of the treaty is said to be of unlimited duration, it is possible to withdraw from the treaty with a three-month advance notice in case a nation's supreme interests are jeopardized. A possible review of the treaty every five years is said to be contemplated. Actually, however, it may be difficult to withdraw from the treaty, thus making it advisable to replace the unequal right of veto of the nuclear-weapon state with an opportunity to reconsider the terms of the treaty once in five years. (July, 1967)

CHAPTER 20

Soviet Policy of Expansionism

IN CONTRAST to the ugly aspects of the situation in Asia today engendered by the war in Vietnam and the Cultural Revolution in Communist China, the situation in Europe is assuredly more hopeful with the thawing of the cold war as a result of the growing rapport between the East and the West.

This great change in Europe was made possible by the gradual consolidation over a period of over twenty years of the consequences of World War II, by the acceptance of the fact that the existing state of affairs can no longer be changed by armed force. Moreover, the policy of President de Gaulle to move from "detente to entente" in France's relations with the Soviet Union and the countries of Eastern Europe has served as a pump to accelerate the process of thawing. Following President Johnson's address in October, 1966, the United States at the same time took a decisive step forward in its policy of *rapprochement* with the Soviet Union and Eastern Europe.

To cope with these changing circumstances, West Germany was forced to make an about-face and move toward the easing of tensions. After installing a high-powered coalition government under Chancellor Kiesinger, Germany embarked on a policy of drawing nearer toward the nations of Eastern Europe. By the end of January, 1967, West Germany had decided to enter into diplomatic relations with Romania, virtually discarding the Hallstein doctrine which had hitherto prevented it from recognizing any nation which had accorded diplomatic recognition to the East German regime. With regard to its relations with East Germany, West Germany is now exploring ways of breaking the present deadlock.

However, this latest trend in Europe should not be viewed with overoptimism. For example, regardless of the progress of mutual *rapprochement* between the United States and the Soviet Union, the basic stand of the United States, as the leader of the free nations, and the Soviet Union, as a leader of the communist bloc, remains unchanged. The United States continues to be watchful of any increase in Soviet influence, and is particularly sensitive to augmentation of Soviet military power. Its reaction to the recent Soviet move to install ABM, or anti-ballistic missile, sites clearly reflects United States determination to give priority to its policy of maintaining its military superiority over the Soviet Union.

On the other hand, the Soviet Union, sticking to its established policy, has turned a deaf ear to President Johnson's approach in October, 1966, insisting that so long as the United States military intervention in Vietnam continued, there could be no progress in the prospects for peaceful coexistence between the Soviet Union and the United States.

In this complicated situation there lurk a number of unanswered questions. Will the nationalism which lies at the bottom of President de Gaulle's policy hinder the further development of European cooperation? Even if West Germany were to align itself to the course of German reunification through the relaxation of tensions, does there not remain the danger that such a policy might result in a permanent dismemberment arising out of the easing of tensions? Will not the feeling of frustration among the people at this permanent partition bring about a resurgence of a dangerous brand of nationalism? And might not the Soviet Union apply a brake to further efforts at reconciliation between the countries of Western and Eastern Europe?

The Soviet Union is reported to be adopting a more generous attitude toward its East European neighbors, assuming a posture of talking as equals with its brother nations. It is further said that the East European countries are moving toward liberalization and restoration of ties with the West European nations. But whether it is "talking" or "liberalization," these are proceeding within the framework of the Warsaw Treaty Organization. As to what would happen in case any of these nations should overstep the bounds, one need only recall the facts of the Hungarian rebellion in 1956 when Soviet tanks were sent into action to crush the "rebels."

The Soviet Union, which during World War II suffered 20 million casualties on the Soviet-German front, has succeeded in extending its political frontiers far to the west of the graves of its war dead. With the coming into existence of eight communist nations and a divided Germany, the present Soviet policy in Europe appears to be based on the maintenance by all means of the *status quo*. And, in order to defend this political frontier, the Soviet Union is insisting, as a minimum demand, on the recognition of both the Oder-Neisse as the borderline separating Poland and Germany and the existence of East and West Germany. This Soviet demand is founded on the firm resolution that the existing states of East Europe shall not stray away from under the Soviet "umbrella."

Although Russia has a long tradition of expansionism, the current case is by no means an exception. In this respect, Tsarist Russia and the Soviet Union are following an identical course, but the appetite for expansionism may be said to be greater in the case of the Soviet Union which has the goal of world communization.

A character of Russian expansionism is that it bides its time in case the opponent is strong, but will not hesitate to resort to aggression backed by direct military action if the opponent shows signs of weakness.

During the days of Tsarist Russia, the policy of southward expansionism carried the Russian armies into Turkey, causing the Crimean War and the Russo-Turkish War. In the east,

Russia also penetrated into the northern territory of China and nibbled farther eastward.

With the advent of the Soviet Union, the Russian forces not only entered Finland and Iran during World War II, but also advanced into the heart of Central Europe as Nazi Germany retreated westward. In the east, in violation of the Soviet-Japanese Treaty of Neutrality, the Soviets launched an attack, overrunning Manchuria and Korea and seizing the islands of Karafuto and Chishima.

At the root of the current Sino-Soviet dispute, besides the ideological conflict between the so-called Soviet revisionism and Communist China's dogmatism, Russia's historical expansionism and China's fear of victimization as well as the latter's traditional way of thinking should always be borne in mind.

When the Cultural Revolution within Communist China was at a feverish pitch, the Soviet Union reportedly strengthened its forces along the long Sino-Soviet border to check the outbreak of any trouble among the national minorities living in the frontier region. The present tension is expected to continue for the time being.

From the very beginning of Communist China's Cultural Revolution, the Soviet Union has kept a very watchful eye on the movement, fearing that it might take on an anti-Soviet flavor, a fear that was later proved to be well founded. Although this confrontation has developed to a point where, under normal circumstances, diplomatic relations would have been severed, the fact that they are both communist countries and have ulterior motives of their own, has prevented them from taking such a drastic step.

The launching of the Cultural Revolution in Soviet eyes is attributed to Communist China's internal and diplomatic failures which have sharpened antagonism within the ruling circles, between the "main current group" led by Mao Tsetung and Lin Piao, and the "group in power" led by Liu Shao-chi and Teng Hsiao-ping.

Thus, the Soviet Union, which views the insane provocative acts of the Cultural Revolution against it as a deliberate policy on the part of the "main current group" is not inclined to become the victim of such a maneuver.

The Soviet Union realizes that any large-scale conflict with Communist China at this time would deal a decisive blow to its policy of aiding North Vietnam, upset her plans to assume the leadership of the international communist movement by calling a conference of communist countries of the world to isolate Communist China, and impair her national prestige.

At the same time, the present Sino-Soviet confrontation and the serious internal confusion within Communist China could also indicate signs of the disintegration of the communist system, nationally as well as internationally. By tightening their solidarity and by leaving no room for any direct or indirect communist aggression, the free nations can hasten their process of disintegration. From a long-range point of view, consolidation among the free nations is also an indispensable element in dissolving the so-called cold war which continues to plague the international scene. (July, 1967)

CHAPTER 21

Japan's Economic
Diplomacy

ECONOMIC issues are today playing an ever greater role in influencing a country's foreign policy. This is particularly true in the case of Japan which has a very limited land area and poor natural resources, not to speak of an overpopulation problem. Having no other means of sustaining such a large population and fostering her economic growth except through development of free and equal trade, Japan rightfully places paramount importance on her economic diplomacy.

Moreover, in a broader sense, the economic issues are inseparable from the maintenance of security. Although the atomic stalemate between the Free World and the communist bloc has engendered a mood of *rapprochement* between the United States and the Soviet Union, their confrontation has shifted to the field of economic competition. Behind the guise of peaceful coexistence, there is a mounting danger that the communist bloc will turn to indirect aggression through economic means.

To counter this danger, it is exceedingly urgent that the gap in the economic levels between the highly industrialized and the developing countries be drastically reduced. Accordingly, the subject of assistance to the developing countries is a matter of high priority in Japan's economic diplomacy.

Needless to say, economic diplomacy in Japan today is designed to harmonize with this major international trend toward closer collaboration among the countries of the Free World.

247

This economic policy has been carried out in the fields of trade and commerce and assistance to underdeveloped countries on a bilateral basis as well as on a multilateral basis, such as through GATT (General Agreements on Tariffs and Trade), IMF (International Monetary Fund), OECD (Organization for Economic Cooperation and Development), and various agencies of the United Nations, notably UNC-TAD (United Nations Conference on Trade and Development). Japanese economic diplomacy has also been active on a regional basis, an example being the Ministerial Conference for Southeast Asian Development.

In looking back over the progress of Japanese economic diplomacy, the country seems to have been blessed by a lucky star, though it is undeniable that she has had to advance relentlessly against a merciless wind. For instance, when Japan was readmitted to the international economic society, the other nations in the initial stage practically ignored her presence. Furthermore, as a direct consequence of her disastrous defeat in World War II, Japan had to overcome tremendous difficulties and handicaps before being considered for readmission to the international economic society.

Although Japan joined the IMF in 1952 and GATT in 1955, there was a period of time when the other member nations of GATT refused to enter into relations with Japan on the basis of the GATT provisions. Having had a feeble economy, Japan was compelled to adopt various protective measures, measures which were severely criticized by the highly industrialized nations of the West which advocated an "open door" policy.

The second stage of Japan's economic development came with the acceptance of the fundamental principles for liberalization of foreign trade and exchange in June, 1960. This process of liberalization was accelerated to a point where in February, 1963, she assumed the status of an Article 11 nation —a status which forbids a nation to impose import controls based on international balance of payments.

In a further move, Japan enhanced her status in the IMF by accepting the role of an Article 8 country in April, 1964, thereby assuming the obligation not to impose currency controls on grounds of international balance of payment difficulties. This step was followed in May by Japan's membership in the OECD (Organization for European Cooperation and Development). On that occasion, Japan retained both the tariff barrier and capital transaction control as her trump card.

In the meantime, Japan concluded the Anglo-Japanese Treaty of Commerce and Navigation in November, 1962, and the Franco-Japanese Treaty of Commerce and Navigation in May, 1963. It is to the great credit of Japan's economic diplomacy that shortly thereafter the countries of Western Europe, including Great Britain and France, agreed not to apply Article 35 of GATT against Japan.

Hitherto, Article 35 of GATT, a stipulation exempting member nations from according the most-favored-nation treatment in tariffs and trade, was applied against Japan as a means of barring the inflow of cheap Japanese commodities.

While the removal of this application was a tribute to the high evaluation of Japan's level of economic progress, this equal relationship alone did not result in the lifting of other economic barriers against Japan, such as import limitations placed on Japanese goods.

Now in the third stage, Japan, as a member nation of OECD (a club of industially advanced nations), is faced with the crucial problem of either relaxing the remaining two protective measures for the sake of world economic development or recklessly plunging into the international economic society without any protection.

The conditions have become substantively more severe. There is also a marked tendency on the part of the industrialized countries to espouse the principles of the "open door" in relation to other countries while, at the same time, maintaining as far as possible a protective policy at home.

This tendency was vividly illustrated by the difficulties encountered by the recent Kennedy Round of negotiations aimed at a general reduction of GATT tariffs on trade. Barriers of national economy and so-called regional economy continued to hamper the smooth progress of the negotiations. Japan's strenuous efforts in the Kennedy Round did yield some excellent results, but the grave issue of capital liberalization remains unresolved.

Initially advocated by the late President John F. Kennedy in January, 1962, the Kennedy Round had as its target a 50 per cent general reduction of world tariff level in five years. This far-reaching proposal, appropriately described as a "grand design," was originally put forward by President Kennedy as a means of breaking the deadlock over bilateral negotiations and to meet the need for broad liberalization in the field of tariffs. The talks were also aimed at accelerating the process of liberalization of import restrictions which has been taking place since the end of World War II.

Of even more importance was the fact that the talks would counter the possible drift toward closed regional economic groupings, such as the EEC (European Economic Community). The so-called regional economic unification was originally regarded as a natural course of development necessitated by modern scientific technology and communications, but there were fears in some quarters that it might well become an exclusive economic bloc.

Placing great hopes on the Kennedy Round, the United States began conducting negotiations for a general reduction of 50 per cent on industrial products. Agricultural products were also included in the wide range of negotiations which attempted to remove nontariff barriers and paid scrupulous care toward the interests of the developing countries. In this respect, compared with the GATT negotiations, the Kennedy Round was a bold and epoch-making decision.

The GATT talks, also epochal in nature, started in May,

1963, at the GATT Headquarters in Geneva. Attended by forty-nine countries, the talks dragged on almost endlessly for five years. However, since the Trade Expansion Act vesting the right of negotiations to the President of the United States was to expire at the end of June, 1967, every effort was made to conclude the negotiations by the end of April. Agreement, however, was not reached until midnight of May 15.

At the stage of presenting the list of exceptions (items not included in the limit of 50 per cent tariff reduction), Japan, as one of the world's leading industrialized nations, formally joined the Kennedy Round as a full-fledged member (a country which is, as a general principle, obliged to reduce tariff by 50 per cent) with nine Western countries in November, 1964. Japan later became one of the four principal members in the steering committee, together with the United States, EEC, and Great Britain, assigned to play a leading role in conducting the negotiations.

A sharp conflict of interests between the EEC and the United States and Great Britain, however, set back the timetable for the negotiations. The position taken by the EEC was constantly opposed to the United States which firmly stood its ground. In this conflict of interests, Japan almost became a bystander. The results achieved under such circumstances were not entirely satisfactory, but the historical significance and benefits in promoting world trade were inestimable.

The balance sheet of the negotiations was disappointing, for in the last stages of the negotiations the leading members, such as the United States, EEC, Great Britain, and Japan successively canceled their "offers" (proposals to reduce tariffs), leaving all of the important items still listed as objects ineligible for tariff reduction.

It appears that the level of tariffs which was to have been cut in half in a period of five years will amount to only about 3 per cent. On the other hand, the fact that the reduction or deferment affected one-fifth of the total annual world trade amounting to $200 billion, or $40 billion covering more than 6,300 items, is of tremendous importance.

From Japan's standpoint, insofar as her industrial products are concerned, the benefits are considerable. The composition of her foreign trade structure reveals that 90 per cent of the export goods are classified as industrial products on which all countries levy duties. However, since most of the imports are fuel, raw materials, and food, of which half are nondutiable, Japan is in an advantageous position.

The retreat on the rate of reduction, unlike excessive advance, may prove to be more effective in forestalling an expansion of the nontariff barrier by the trade protectionists in the various countries.

As far as agricultural products are concerned, Japan is an importing nation. Since it is unlikely that she can in the future be able to increase her rate of domestic self-sufficiency, Japan is on a creditor footing in relation to other countries, promising an expanding import market.

On the question of food assistance to the developing countries, in view of her position as an importing country, Japan opposed the incorporation of obligation to be assumed under the international grain agreement. Eventually, however, in approving the allotment of 5 per cent of the total amount of assistance, Japan agreed to substitute this aid in the form of fertilizer and agricultural implements rather than in wheat or its equivalent in foreign currency.

On the other hand, even if tariffs are reduced by the Kennedy Round, the prospects for Japanese trade can hardly be described as bright so long as discrimination against Japan remains. There is even speculation that the conclusion of the Kennedy Round may even make it more difficult to abolish the discrimination against imports from Japan. Moreover, there is no assurance that the increased exports of countries not subject to discrimination, equivalent to the amount of tariff reduction granted by the Kennedy Round, will not seriously encroach on Japan's vital export markets, making it, ironically, more advantageous not to lower tariffs.

Japan has not been neglecting her persistent efforts, either through GATT or bilateral negotiations, for the removal of discriminatory trade practices against Japan. When the Kennedy Round of negotiations reached a critical stage in the fall of 1966, Japan adopted a firm policy directed at removing these trade barriers. In conducting bilateral negotiations with various countries, Japan gave notice that she would not be bound by tariff reductions under the Kennedy Round in case any country continued its discrimination.

Before such bilateral talks could positively get underway, Japan was willy-nilly compelled to conduct general negotiations, as a result of which she accepted the mechanical reduction of tariff rates which did not take into account the existence of such discriminations.

The number of export commodities from Japan on which import restrictions continue to be enforced is still very substantial. For example, the number of items on which West Germany continues to clamp restrictions is 19, France 71, Italy 104, the three Benelux countries 28, Great Britain 57, and Canada 17. While not strictly in the category of import restrictions, the practice of having Japanese industries exercise voluntary control on the export of cotton textiles to the United States and Great Britain is another striking example of effectively checking the export of Japanese commodities.

Thus, the spotlight of economic diplomacy is again being focused in the direction of these discriminations against Japan. In the series of bilateral negotiations, Japan has offered to liberalize trade on certain commodities if her counterparts would also abolish discriminations on specific items. However, during the Kennedy Round, Japan had, for all practical purposes, exhausted almost every negotiating card in her hand.

Consequently, Japan should adopt a more independent economic policy in the future, negotiating in the spirit of GATT for the abolition of discriminatory practices or conducting bilateral talks for the expansion of trade on idealistic terms.

Special attention should be paid to Japan's relationship with the United States whose market absorbs 30 per cent of Japan's export trade, the highest ratio of dependence of any highly industrialized nation on American trade. Although this Japanese-American trade has for long been marked by an excess of imports on the part of Japan, it registered a favorable balance of over $100 million in 1965. In 1966 this excess in exports rose to over $300 million, representing a 20 per cent growth in the volume of exports. With business receding in the United States in 1967, it is feared that the trend in the future will be toward a contraction in the amount of exports.

In addition, private American business interests are gradually advocating stronger trade protectionism. For example, voices are even being raised in the United States Congress to levy a surcharge on steel imports—a branch of Japanese industry which has been the leading exporter to the American market for the past two years.

This trend in the United States appears to be related to the deterioration in America's balance of payments, particularly the falling volume of exports over imports. The favorable balance of $6.7 billion in 1964 fell to $4.8 billion in 1965, and declined to $3.7 billion in 1966. While the main cause of this worsening situation in the trade pattern is attributable to the heavy military expenditures connected with the Vietnam war, the steady aggravation in the balance of payments is causing a greater drain on America's gold reserves and endangering the position of the dollar. This situation is giving rise to signs of protectionism reviving in the United States.

In the latest Kennedy Round, Japan had laid major stress on negotiations with the United States, but there were increasing indications of trade protectionism on the American domestic scene.

Regarding the reduction of tariffs, the United States substantially reduced its original proposals during the course of the negotiations, even withdrawing its offers on steel products and synthetic fibers. In view of America's grim stand, Japan also withdrew its offer to lower tariffs on paper and certain types of machines.

During the final stages of this negotiation, the United States began applying direct pressure on Japan for the acceptance of the food assistance provisions under the grain agreement. Although Japan's stand was finally accepted, it marked one of the rare occasions when Japan took such a firm stand and won its point in negotiating with the United States. It may also be said that the United States bowed to Japan's stand because of its desire to honor its declaration that Japan was an equal partner of the United States.

The stage has now been reached when Japan should reexamine her posture—learning from her experiences in the Kennedy Round of negotiations—if she is to carry out her economic diplomacy toward the United States in a spirit of equality.

Meanwhile, at the insistence of the United States and other advanced nations of the OECD, Japan is wrestling with the difficult problem of liberalizing capital transaction. The repeated demands for liberalization made at the Japan-America Trade and Economic Joint Committee in the summer of 1966 and at the BIAC (Business Industry Advisory Committee), an agency of the OECD, in the autumn of the same year have placed Japan in a position where she can no longer indefinitely ignore the problem.

Compared to the liberalization of trade, the liberalization of capital will have a far deeper and wider effect on the Japanese economy. In the case of trade liberalization, it will be possible to counter the inroads of foreign products by tariff barriers. Cushioned by the national economy, the effects can be temporary.

However, once capital is liberalized, the capital and technology of a foreign state will become semipermanently entrenched in the country, their roots sinking deep into the national economy. By being directly linked with foreign markets, this state of affairs will sweep away the national boundaries. Furthermore, should the huge foreign capital power, superior technology, and international marketing network overwhelm the domestic enterprises, they are bound to cause serious repercussions.

On the other hand, apart from the urgings of other countries, the question of liberalizing capital transaction will have to be faced some day in the light of Japan's own industrial as well as international economic policy.

Japan should tackle this problem with a forward-looking attitude, expanding further the sphere of her industrial activity within a liberalized economic structure for the greater welfare of the nation. At the same time, Japan should henceforth adopt a policy that would give her a more effective voice internationally.

While Japan should make every effort to accede as soon as possible to the request of the member nations of the OECD to bring about a level of liberalization comparable to that of the Western countries, it is common sense to expect that the time for adopting such a policy will have to be three to five years from now. However, the exact timing should be based on Japan's own judgment and initiative, taking into account her national interests.

The government which is presently laying the groundwork for liberalization, appears to be held up by the problem of arranging the final stages of industrial classification, but it is essential that the situation be painstakingly studied and for the liberalization to be of a progressive character.

With the progress toward liberalization in the future, it is natural that Japanese enterprises will become involved in severe competition with the world's giant business concerns. At the end of 1964, American enterprises, which hold a dominant position in the world, had overseas investments totaling $44.3 billion. The massive business group known as the

World Enterprise has, either through joint management with local companies or the establishment of 100 per cent-owned subsidiary, made notable inroads into the European market in the 1960's, following similar successes in Canada and Latin America.

The West European countries are not, however, looking on with folded arms at the activities of these aggressive American enterprises. The EEC is contemplating the establishment of a "European Enterprise" to counter the "World Enterprise" on an equal footing.

The various governments are also preparing various measures to encourage the merger of enterprises in view of the pressing need to institute industrial reorganization.

Insofar as Japan is concerned, she should make a detailed study of the developments now taking place in the countries of Western Europe which have been quick to proceed with capital liberalization. This will enable her to learn from their experiences and to gauge subsequent events in formulating her own policy.

Notwithstanding these circumstances, the United States has, in the process of accelerating trade liberalization, imposed a stringent voluntary restriction on the exports of steel and cotton products to the United States. Therefore, in connection with the liberalization of capital, it is necessary that Japan should insist that America agree to controls on enterprises entering the country to ensure that they do not disrupt Japan's financial and monetary policies.

Thus, the new task facing Japan's economic diplomacy is to control, through political and diplomatic means, the managerial policies of these gigantic enterprises backed by America's capital and technological power operating in Japan. (July, 1967)

CHAPTER 22

Assistance to Developing Nations

THE PROBLEMS which today confront the developing nations of the world are similar to those which faced Japan at the time of the Meiji Restoration. The rapid economic recovery and development of Japan from the utter ruins of World War II is often described—along with the recovery of West Germany—as one of the miraculous achievements of the postwar world. This phenomenal growth, however, should not be too surprising against the background of development which began with the Meiji Restoration a century ago.

During the half century since Japan emerged from the status of a developing into a developed nation in the latter part of the Meiji era, the growth rate of the Japanese economy has surpassed the rate of economic growth of the United States during the same period and the record of the Soviet Union in the forty years since the Russian Revolution.

With very little natural resources and capital to sustain such a development, Japan has had to rely on mass education, boundless energy, strong sense of national service, and the courageous spirit of her people to provide the generating power behind this remarkable economic expansion. The developing nations of the world might profit from the lessons and experience of Japan.

While the developed nations of the world have continued to maintain their steady economic growth and development in recent years, the developing countries, plagued by an annually increasing population, have been hard pressed to provide even the basic requirements of life—food, clothing, and housing.

The population of the developing nations of the world presently totals 1,250 million. If the 700 million of Communist China are added, it means that three-quarters of the world's population are still in the so-called developing stage. If the developed countries of the world do not extend effective economic cooperation or assistance, there is the danger that the dissatisfaction and frustrations of the peoples in these countries will create political instability endangering the peace of the world.

The developed countries, for their part, have since the end of World War II tackled the problems of postwar reconstruction and rehabilitation in the war-ravaged countries. In order to maintain their economic growth, high standard of living, and full employment, these countries have also come to realize that their well-being relies on a healthy world economic development and prosperity, including the developing nations.

It is natural, of course, that Japan, which had to recuperate from her heavy defeat in World War II, was unable to join the other developed nations in extending aid to the developing countries in the early years. It was only in 1950 that Japan was able to make investments overseas. Although the country regained sovereignty in April, 1952, Japan was unable to cooperate with the developing nations in the field of foreign investments beyond an average of $18 million a year.

However, since she joined the Colombo Plan in October, 1954, she has gradually increased and strengthened her assistance which is now no longer limited mainly to technical cooperation as in the earlier years.

It is interesting to recall in this connection the dramatic speech which the then Japanese Prime Minister Shigeru Yoshida delivered before the National Press Club on November 8, 1954. Speaking about the problems of Southeast Asia, he urged the developed nations to make an immediate economic assistance of $40 billion to the developing nations in the region.

In making his plea, the Japanese Prime Minister warned that "if the economic development of Communist China should substantively surpass that of the Southeast Asian countries in the next few years, the latter would not be able to resist the consequent pressures and might easily succumb to communism. In order to increase its economic strength, Communist China was undertaking large-scale investments, at least double that of Southeast Asia in terms of per capita.

"If we are to meet this challenge in time," warned Yoshida, "external assistance must be provided as the free countries of Southeast Asia do not have sufficient developmental capital. Although there are a number of specialized agencies to provide capital to the developing countries, they are providing no more than $400 million annually to Southeast Asia. But this is only one-tenth of the amount required to compete against Communist China.

"It is for this reason that it is essential," the Japanese Prime Minister went on, "for governments and international financial institutions to greatly expand their supply of capital. In order to make this scheme successful, the people of Japan are prepared to spare no efforts."

This speech made a deep impression on the American audience. Shortly thereafter, Prime Minister Yoshida resigned, and his bold and imaginative plan for Southeast Asia never materialized. Since then the world situation has undergone profound changes, but the need for such a plan has become even more acute.

With the death of Stalin, the Soviet Union entered the so-called Khrushchev era, an era which was marked by a new Kremlin policy of peaceful coexistence and economic competition as well as a call for complete disarmament. The rivalry between the noncommunist world and the communist world shifted from the military to the economic front. The cold war took the shape of a race to extend economic assistance to the developing countries of the world. The battle to win the goodwill of these countries covered vast areas of Asia, Africa, and Latin America.

Since then Japan's economic assistance to the developing nations has included a yen loan the equivalent of $50 million on a government basis to India in 1958. Japan has also joined the creditor nations conference set up by the World Bank for India in 1958 and for Pakistan in 1960. Thus, Japan has been providing an increasing amount of capital investments to the developing countries.

When in March, 1960, the industrialized nations of the West established DAG (Development Assistance Group) to coordinate assistance, Japan also became a member. By 1961, the flow of capital from Japan to the developing regions of the world exceeded $380 million, placing Japan fifth among the DAG members, following the United States, France, Great Britain, and West Germany.

Parallel with this increase in aid volume, Japan established the Overseas Economic Cooperation Fund in March, 1961, and the Overseas Technical Cooperation Agency in June, 1961, in an effort to extend more effective assistance and to improve the structural organizations through which such aids are channeled.

Since October, 1962, when DAG was reorganized as DAC (Development Assistance Committee) under the OECD (Organization for Economic Cooperation and Development), Japan has played a positive role as one of the leading members.

Within the context of the question of assistance to developing countries, symbolized by East-West relations between the noncommunist and communist blocs, there is the so-called North-South division. The term "North-South" refers to the mutual relations between the industrially advanced nations of the Northern Hemisphere and the agricultural and less industrialized countries to the south.

The problem is, however, complicated by what has been referred to earlier as an extension of the cold war by the Free

World and communist bloc in the region to broaden their respective spheres of influence. Consequently, the North-South problem is also impregnated with the East-West problem.

It was against this background that the late United States President John F. Kennedy proposed in the spring of 1962 that the United Nations designate the 1960's as a decade of development. At the 17th General Assembly, which met later in the autumn, a resolution embodying this proposal was adopted. The resolution set as its target a minimum annual growth of 5 per cent in the national incomes of the developing countries by 1970.

As a part of the United Nations ten-year development program, the first meeting of UNCTAD (United Nations Conference on Trade and Development) met in Geneva for about three months from March 23 to June 15, 1964. Countries participating in the conference included all the members of the United Nations as well as West Germany, Switzerland, Monaco, and others who are members only of the specialized agencies of the United Nations, totaling 121. Observers from GATT, EEC, COMECON, and other organizations swelled the number of delegates attending the mammoth conference to 1,500.

The significance of this conference, summoned to discuss a dynamic world-trade policy to meet the problems of the North-South division, was in many respects epoch-making. It agreed to make UNCTAD an agency of the United Nations which would meet once in three years. A permanent executive committee composed of delegates from fifty-five countries was established, together with three committees to deal with primary products, manufactured goods, and investments.

The tempo of economic assistance and cooperation by developed nations has accelerated since the conference, increasing from $9.9 billion in 1964 to $11 billion in 1965. Japan has also recently become more positive in its attitude toward cooperation. Despite a slight fluctuation in the intervening period from the peak year of 1961, the country's aid in 1965 was $485 million, nearly 60 per cent higher than in the preceding year, or 0.7 per cent of the national income.

It should be emphasized that Japan has adopted positive measures since 1966 to increase her economic cooperation with countries in the Asian and Pacific region, convinced that such regional cooperation is essential for promoting and increasing the effectiveness of development aid to these countries.

As a result, a number of organs for regional development and economic cooperation have been formed in 1966, such as the Ministerial Conference for Economic Development of Southeast Asia, Ministerial Conference of the Asian and Pacific Region, the Asian Development Bank, and the Southeast Asia Agricultural Development Conference. Other important events in the field of development cooperation have been the 20th-anniversary meeting of ECAFE in Tokyo in April, 1967, and the meeting of ASA (Association of Southeast Asia) which was revived in August, 1966.

The 23rd session of the United Nations Economic Commission for Asia and the Far East, which met in Tokyo, was of special significance in view of the next ECAFE conference scheduled to take place in New Delhi in February, 1968, followed by the second UNCTAD to be held also in the Indian capital. These conferences are highly important in focusing world attention on the question of North-South division and the need for greater cooperation between the developed and developing states of Asia.

Although this was the third time that ECAFE had held its sessions in Tokyo, it marked the 20th anniversary of the organization. During the two-week session from April 3 to 17, 1967, the developing countries stressed the need for preferential duties and a commodity agreement on primary products.

These problems are likely to assume major importance at the GATT (General Agreement of Tariffs and Trade) meetings after the conclusion of the Kennedy Round of negotiations for tariff reduction.

In preparation for the second UNCTAD, the secretariat of the organization has taken great pains to coordinate the views of the seventy-seven nations participating in the Algiers conference into a charter to be presented to the conference in New Delhi in February, 1968.

Underlying the demand of the developing countries for preferential duties is the strong desire for "trade rather than aid." The developing nations, burdened by a growing volume of debts, which totaled $10 billion in 1955 and had grown to $35 billion in 1965, are making little progress to improve their economic positions. The only way to repay the massive debts was to expand exports and earn foreign exchange, but the success of this effort depended on the rate of economic development in the developing countries. Therefore, the solution of the question of preferential duties to promote exports has become a prerequisite for the future prosperity of the countries in the stage of development.

On the other hand, the granting of preferential tariffs runs counter to the postwar trend of world trade as evidenced by the GATT policy of nondiscrimination (allowing of most-favored-nation treatment) and the principle of free trade. However, in June, 1966, even the developed nations of GATT, in an attempt to remove tariff and other trade barriers confronting developing countries, adopted a provision not to expect reciprocity. The OECD is also adjusting the views of the industrially advanced nations.

Australia has already decided to give preferential treatment, and the Netherlands is also expressing similar views. Although the United States response was initially negative, President Johnson in a speech before the conference of the leaders of the American states in Punta del Este in April stated that after the completion of the Kennedy Round of talks, he would consider the problem of preferences on a world scale.

Thus, the granting of preferences to the developing nations

is being rapidly acknowledged, and after the Kennedy Round the Johnson Round of negotiations is expected to be inaugurated.

As far as Japan's attitude is concerned, although this was rather passive at the ECAFE session, there is a realization that if the extension of preferential treatment should benefit the development of the developing nations this in turn would eventually increase Japan's export markets in these countries. At the same time, the country favors a time limit to the granting of preferential duties, and hopes that in time the principle of nondiscrimination adopted by GATT will be restored.

For Japan there is a debit side. With a dual structured economy, consisting of super industrial establishments and small and medium industries, of which some are in a backward state, any large-scale import of primary products and manufactures and semimanufactures from the developing countries will place the domestic agricultural and medium and small industries in a dilemma. The country must, therefore, adopt a two-pronged policy aimed—on the one hand— at the rationalization or conversion of backward industries while—on the other—making every effort to meet the requirements of the developing nations.

The commodity agreement on primary products to cover such items as rubber, jute, tea, sugar, and copra has been proposed to stabilize fluctuating international prices of these commodities and to remove the obstacles to greater exports by the countries of Asia. The commodity agreement is aimed at stabilizing world demand and preventing sagging prices of primary products. One of the problems is how to include the establishment of buffer stocks in the agreement.

Although the function of the buffer stock is to purchase commodities when prices decline and release stocks when prices increase, problems connected with the types of commodities, the volume of stocks, prices, and financial support are still under consideration.

After studying the effects of such an arrangement on the

national economy, Japan will have to decide on a definite attitude. Where the developed nations must make "sacrifices" as in the case of granting tariff preferences, this is actually easier said than done. In this connection, Japan has many difficult problems which cannot be brushed aside lightly. The time of adjustment has come for Japan, in the light of her economic relations with the developing countries, to take up seriously the question of reorganizing her industrial structure. In any event, the problems which will face Japanese economic diplomacy in the future are of a nature that can no longer be solved by a policy of expediency.

An unusual event of the ECAFE session was the adoption of the joint resolution, known as the "Tokyo Declaration," jointly sponsored by fifteen countries, including Japan, the United States, Great Britain, Malaysia, India, and Indonesia. The Declaration called for the effective mobilization of indigenous resources of the developing countries of the region and stressed the need for the developed nations to extend the maximum assistance to the less industrialized states. It is very uncommon for a declaration adopted at an ECAFE session to refer to a specific area. This declaration is also unique for having quoted the words of Prime Minister Sato who had addressed the opening session.

It is clear that Japan, as the only highly industrialized nation in the ECAFE region, must assume heavier responsibilities in the field of developmental assistance. The session also approved resolutions concerning the ministerial conference of the nations of the region, establishment of the Asian Statistical Institute in Tokyo, development of the coconut industry, the Asian International Trade Fair, standardization activities, housing plan, population conference, Asian Industrial Development Council Meeting, development of mineral resources, and preparations for the second UNCTAD meeting.

In a concerted drive to provide assistance, the delegates of the industrially advanced countries to the first UNCTAD resolved to allot 1 per cent of their respective national incomes to assist the developing nations. During the same year, the members of the Development Assistance Council of OECD adopted a resolution for the developed nations to extend very liberal terms on their loans to the developing nations of 3 per cent interest and a repayment period of more than twenty-five years. However, Japan has not yet been able to carry out either of these resolutions.

Recognizing the fact that the economic rehabilitation of Indonesia directly affected the stability of Asia, Japan in April, 1967, decided to extend a fresh credit totaling $60 million to Indonesia, but the terms of interest and period of repayment have yet to be worked out. The Japanese government, in an effort to keep the real interest below 4 per cent, is considering a formula of including grants in addition to the yen credit in the assistance program. The time is ripe for Japan to review its entire system of external economic cooperation.

At present, Japan relies mainly on the Export-Import Bank. About one-third of the budget of the bank in 1967 was earmarked for economic cooperation. Hitherto, Japan has extended assistance in the form of joint-financing to the developing countries through the Export-Import Bank and commercial banks at the rate of 8 to 2 in which the average interest rate has been 5.75 per cent. The interest rate of the Export-Import Bank alone is 5.5 per cent. Since the bank's capital is partly acquired through treasury investment and loan, there are factors, such as balancing of accounts, which prevent further reduction in interest rate.

On the other hand, according to estimates of the United Nations, the developing nations have had to set aside $2 to $3 billion out of the total of $6 billion borrowed in 1965 for the repayment of interest. The question of interest burden has, therefore, become a very critical problem.

Lately, in a growing number of cases the developing nations—as in the case of Indonesia—have sought loans not for so-called project assistance, but rather for checking inflation and solving the foreign-exchange shortage. The Overseas Economic Cooperation Fund is able to offer a low interest rate of 3.5 per cent, but according to the laws governing the fund the credits can be provided only for project assistance.

In order to bring the nature of the assistance and the conditions of interest in line with international trends, it will be necessary either to revise the laws of both the Export-Import Bank and the Overseas Economic Cooperation Fund or improve the method of raising capital.

The Development Assistance Committee of OECD has pointed out on a number of occasions that Japan has not yet attained the average level of 1 per cent of the national income —the amount mentioned in the resolution of UNCTAD— which other members of DAC are spending on overseas economic assistance. Furthermore, the amount of grants, liberal terms of credits, and technical assistance offered by Japan are less favorable than those offered by the other members of DAC.

With the gradual improvement of her international position and development of economic strength, it will become incumbent on Japan to increase the quantity and quality of her assistance to the developing nations.

Although the use of a yardstick based on allotting a certain percentage of the national income to foreign assistance is one method of sharing the cost, certain problems present themselves when the same yardstick for highly industrialized nations of the West is adopted for Japan which has only one-third to one-quarter of the per capita national income of the latter.

For example, in Japan there is a very strong domestic demand for capital, particularly among the small and medium industries and in the field of agriculture where modernization has become a pressing problem. The demand for low-interest long-term credits at home necessarily places a ceiling to any substantial improvement in the conditions of credit facilities for overseas assistance.

Unless the quantity and quality of assistance are scrupulously based on the scale of national finance, the requirements of social development, the volume of capital accumulation and the stability of the international balance of payments, it would be unwise to risk any sharp increase in external expenditures merely for the sake of achieving an international ratio of assistance.

Needless to say, there is a limit to the obligations which Japan can assume for Asian development and economic cooperation. In view of the fact that aid by industrialized countries to Asia is lagging behind the assistance given to the developing nations in Africa and Latin America, Japan has the important task of extending that pipeline of economic cooperation of the developed nations to this region of the world. It is to fulfill this mission that Japanese diplomacy since 1966 has been vigorously directed toward materializing the vision of an Asian-Pacific sphere of economic cooperation. (July, 1967)

CHAPTER 23

Essential Elements
of the New Diplomacy

New Diplomatic Attitudes

WITH THE miraculous development of science and technology, the world of today is at the threshold of the space age, or in the initial stage of the nuclear age. Viewed from the standpoint of international relations, the progress made in the fields of transportation and communication has sharply reduced distances and has greatly increased the interchange and close contacts between the nations of the world.

For example, if we take the relations between Japan and the United States, in 1935 only 1,100 Japanese visited the United States, and 9,100 Americans came to Japan. In 1965, however, the number of Japanese visitors to the United States had risen sharply to 55 thousand, and Americans visitors to Japan had likewise increased proportionately to 185 thousand. This outstanding growth in exchange visits has been made possible as a result of the modernization of the means of transportation.

This international exchange has been notable not only in the fields of politics, economics, and military, but also in the fields of learning, culture, arts, sports, etc. Consequently, there has been a rise of internationalism, especially among the younger generation, and a growing consciousness of a world community.

270

Thus, when we speak about the essential elements of the new diplomacy, we find that the development of transportation and communication has introduced other forms of diplomacy, besides that of the conventional diplomatic channels, such as exchange of ideas at the highest political levels, as well as the regular international conferences and meetings of experts.

In other words, it has become customary for heads of state, prime ministers, and presidents, to exchange visits, and for two or more countries to annually hold foreign minister's conferences or other ministerial gatherings.

Since diplomacy cannot be conducted without a person-to-person contact, it is undoubtedly imperative that responsible government officials, such as the prime minister and the foreign minister, should make occasional visits to leading nations of the world. Meanwhile, the frequent meetings of the United Nations and various international organizations have become a part of the so-called conference diplomacy of our times.

While it is true that present-day diplomacy has been elevated to a high level, characterized by many facets, the basic principle of national interests continues to remain the *sine qua non* of all diplomatic endeavors.

Owing to the phenomenal development of modern science and technology, the old interpretations of "independence" and "self-sufficiency" within the context of national interests have become outdated. In its place has come the idea of a regional collective organization which the nations of today are willy-nilly pursuing in their national interest. It is in the light of these circumstances that I have been advocating for many years that Japan's diplomatic objective should be the formation of an Asian-Pacific collective organization within the framework of the United Nations.

While the national interests of the various nations are determined after giving due thought and judgment on an individual basis, the new diplomatic ideal—the regional collective organization—rests on the interwoven and common interests of these nations. To achieve this, it is necessary to nurture and promote regional community consciousness and recognize the value of the regional collective organization. In other words, realize that regional interests are an integral part of the national interests common to all the countries of the region. Moreover, the common interests of these various states will no doubt continue to expand in the future and branch out anew.

This ideal originated about forty years ago in the form of the Pan-Europe movement advocated by Count Richard Coudenhove-Kalergi of Austria. In his famous book *Pan-Europa,* Count Coudenhove-Kalergi stressed "technics and politics," pointing out that the world is daily becoming smaller and smaller, and with the development of transportation and technology the relationship between the cities was becoming increasingly closer. In the same sense, the nations of the world were also becoming smaller and bridging the distances between them.

The distinguished Austrian diplomat sounded a warning that dreadful consequences would ensue if the world failed to keep political techniques abreast with the progress of communication techniques. To avoid a collision between neighboring peoples, brought into closer contact by the radical shrinkage of time, the peoples must make similar progress in their political relations.

It is worth noting that America, the most advanced region in the field of technology, stands foremost among the nations equipped with a system of federation of peaceful nations, imbued with the highest ideals of the Pan-European Union and the League of Nations.

The individual nations which passed through historical developments are too small to maintain their independent existence in the future. They must be molded into a supranational federation and expanded. The leading nations of the world today are the federated states of the Soviet Union, Great Britain, and the United States of America.

The Pan-American Federation which is on the verge of establishment is unique in that it is not directed against another federation of states, but is devoted to opposing war and to the promotion of common cultures. Europe should learn from that living example, otherwise it will be recklessly thrown into a fresh war, running the risk of suffocating to death in a sea of lethal bombs.

Although the Pan-European movement of Count Coudenhove-Kalergi suffered a serious temporary setback with the rise of Nazism in Germany, it has risen from the ashes of World War II and is now outstandingly developing as the EEC (European Economic Community) of today.

There are growing signs that the EEC, now moving from economic integration to a new concept of political unification, will soon see the participation of Great Britain and its merger with EFTA (European Free Trade Association). In addition, President de Gaulle of France, an insistent advocate of European unity, is also increasing contacts with the Soviet Union and the East European bloc. On the otherhand, with the modernization of NATO, President Johnson is accelerating the consolidation of the Atlantic collective organization.

In Asia, too, the concept of a collective organization has been steadily growing. In this connection, I think it would be pertinent to quote from Mr. Takeo Miki's speech on assuming the post of Foreign Minister. He declared: "Throughout the entire region of Southeast Asia, there is a new tendency to promote economic cooperation in a sober manner. They lay great store in Japan as an advanced nation. Moreover, the United States, Canada, Australia, and New Zealand, inspired by the spirit of the Pacific region, are showing greater interest in Asia. Together with these nations, I should like to see Japan contribute toward the development and advancement of Asia. There is a limit to what Japan can do alone. I think the time has come when we must think of the development of Asia on a broader scale. In this sense, I wish to emphasize the advent of the so-called Asia-Pacific Age!"

The ideal of a world collective organization took positive shape after World War I in the establishment of the League of Nations and its successor, the present United Nations. However, even in the case of the United Nations, before it can act effectively to fulfill its primary function as a world peace-keeping body, it must surmount a number of difficult problems. It is quite natural that all the member nations of the United Nations, upholding the principles of the United Nations as the basis of their foreign policy, are dedicated to the solidification of the United Nations as their diplomatic goal.

The formation of the regional collective organization in the present stage of international politics should be given preference. All signs are that history is also relentlessly moving in this direction.

Space and Nuclear Diplomacy

Although the so-called space age was inaugurated by the Soviet Union which sent two artificial satellites into orbital flight, space development is now shared by both the Soviet Union and the United States. Mobilizing every available scientific and technical resource, the two nations are currently engaged in a fierce race to be the first to leave the footprints of man on the moon, a colossal undertaking which they expect to accomplish within two or three years.

Another characteristic of the world is that of the nuclear age. With the boundless possibilities of nuclear fusion and fission still relatively untapped, nuclear energy is now in the process of revolutionizing the source of energy in the world. Owing to this scientific progress, the possibility of man to travel and communicate through space is no longer an idle dream.

On the other hand, it cannot be denied that mankind is faced with the agonizing problem arising from the utilization of outer space for military purposes and the development of nuclear weapons. While we are living in a century of tremendous developments, we are also confronted by exceedingly complex problems, problems which are associated with the use of the words "space diplomacy" or "nuclear diplomacy" in the field of international politics.

In the field of space diplomacy, both the United States and the Soviet Union have been faced with the question of restricting the outer space activities for peaceful purposes and not for military aims. As a result, at the end of 1958 the Committee on the Peaceful Uses of Outer Space was set up in the United Nations by the resolution of the 13th General Assembly.

Later in 1963, the 18th General Assembly adopted "the proclamation concerning the principles for restricting exploration and use of outer space" (to be stipulated in the peaceful uses of outer space) and "the resolution regarding the ban on placing in orbit around the earth any objects carrying nuclear weapons or any other kind of weapons of mass destruction."

Space diplomacy also received a positive impetus with President Johnson's proposal on May 7, 1966, for an early inclusion of a treaty on the peaceful uses of outer space in accordance with the United Nations declaration of 1963. On June 16, President Johnson presented the American draft proposal to the United Nations through the United States Ambassador to the world body, Arthur Goldberg. While the Soviet Union responded to President Johnson's call by tabling its draft proposal concerning the conclusion of an international agreement for a "basic law to utilize the moon and other celestial bodies for peaceful uses only."

The *New Tork Times,* in commenting on the President's May proposition, warned that if human genius triumphs before the conclusion of an international treaty on the peaceful uses of outer space, the world of the future would take on increasing complexities. Emphasizing the importance of diplomacy keeping pace with technological advances, the paper pointed to the fact that the problem is quickly approaching a crucial stage.

These two drafts were discussed from July to August by members of the Judicial Sub-Committee of the United Nations Committee on the Peaceful Uses of Outer Space in Geneva, composed of twenty-eight nations, including Japan, and were transferred to the United Nations Headquarters in September for final deliberation.

Finally on December 8, President Johnson announced that the United States, the Soviet Union, and other countries had reached an agreement on the treaty for the peaceful uses of outer space.

This outer space agreement, formally defined as "a treaty concerning principles restricting national activities in regard to exploration and use of outer space including the moon and other celestial bodies," can be summed up as follows:

1. The moon and other celestial bodies are open to all countries, and no nation can claim sovereignty thereto.

2. The moon and other celestial bodies shall be used only for peaceful purposes.

3. Military utilization, such as the construction of military bases, facilities, etc., and testing of nuclear weapons, shall be forbidden.

It is expected that the Judicial Sub-Committee will shortly submit a resolution to the Political Committee of the United Nations, requesting the nations to sign and ratify the treaty, and that after passing the Political Committee it would be approved by the 21st General Assembly.

It is further anticipated that, following its approval by the General Assembly, the treaty would be signed in Washington, Moscow, and London around next January and that the treaty would go into effect toward the latter part of 1967, following ratification by at least five nations, including the United States, Great Britain, and the Soviet Union.

The importance of the treaty lies in the fact that for the first time mankind has a law pertaining to the use of outer space. As President Johnson has pointed out, it can certainly be looked upon as "the most important arms control development since the 1963 partial nuclear test ban treaty."

Although at one time difficulties were reported in the negotiations between the United States and the Soviet Union, it is worth noting that the Soviet Union decided to come to an agreement with the United States despite the continuance of the Vietnam war.

Actually, however, military utilization of outer space is still continuing, either in the form of intercontinental ballistic missiles which travel beyond atmospheric range, reconnaissance satellites, navigational satellites, military communication satellites, or the manned orbital laboratories.

All of these vehicles are not prohibited by the treaty, but the treaty is nevertheless promising in that it firmly bans the launching into orbit of nuclear weapons without the provisions for inspection and verification. Moreover, like the 1963 Partial Nuclear Test Ban Treaty, the outer space treaty is open to nonmembers of the United Nations as well.

Under these circumstances, at a time when the United States and the Soviet Union are competing in space development with their national prestige at stake, it is abundantly evident that people all over the world are deeply concerned that the achievements of 20th-century science shall be devoted to the happiness and prosperity of mankind.

Japan, too, has from the very outset advocated that outer space should be restricted exclusively to peaceful purposes, and has proposed that all launchings of space objects should be notified beforehand. Her research program has not only been hampered by the lack of financial resources, but interministerial differences have hitherto delayed progress.

Although space development requires a colossal amount of

money, materials, and personnel, needless to say Japan should conduct research into this field as an important national undertaking. She must not lose sight of the long-range objectives, and bitterly regret her failure to act now.

There are certain areas where the so-called nuclear diplomacy interlaps with space diplomacy, but here let us confine ourselves to the great weight given to nuclear power in international politics. No doubt, the main motive for France and Communist China deciding to develop nuclear weapons was to acquire a greater voice. It is also suggested that the reason for West Germany's insistence that she be allowed to participate in NATO's nuclear force is in order to acquire a diplomatic trump card.

The total elimination of nuclear weapons is the deepest desire of mankind. However, in the field of nuclear disarmament, progress was made only in reaching an agreement on a Partial Nuclear Test Ban Treaty in 1963. Prospects of reaching an agreement on the treaty of nonproliferation of nuclear weapons are still uncertain despite two years of discussion.

As the only nation to have received the baptism of atomic destruction, Japan is firmly determined to renounce nuclear armaments. Furthermore, it has no desire whatever to acquire any such diplomatic advantage in international politics from the acquisition of nuclear power.

Through utilization of nuclear energy for peaceful purposes, Japan and West Germany, Italy, Sweden, Canada, as well as India—although possessing no nuclear weapons—are capable of producing atomic arms. Japan should continue to possess such a capacity technologically, scientifically, and economically, at all times.

Especially at a time when Communist China is proceeding relentlessly toward becoming a great nuclear power, Japan can only maintain peace in the Far East by possessing this capacity, enabling her also to stand up to Communist China's voice in world affairs.

To realize genuine peace in Asia, it is the mission of Japan to cooperate in the economic development and improvement of the standard of living of the Asian countries, striving to the best of her ability to build up a solid foundation through such a cooperation. This should undoubtedly be the great path along which a developed nation of Asia should tread.

Value of the Hot Line, Balance of Power, and Importance of History

When speaking of the new age of diplomacy, attention is often focused on the hot line, or direct line of communication, between the White House and the Kremlin. This line was established after the Cuban crisis at the end of November, 1962, when a mood of detente began to characterize Russo-American relations. It was one of the outcomes of the so-called nuclear diplomacy.

Learning from the Cuban crisis, the two powers signed a treaty of communication in August, 1963, as a means of avoiding an all-out nuclear war, an accidental war, or an international crisis. The hot line, consisting of a cable line under the Atlantic Ocean and a wireless link via Tangier, came into operation in September of the same year. In an emergency the leaders of the two countries will be able to exchange views or to either send or receive messages through the hot line.

In June, 1966, when President de Gaulle of France visited the Soviet Union, it was decided to set up another hot line between the Elysée Palace and the Kremlin. An agreement between the two countries was signed in November for the establishment of direct communications. With the possibility that the world can be plunged into the terrible horrors of a nuclear war with the press of a button, the leaders of the two countries hope this catastrophe can be avoided through discussion whenever a dangerous situation arises.

The value of the hot line seems to symbolize the agonies of

mankind in the nuclear age, an age which should not be allowed to overshadow everything else. Any faltering or self-righteous attitude on the issue of the day, such as ignoring the principle of balance of power and refusing to take note of the lessons of history, is dangerous.

Even in the nuclear age, the principle of "balance of power" remains a decisive factor in international politics. During the Cuban crisis of 1962, the late President Kennedy warned Soviet Premier Khrushchev that the United States could not permit the balance of power to be upset, even at the risk of a nuclear war.

Since that time, the basis of American-Soviet coexistence has been strengthened and the risk of a third world war is regarded to have lessened.

Last November, when Japan's Ambassador to the United Nations, Akira Matsui, spoke to the General Assembly on the question of Chinese representation, he said, "an attempt to change Chinese representation by ousting one of the parties to the dispute [Nationalist China] will upset the balance of power in the Far East and increase tensions." He repeated Japan's opposition to the resolution to unseat Nationalist China and to invite Communist China.

A close study of the realities of international politics will clearly bear out the fact that the maintenance of the balance of power is an indispensable factor in preventing war and preserving peace. It can never be overemphasized that an inadequate evaluation of the balance element is not only superficial but also dangerous.

From a historical point of view, each age has its historical characteristics as does international politics. The object of diplomacy should be not only to properly recognize and grasp the current of the times but also to ensure the security and development of the country in accordance with this current. To do this, it is essential to study present as well as past history, and to make a calm and correct appraisal.

In addition, the present-day world is composed of national

states, each with different characteristics founded in their respective histories. Since the life of each race pulsates within its own history, it is important to understand and to consider nationalism. There is no other way to reach such an understanding except through a study of history.

Although it has been some time since voices were raised to reconsider Japan's diplomacy, it is possible to find many indicators and lessons for the basis and method of diplomacy from Japan's history, particularly its diplomatic history.

In this connection, the great Japanese statesman of the Ministry of Foreign Affairs, the late Viscount Kikujiro Ishii, wrote: "If I were asked what would be the guiding principles of diplomacy, I would answer 'history,' diplomatic history. Since history repeats itself, learn from past lessons."

Failure to look back on history hinders the nurturing of patriotism among the younger generation. The late statesman and politician Shigeru Yoshida wrote in his book *The World and Japan* that "the young people of Japan today generally know little about the history of their country and do not correctly evaluate the accomplishments of the leaders of the Meiji era. The sagacity and efforts exhibited by our past leaders in dealing with a series of crucial issues, such as the Sino-Japanese War, the Tripartite Intervention, and the Russo-Japanese War, are highly evaluated internationally. A people which do not have justifiable pride in their nations' history can hardly accomplish anything great." (December, 1966)

CHAPTER **24**

Japan's Diplomacy and Political Parties

Role of Political Parties in Japan's Diplomacy

BASICALLY the political ideas of free nations are expressed through parliamentary democracy in which the political parties shoulder the responsibility. Accordingly, the duties which these parties must discharge through parliamentary procedure in both domestic and foreign affairs are manifold and the responsibility which they bear is extremely heavy.

In the field of national diplomacy, although it goes without saying that diplomacy is the prerogative of the government, unless the governing party positively and energetically participates by offering advice and guidance when the need arises, it would be impossible to formulate a people's diplomacy.

Similarly, since the target of any political party is to seize the reins of government, the opposition parties should always possess a responsible program in the field of diplomacy and be prepared to assume responsibility.

Furthermore, in the light of the fact that a nation's diplomacy is intimately linked with the very basis of its existence and its international confidence, a serious problem would arise if a political party which has newly assumed office were to pursue a policy lacking both consistency and continuity.

Consequently, the government and opposition parties should not only rise above party interests but also be guided

282

by national interests, the basis of guiding diplomacy, in the pursuance and consideration of a nation's foreign policy. While devoting themselves diligently to the execution of the nation's diplomacy, it should be the duty of politicians, whether of the government or opposition parties, to work for the realization of the so-called supraparty diplomacy.

Some of the salient points defining the government's diplomatic rights and the participation of political parties in a nation's foreign policy may be summed up as follows: First, it being imperative that a nation's will be unified in the field of foreign relations, the diplomatic right is in the hands of the government.

Second, the government's diplomatic rights extend over two fields, namely of negotiations with foreign powers and the framing and deciding of a diplomatic policy. Negotiations with foreign countries are carried out solely by the government, and only in very exceptional cases is a political party invited to participate. Nevertheless, it is naturally within the rights of every member and political party of the National Diet to criticize the government regarding the negotiations from the standpoint of probing into national affairs.

Members of the Diet and every political party also have the right and duty to positively participate in the deliberations in the National Diet on matters affecting the decision or alteration of the nation's foreign policy and on the ratification of an international treaty. The question of supraparty diplomacy arises principally in this field.

Although every political party has an organ which coordinates the survey, study, deliberations, and views of the party on diplomatic questions, the Liberal Democratic Party has established the Foreign Relations Research Committee under the Political Affairs Research Committee.

I assumed the post of vice chairman of the Foreign Relations Research Committee in 1953, and have served five years as chairman of the said Committee since 1961. During this entire period, I have devoted myself wholeheartedly toward the survey and study of Japan's foreign policy from a national and long-range point of view. Every effort was made to encourage a just and sincere discussion of diplomatic issues.

While chairman of the Foreign Relations Research Committee, I compiled reports on "The Development of EEC and Japan" in 1962, and on "Supraparty Diplomacy" in 1964. The former report took up in detail the problems of EEC, a development which would mark a turning point in world history, and its future influence over Japan and Asia, while the latter report, stressing the necessity and importance of supraparty diplomacy, was a survey of supraparty diplomacies in foreign countries.

Meanwhile, the Sato Cabinet has been endeavoring to modernize the conservative party by dissolving factionalism, but the primary need is to strengthen and respect the party organs. In the case of the Foreign Relations Research Committee, while it is beneficial for the members of the National Diet to have their own various organizations relating to research into diplomatic problems, the members should express their views to the public only after the views have been fully deliberated by the Foreign Relations Research Committee, the official organ of the party which should also serve as their mouthpiece.

It is also not surprising that on certain issues it is impossible to reconcile the views of the minority, but in such cases it is the practice to include the minority view in the announcement.

In connection with party activities on foreign affairs outside the Diet chamber, especially those of the opposition, it is often stated that present-day diplomacy should be fully backed by the people, that the government's diplomacy and the people's diplomacy should be like two wheels of a cart. Needless to say, that is as it should be, for nothing can lend weight to a nation's diplomacy more than unity and cooperation of its people. Notwithstanding, this does not countenance the type of arbitrary diplomatic activities engaged in by Japan's opposition party, such as the Socialist Party, particularly in relation to Communist China. A nation's diplomatic rights are unquestionably the prerogative of the government, and it must not be forgotten that there is a limit to the diplomatic activities of opposition parties.

In special cases, where a political party becomes involved in diplomatic activities, it is usually in order to supplement a role which a government cannot undertake on a governmental basis. Such an involvement should be predicated by national interests in which assistance is rendered in the form of direct or indirect cooperation with the government. Whatever the nature of the diplomatic activities of the opposition party, it is necessary for the government to be receptive if they are to be materialized. In other words, the diplomatic activities must be of a type and content that the government can accept.

As a matter of fact, the Socialist Party in activities outside the National Diet stirred up the masses to agitate against the Japan-United States Security Treaty in 1960 and the ratification of the Japan-Korea treaty in 1965. Although the effort of a political party to disseminate its views among the general public may be taken as a matter of course, it should always be remembered that excesses committed in the name of a popular movement may endanger the very foundations of democratic government. The establishment and development of a democracy founded on a sound parliamentary system can hardly be expected if political parties pay scant attention to deliberations in parliament, the cornerstone of democratic government, and devote their main energies to mass movements outside the National Diet.

Supraparty Diplomacy

As a general rule, diplomacy should always be guided by national interests, and it is the mission of political parties to prevent the government from deviating from that course.

Every party, either government or opposition, should be fully aware of its mission, and make every effort to carry out a diplomatic policy that is in the national interest and in harmony with the ever changing current of history.

It is true that the present-day world is still antagonistically divided into the Free World and the communist bloc, and there is no difference in the substance of the foreign policies of the free nations in dealing with this confrontation. Moreover, there is also no striking difference of views among the political parties of the various countries concerned.

For example, the Democratic and Republican Parties follow a bipartisan policy regarding United States foreign relations, while the Conservative and Labor Parties in Great Britain and the Christian Democratic and Social Democratic Parties in West Germany are not sharply divided on issues of foreign policy. Except for the extreme right and extreme left parties in France and Italy, the center parties are generally cooperative in matters of diplomacy.

In these countries, the opposition parties adopt a responsible attitude toward policies they hope to realize, and in the fields of diplomacy they cooperate in promoting national interests as much as possible, never permitting their political squabbles to get out of hand.

In sharp contrast, in Japan the views of the Liberal Democratic Party and the Socialist Party on key matters of foreign policy or national defense are completely at variance, and it is almost impossible for them to compromise or to hold fruitful consultations on these issues. The reason is the strong tendency of the Japanese Socialist Party to bandy the Marxist line of world outlook, and not a few members openly admit their Marxist leanings. This fact is a fatal handicap for Japan's diplomacy, and to the United States and other countries which entertain great hopes in Japan this handicap is a source of uneasiness and is difficult to dispel.

Since Japan's future would be placed in jeopardy if we were to abandon all hopes of a supraparty diplomacy, I have never tired over the years in my efforts to stress the importance of realizing this cooperation, not only in my speeches in the National Diet but also in lectures, broadcasts, and commentaries. I have urged that every avenue should be explored to find a common ground for compromise between the Liberal Democratic Party and the Socialist Party, failing which the Liberal Democratic Party should at least attempt to realize a supraparty position with the Democratic Socialist Party.

In response to a strong call by Mr. Suehiro Nishio, Chairman of the Democratic Socialist Party, for a supraparty diplomacy three or four years ago, I referred to his advocacy during my interpellations in the Budget Committee of the Upper House on March 6, 1964. The highlights of my questions and the answers of Prime Minister Hayato Ikeda and Foreign Minister Masayoshi Ohira are as follows:

In reply to Mr. Nishio's call, I urged that (1) regarding important diplomatic problems, efforts should be made to hold frequent talks between the leaders of various political parties, and there should be a common understanding on vital information, (2) opposition party leaders should attend formal diplomatic functions, and (3) participation of opposition parties should be sought at international conferences in a form and within limits which will not compromise the diplomatic privileges of the government.

Foreign Minister Ohira, in reply, stressed the necessity of building up confidence between the leaders of the government and opposition as proposed by Mr. Nishio, and explained that it was this spirit which prompted the government to invite the members of the opposition political parties to join the government delegates at the General Assembly meeting of the United Nations in the autumn of the previous year. The invitation was rejected by the Socialist Party.

Shortly after becoming Prime Minister, Mr. Ikeda for his part had even suggested a mealtime discussion with members of the opposition parties, but was also rebuffed. The prime minister further revealed that whenever he had invited a foreign head of state or a leading foreign politician to visit Japan, he had extended invitations to Japanese opposition party leaders to the functions.

Concerning the sending of observers to the United Nations as proposed by Foreign Minister Ohira, Mr. Ikeda said that he would welcome such a participation by the opposition parties.

After voicing satisfaction over the explanations to proposals 2 and 3, and requesting further elucidation of proposal 1, Foreign Minister Ohira added that he sincerely desired to gradually build up relations of mutual confidence between the government and opposition parties and ultimately to create an atmosphere of confidence.

Continuing my interpellations, I drew attention to the fact that in the United States and in Europe a supraparty attitude regarding national defense and the need to maintain continuity in diplomacy was being generally observed. However, in Japan, there existed a wide gap in the views of the government party and the opposition concerning such important problems as defense foreign policy. Emphasizing that a repetition in the future of the events surrounding the security pact disturbances would pose a threat to Japan's security, I expressed my firm belief that it was the duty of politicians to reach a supraparty understanding, whatever the seemingly insurmountable obstacles.

The prime minister, who regarded the party relationships abroad with envy, pointed out that in prewar Japan there were many examples of party leaders meeting to discuss foreign affairs. He deeply regretted the postwar period political confrontation, but promised to make efforts in the future to alleviate the situation.

A summarized version of the interpellations with the prime minister follows:

Morinosuke Kajima: If supraparty diplomacy is to be taken up, it is necessary that such questions relating to national defense and security which divide the nation should be considered from a long-range point of view. Should an understanding be difficult between our party and the Socialist Party, then I feel that the reaching of some kind of understanding with the Democratic Socialist Party, an advocate of supraparty diplomacy, will contribute toward the lessening of the present tension.

Prime Minister Hayato Ikeda: At the present time, any such approach to the Democratic Socialist Party might well aggravate the political situation by allowing emotions to run high in addition to the already existing differences of opinion.

From the point of view of supraparty diplomacy, I think that we can attain our objective quicker if all the parties moved together in the desired direction.

Morinosuke Kajima: In order to realize supraparty diplomacy, would it not be advisable to establish a secretariat to handle preparations or, if a less formal organ is desirable, some organization or body?

Prime Minister Hayato Ikeda: I am endeavoring to proceed in the direction to which I alluded earlier, but I believe that the government should not take the lead, but that all the party factions in the Diet should get together to discuss the issues involved. The government will naturally exert its efforts in the future, but if matters are taken up within the Diet progress would be very much smoother.

In the interval, I had published a report on supraparty diplomacy on June 25, 1959, following full investigation and deliberation for six months from January, 1959, in the Foreign Relations Research Committee of which I was chairman. Attached to the report were the materials and data compiled by the Foreign Office, the National Diet Library, and leading authorities relating to foreign countries. Readers will certainly find these of deep interest.

The question of supraparty diplomacy has continued to be eagerly debated even after the inauguration of the cabinet led by Prime Minister Sato. The issue became lively prior to and after the visit of Prime Minister Sato to the United States in January, 1966. Public opinion appeared to favor such a diplomacy.

It is interesting to note that two tea parties, attended by leaders of the Liberal Democratic Party, the Socialist Party, and Democratic Socialist Party, as well as leaders in various walks of life, were held in a very congenial atmosphere in which the question of supraparty diplomacy was discussed. Though the talks did not take a major step toward actually realizing supraparty diplomacy, it is a highly significant first step in the right direction.

It is unfortunate that supraparty diplomacy retrogressed over the questions of normalizing Japan-Korea relations and the war in Vietnam, sharpening the clashes between the government and opposition parties. In order to be able to cope with the current international situation, especially the fluid conditions in Asia, and the approaching crucial year of 1970, it is becoming increasingly important for Japan to adopt a supraparty diplomatic approach based on national interests. (March, 1967)

CHAPTER **25**

Path to Peace

My Concept of Neopacifism
—Political and Religious Pacifism—

PEACE is not only an eternal ideal of all mankind, superseding beliefs and ideologies, but it is also man's most desirable objective today. While postwar Japan is dedicated to the ideals of peace, as enacted in the so-called Peace Constitution, this dedication is based on her defeat in war and the three million compatriots who sacrificed their lives.

In its Charter, the United Nations has responded to the wishes of all mankind by stipulating in the preamble that "We the peoples of the United Nations determined to save succeeding generations from the scourge of war, which twice in our lifetime has brought untold sorrow to mankind . . ."

By their terrible sufferings in World War I and II, the living generations of today should have had enough of the calamitous effects of war. Furthermore, in the nuclear age, if they should repeat the tragedy of another all-out war, the whole of mankind faces the threat of total annihilation.

However, in the present extremely fluid international situation, besides the threat of an all-out war the world is constantly plagued by so-called local and limited wars as a result of the confrontation between the East and West and the problems between North and South, the principle of self-determination of peoples and territorial questions.

291

Among the more serious conflicts that have disturbed world peace are the Korean War, the Suez conflict, the Algerian War, disturbances in the Congo, the Indo-Pakistan War over Kashmir, and the Indonesian-Malaysian confrontation. The current Vietnam war has been continuing for more than five years ever since the United States has become actively involved, and there are no indications when the hostilities will end.

It is, therefore, apparent that no international issue is more important than peace not only to the countries affected, but to Japan as well.

It is a matter of sincere regret that pacifism as it is understood in Japan is utopian, unrealistic, and negative. For this reason, I repeatedly clarified in the years following the end of the war my thoughts on neopacifism which have been generally supported by the people and adopted in the policies of the Liberal Democratic Party and the government.

Later, during my interpellations in the Upper House plenary session on January 28, 1965, as a representative of the Liberal Democratic Party, I took up the issues of peace and security. On this occasion, I emphasized the main points of neopacifism, principles of which apply today as they did then. These principles to which I firmly adhere were outlined in the following summation.

At the outset of my statement on neopacifism, I stressed that, while there are differences of interpretation regarding peace among politicians, thinkers, and religious leaders, the important thing is to consider the question of peace in the light of the international situation confronting Japan.

As methods of preserving peace, there are those who advocate complete disarmament or reduction of armaments, and those who insist on armaments expansion, but I strongly insisted that neither the present level of Japan's defensive strength nor a military buildup at the sacrifice of the people's standard of living would lead toward peace.

I then pointed out that the so-called pacifism of today had

many serious deficiencies. First, the so-called peace doctrine is quite unrealistic and politically unsound, and too many of its leading advocates are dreamers and gimcrack politicians. Consequently, the peace doctrine becomes tinged with religious and dialectical flavorings, making it impossible to view domestic and international situations in their right perspective. Often, such a premise leads to erroneous conclusions.

Second, since they seek instantaneous results in the idle pursuit of lofty ideals, without placing any limit on the goals for the peace doctrine, they end up achieving nothing at all. Consequently, they cling vainly to future hopes, unperturbed, while leaving everything in the hands of those who are opposed to the ideal.

Third, even though the objectives of the peace doctrine may be rational, the methods chosen to attain the objectives are often irrational. They devote their entire energy only toward opposing war, and lack any organized plan to realize the peace they purportedly seek. However lofty the objective may be, there is a positive lack of planning.

In conclusion, I emphasized that a new age requires neo-pacifism, and that religious pacifism should be replaced by realistic, political pacifism. In order to achieve the goals of neopacifism, a limit should be established and all energies should be concentrated toward the fulfillment of this limited objective.

The reason for this stand is that peace can only be achieved step by step, and a realistic step forward is worth more than a thousand imaginary steps.

"Si vis pacem, para bellum"
Its Relation to the So-called Peace Constitution

For further clarification of my ideas concerning neopacifism, I should like to take up the relationship of peace and armaments.

Needless to say, under the present international situation, Japan's current state of disarmament and defenselessness under neopacifism does not necessarily contribute to the preservation of peace. The old saying, *si vis pacem, para bellum,* or "if you desire peace, prepare for war," is a timely reminder that lack of defense and cries of peace alone do not ensure peace.

Although war does not break out today as heedlessly as in the past, it is essential for nations to make adequate preparations to avoid an easy crossing of borders and conquest of territory. Since Japan cannot defend herself against either the Soviet Union or Communist China, she has entered into the Japan-United States Security Treaty which has been the instrument for preserving her security.

Among the measures to preserve peace, there are those which I describe as an absolute peace line and the religious peace line. However, since the statesmen in power are not religious men, it is essential that their political thinking consider the inevitability of war without being prepared. Among the Japanese statesmen, there is a lack of awareness of this fact within the Komeito not to speak of the Socialist Party.

On the basis of the Peace Constitution, Japan's defensive power has been built up on an easy purchase system, as it were. With the outbreak of the Korean War, Japan gave up her former policy of possessing no military establishments whatsoever and inaugurated the National Police Reserve. This force was later transformed into the Ground Self-Defense Force, the Maritime Self-Defense Force, and the Air Self-Defense Force. In addition, although the first, second, and third defense build-up plans have been successively promoted, there is still a tendency on the part of the people to show a lack of interest in the self-defense forces and Japan's defensive strength.

We shall be only too pleased to welcome the day when the peoples of the world can negotiate the realization of complete disarmament in a peaceful atmosphere. But reality is very far from this state of affairs, and the present-day world situation does not guarantee the people of Japan that the preamble of its Peace Constitution, "trusting in the justice and faith of the peace-loving peoples of the world," can be relied upon.

The old type of aggression and expansion has disappeared as far as the advanced nations of the world are concerned, but a new type of aggression, distinguished by the slogans of "progress," "liberation," and "peace," is still attempting to control the territories of other nations and attempting by aggressive action to obliterate human freedom. The danger of such a localized armed aggression exists even in the environs of Japan.

Even Article 9, the so-called peace provision, of the Japanese Constitution, renouncing the use of force as a means of settling international disputes, does not deny the inherent right of self-defense possessed by all nations. Moreover, the second clause denying the maintenance of war potentials and the right of belligerency of the state is not generally interpreted as forbidding the maintenance of any armed forces.

In this connection, the late Shigeru Yoshida, one-time prime minister who was responsible for the enactment of the Japanese Constitution, stated in his book entitled *World and Japan:* "It is true that so far as I was concerned, the original intention of stipulating the second clause of Article 9 of the new Constitution disavowing war potentials, was mainly political, aimed at enabling Japan to return to the international community of nations as soon as possible and to wipe out the stained reputation of Japan as an aggressive and militaristic nation. Therefore, if Article 9 is to be interpreted in a narrow sense so as to outlaw even the self-defense force, it would set Japan adrift from the realities of the world and be the cause of political turmoil."

Referring to the Keitei Incident in the National Diet, Prime Minister Sato on March 31, 1967, clarified the unified view of the government, declaring that "it has been the consistent view of the government's interpretation of the constitutional theory that the existence of the self-defense force is not a violation of the Constitution."

Incidentally, whereas the first Japan-United States Security Treaty expressly provided in the latter part of the preamble that "the United States . . . is in the expectation that Japan will itself increasingly assume responsibility for its own defense . . . ," the revised treaty stipulated in Article 3 that "the parties, by means of continuous and effective self-help . . . will maintain and develop, subject to their constitutional provisions their capacities to resist armed attack."

In its interpretation of the Japan-United States Security Treaty system, the Supreme Court in 1959, in giving a ruling on the Sunakawa Incident, said that "the peace doctrine of our Constitution did not lay down a rule of defenselessness or nonresistance. To be able to take necessary measures of self-defense is not only natural but an inherent national right. Such measures may include a common defensive system with a specified country."

In the meantime, for the attainment of world peace, Japan, an industrialized nation, should within the limits of her economic power not only assist the developing nations to raise their standards of living, but should also contribute toward the defense of freedom against the threats of the forces of aggression.

The poverty, ignorance, prejudices, and disease prevalent in the developing countries are all enemies of peace, and the existence of these negative factors have added fuel to the ideological struggle between East and West.

On the other hand, if Japan as a member of the United Nations seeks only to benefit from the organization without lending a helping hand to maintain peace, she can hardly hope to escape from the charges of irresponsibility.

Peace and Regional Collective Organization

It would naturally be ideal if the United Nations can firmly guarantee world peace. Article 10 of the Japan-United States Security Treaty alludes to the role of the world organization as follows: "This treaty shall remain in force until in the opinion of the governments of Japan and the United States of America there shall have come into force such United Nations arrangements as will satisfactorily provide for the maintenance of international peace and security in the Japan area."

Judging by the present international situation, it is indeed impossible to foresee when the United Nations will be in a position to fully function as an effective peace-keeping organization. It still remains an ideal of the United Nations.

I believe that it is a matter of urgency to form regional collective organizations which are linked with a world organization like the United Nations. This is because the existence of such regional collective organizations is indispensable for the peace and security of the member states.

As a matter of fact, the Charter of the United Nations encourages the development of regional arrangements or agencies within the framework of the world body.

Consequently, it is strongly hoped that Japan, while adhering to the Japan-United States security system, will enter into regional cooperation, collaboration, and association with the free countries of Asia. In effect, this envisages the creation of a Free Asia, the realization of which I have advocated for many years. Recent signs of acceleration in the direction of this goal fill me with feelings of great elation. Simultaneously, Japan has been displaying more initiative in her foreign policy to promote the idea of Asian-Pacific solidarity, a goal which I have been consistently championing.

I should add here that the formation of a Free Asia is not aimed at confronting the communist influence in the Asian-

Pacific area. The idea is entirely the same as that advocated by Count Richard Coudenhove-Kalergi some forty years ago when he launched the Pan-Europe movement. Nonetheless, it should not be overlooked that the Pan-Europe movement was proposed as a means to safeguard Europe from the growing political and military threat of the Soviet Union. He has referred to this threat immediately after World War I as well as World War II.

The ideals of Count Coudenhove-Kalergi were recently revealed in an open letter which he sent as president of the Pan-European Union to Mr. Willi Brandt (currently Foreign Minister of Federal Germany) of the Sozialdemokratische Partei Deutschlands (SPD) when he was nominated by his party as candidate for the chancellorship in 1960.

In his open letter, Count Coudenhove-Kalergi attempted to discourage Mr. Brandt, who was then Mayor of West Berlin and known as a valiant fighter on the frontline of Free Europe, from becoming a candidate of a political party whose platform was incompatible with Pan-Europeanism. The SPD manifesto, although acknowledging the necessity of a regional security organization, asserted that a unified Germany should be a member of the European security system and should support economic collaboration in Europe.

Count Coudenhove-Kalergi pointed out that no reference was made to West Germany's efforts to work for integration with other free nations, and that it is meaningless merely to harp on economic cooperation.

Comparing the platform of the SPD regarding European policy with that of the Christlich-Demokratische Union (CDU) led by Adenauer, who was then Chancellor, Count Coudenhove-Kalergi expressed satisfaction that the latter party was taking measures, step by step, for the integration of Free Europe in the economic, cultural, and defense fields, and was also cooperating with the United States.

He believed that such a Pan-European policy would not only guarantee the freedom, peace, human rights, and happiness of Europeans, but would also be a preparatory step for exercising the right of self-determination by Europeans on the other side of the iron-curtain and pave the way for the reunification of East and West Germany.

The count urged Mr. Brandt to declare openly and in no ambiguous way that he would continue to develop and promote the European policy of Chancellor Adenauer. This declaration from the mouth of a major opposition party candidate for chancellor would serve to convince the entire world that European integration was not a problem affecting a single political party but the united demand of the people of West Germany.

Subsequently, the SPD, supporting the stand taken by Count Coudenhove-Kalergi, has taken a policy identical to the CDU in relation to European integration.

On forming a coalition cabinet with the CDU in December, 1966, the SPD proclaimed that the stalemate in the move toward European integration must be broken, and that efforts should be made toward consolidating the European collective organizations, abolishing customs barriers between the nations belonging to EFTA (European Free Trade Association), and fostering a new relationship between Germany and France. The party also confirmed that the West German government would effectively support the efforts of Great Britain and the other EFTA members to join the EEC.

On December 13, 1966, Chancellor Kiesinger of the coalition cabinet, speaking of government policy on the question of European integration, said that it is our firm belief that the economic and political integration of Europe is not only in the interests of the European nations, but also the United States of America. The German chancellor then expressed the view that some day the Soviet Union will conclude that an integrated Europe is an essential element of world peace.

There is in Europe today an indication that the pace of development from economic integration based on the EEC to political integration has recently quickened. For the formation of Free Asia, there are a number of lessons which can be drawn from the European example.

In the meantime, Count Coudenhove-Kalergi is advocating a political cease-fire between the member nations of the North Atlantic Treaty Organization and the Warsaw Treaty Organization, to be followed by compromise and cooperation as a path to world peace. Because of their distrust of the communist bloc nations, the Western nations are hesitant to accept this idea. It is for this reason that the count has stressed the importance of unifying Europe.

A similar situation prevails in Asia. Though I earnestly hope that some day a collective security system guaranteed by Japan, the United States, Communist China, and the Soviet Union will come into being, I think that the prompt formation of a Free Asia is a prerequisite. (April, 1967)

CHAPTER 26

1969:
A Year of
Mounting Crises

Choice Between Collective Security and Neutralism

THE MOST vital issue confronting Japan's foreign policy is the question of national security. This can be clearly discerned from the fact that, with the so-called time for re-examining the security treaty in 1970 rapidly approaching, the domestic situation has become increasingly tense and disturbed.

Needless to say, the core of Japan's security is the collective security system between Japan and the United States. The validity of the Japan-United States Security Treaty, limited to a fixed period of ten years, expires on June 23, 1970. Although, on the one hand, the treaty will become automatically extended beyond that date, it can, on the other, be abrogated at any time by giving a year's prior notification of its termination. In this context, the nature of the security treaty takes on a different significance.

In order to cope with this so-called 1970 issue, the government and the ruling Liberal Democratic Party have been renewing their pledge to adhere to the policy of supporting the Japan-United States Security Treaty.

In this connection, the majority of the Japanese people have demonstrated their clear support for the treaty, as evidenced also by the results of the Upper House elections in July, 1968.

301

Among the opposition parties, the Democratic Socialist Party and the Komeito favor cancellation of the treaty by gradual stages, while the Socialist and Communist parties demand outright abrogation of the treaty.

In either ease, the opposition is taking up a position of confrontation against the government and the Liberal Democratic Party in developing the so-called 1970 struggle which is now unfolding.

Essentially, in order to maintain its existence, development, and prosperity, the state has the supreme obligation to safeguard national security. However, it is deeply deplorable that public opinion in Japan should be so divided on such an important issue. On the other hand, the situation, however regrettable, having already advanced to the extent, is extremely difficult, if not impossible, to remedy.

The situation having come to such a pass, the only course left open to the government and the Liberal Democratic Party is to firmly maintain the Japan-United States Security Treaty as a farsighted national policy.

In the United States, a new Republican Administration under President Richard M. Nixon will be installed in the new year. While it appears to be keeping an eye on developments in Japan, it has not yet shown any indication that it is seriously concerned with the problems that are shaping up in this country.

In this connection, it is worth noting that Mr. Nixon, who will assume office as the 37th President of the United States, made certain references to his policy toward Japan in an election campaign pamphlet on domestic and foreign policies published last October 28.

In it, he stated: "One must recognize that it simply is not realistic to expect a nation moving into the first rank of major powers to be totally dependent for its own security on another nation." He went on: "Not to trust Japan today with its own armed forces and with responsibility for its own defense would be to place its people and its government under a disability which . . . ill accords with the role Japan must play in helping secure the common safety of noncommunist Asia."

He further stressed: "I think it is vitally important for us to recognize that we have no real collective security in Asia without Japan being a part of it. The interests of Japan and Asia of a free, strong Japan are the interests of a free, strong United States in the Pacific. And I think that once Japan assumes the role of leadership, Okinawa certainly could be returned."

The irreconcilable positions taken by the ruling Liberal Democratic Party and the four major opposition parties in Japan on the problem of 1970 are basically rooted in principles: the principle of collective security as reflected in the maintenance of the Japan-United States Security Treaty by the former and the principle of neutralism as reflected in the policy of the latter to gradually dissolve or abrogate the treaty.

However, in the present nuclear age, it can be said that there is no nation on earth which does not regard collective security as an almost absolute necessity. In other words, due to the awesome capability of nuclear weapons, all countries without exception realize that defensive action can no longer be confined within national boundaries. They also recognize the fact that it has become impossible for any single nation to build up a completely adequate self-defense system.

Moreover, it is believed unlikely that the United Nations, the machinery for the maintenance of world peace, will be able to fully and effectively discharge its role within the foreseeable future. It is in order to supplement the role of the United Nations that collective security, either bilateral or multilateral, is necessary.

As for the case of neutralism, it is unlikely in the present-day situation that the neighboring countries will allow Japan, occupying as she does a position of geographical importance and industrial eminence, to remain neutral. Furthermore, it is not a policy which she should choose to pursue.

In this complicated situation, I must warn against the dangers posed by the opposition parties, attempting to take advantage of the pacifism of the people, to push their policy of neutralism. There are signs that a certain segment of the population is being misled. It is, therefore, a matter of deep concern that the Socialist Party, the leading nongovernmental party, is advocating a policy of "unarmed neutrality" and the Komeito is pressing for "complete neutrality."

The Socialist Party is proclaiming that its platform of "unarmed neutrality" is the forerunner of a new form of security which is at the same time the most realistic.

Admittedly, there is hardly any country which has to this date "tested" the efficacy of being totally "disarmed" either practically or historically. A glance at past history—or from the viewpoint of international law, for that matter—reveals that armed power was necessary to maintain neutrality and to prevent aggression.

The Komeito bases its stand on "complete neutrality" as being nonparticipation in any military alliance and the maintenance of a position of equal distance with other nations. In this respect, the party points out that its neutrality differs from the parties, such as the Socialist and Communist parties, that lean toward the communist bloc. To uphold this policy, it regards the "maintenance of an absolute minimum force of national guards" as being unavoidable.

In expressing views on either "unarmed neutrality" or "complete neutrality" I don't think that either of them can escape the criticism of being, at best, "visionary pacifism."

In the case of the Democratic Socialist Party, although it calls for the gradual cancellation of the security treaty, it might be unduly extreme to link this policy immediately to neutralism. Whereas the Komeito is pressing for the early cancellation of the treaty, if possible during the 1970's, in order to realize its policy of "complete neutrality," the Democratic Socialist Party has not put any timetable for its policy of gradual cancellation.

Be that as it may, the Democratic Socialist Party is currently advocating a revision of the Japan-United States Security Treaty in 1970 in order to achieve the party's so-called "security without retention of the U.S. Forces in Japan." Knowing that the time is not yet ripe to advocate self-defense, the party's policy can only be described as underestimating the need for collective security in the world of today.

While the Communist Party campaigns for "armed neutrality," it must not be forgotten that by advocating their brands of neutralism both the Socialist Party and the Communist Party are only endeavoring to camouflage their intentions of carrying out a socialist revolution to seize the reins of government.

Trend Toward "Automatic Extension"

One of the problems connected with the policy of maintaining the Japan-United States Security Treaty is whether the treaty should be based on "automatic extension" or "fixed period of extension." With regard to this question, I have long pointed out that the conclusion of the Japan-United States Security Treaty, founded on the principle of maintaining a power balance in international politics, counterbalances the Sino-Soviet Treaty of Friendship, Alliance, and Mutual Assistance.

Furthermore, since the Sino-Soviet pact of alliance has been designed to remain in force until 1980, it has been my desire to see the Japan-United States Security Treaty similarly extended for a fixed period of another ten years.

Faced with the need to deal with this question, the Security Committee of the Liberal Democratic Party, which has been positively studying the "problem of 1970" since December, 1965, published its interim report in June, 1966. In the report the committee strongly urged that the treaty be extended for a fixed period of ten years, a position supported by an over-whelming majority of the members of the party.

Nevertheless, since 1967, owing mainly to two reasons, the trend in government and party circles has been gradually shifting in favor of "automatic extension." The first reason for this trend is founded on the reported hesitancy of the United States government, which feels that it would be difficult to obtain the ratification of the Senate to a ten-year extension of the present treaty.

The second reason is the desire to avoid a repetition of the disturbances which took place in Japan during the previous revision of the security treaty, thereby sidestepping the struggle against the security treaty launched by the Socialist Party and other so-called renovationist forces.

In the United States, the lack of enthusiasm stems from the feeling that the nature of the present security treaty lacks reciprocal obligations, favors Japan unilaterally, and is disadvantageous to the United States. The points at issue concern the agreement of prior consultations relating to the execution of Article 6 of the treaty and the question of the geographical limits of the treaty's application.

Actually, the United States Senate was greatly dissatisfied with these points at the time the treaty was concluded in 1960. Notwithstanding, as a result of its deliberations the Senate unanimously approved the treaty 90 to 2 with 1 abstention and 6 absentees. It is well to remember that the treaty was signed against the background of a grave international situation, caused by the confrontation between the Free World and communist blocs.

It was vitally important for America's world policy to keep Japan firmly tied to the Western world. Even in the current international situation, that requirement remains unchanged. In Europe, the tensions which had been easing have again been revived by the entry of Soviet forces into Czechoslovakia. In Asia, too, even the progress in the Vietnam peace talks offers no ground for optimism.

Moreover, the statement delivered in the United States by Senator Fulbright, Chairman of the Foreign Relations Committee, during the deliberations on the security treaty is still valid today. He declared then that our (United States) objective is to retain Japan as the strongest bastion of free people in the Far East. In other words, he warned that if the strength of Japan were added to the strength of Communist China, the industrial capacity, scientific know-how, and extensive technology of the Japanese people would add immeasurably to the manpower resources of Communist China. For the Free World, particularly to the United States, this would create a very dangerous power.

Nonetheless, if the United States were to raise anew the issues referred to earlier, that is "prior consultation" and "area of application," it must not be overlooked that there is a major underlying current of fear about the actual extent of American understanding of the Asian situation and the so-called Japanese public opinion as reflected in the United States.

Although this fact leads to the question of the nature of Japan's mass media which manipulates "public opinion," should public opinion in Japan realize that the peace and security of Japan are inseparable from the peace and security of the Far East, it is felt that the United States will not make such an issue of the problem.

It is hardly necessary to explain the theory of "evasion" in Japan itself. On the other hand, it is hardly conceivable that the policy of "sidestepping" the re-examination of the 1970 security problem will pass off peacefully, especially in view of the fact that the major opposition party, the Socialist Party, together with Sohyo, the General Council of Japanese Labor Unions, is desperately attempting to mobilize the struggle against the security pact in 1970 by linking it with the anti-Vietnam war struggle, return of Okinawa, restoration of Japan-Communist China diplomatic relations, abolition of the American military bases, etc.

Recently, even the struggle against the "establishment" by the so-called student power has been directly linked to the anti-1970 security treaty movement. While the struggle may be confined to only a section of the younger generation, their lack of sound ideals and reckless behavior have become scandalous. I cannot but urge the students and youth in general— the future leaders of the nation—to carefully reflect and to arouse themselves against this trend.

The Importance of Economic Problems

Needless to say, although the question of security is not simply military but extends to the political, social, cultural, and other fields, its effects in the economic field are particularly important.

Of course, in Article 2 of the current security treaty there is a reference to economic cooperation, the so-called stipulation on economic collaboration.

In contrast, military matters predominated in the original security treaty. If the security treaty were purely military, it would be best if its provisions were never put into force. For the treaty to be widely supported by the people and exist for a long period, it is necessary to pursue economic and political cooperation. Hence, such provisions were clearly stipulated in the NATO Treaty, the SEATO Treaty, the Sino-Soviet pact of alliance, and other similar treaties.

Accordingly, when the current security treaty was being revised, I pointed this out to the then Prime Minister Nobu-suke Kishi and the then Foreign Minister Aiichiro Fujiyama. With the support of other influential persons and leaders in business circles, the economic provisions were inserted in the present security treaty.

It is now a matter of public knowledge that since that time, by effectively executing the economic provisions, economic relations between Japan and the United States have rapidly developed, resulting in greater trade, technical cooperation, capital investments, assistance to underdeveloped countries, etc. Within the Japan-United States security system, the importance of such economic collaboration can never be overemphasized.

Therefore, if the security treaty is abrogated, there will be grave effects on the economic field. During the recent inauguration of the new leadership of the Socialist Party, the Secretary General of the party, Saburo Eda, voluntarily made the following painful admission to newsmen: "If the security treaty is abrogated, the United States might resort to economic retaliation. In that event, we have not conducted enough study to convince the people about what would happen to the Japanese economy."

In order to protect the dollar, the United States strongly desires that Japan play a more positive role in the preservation of economic cooperation. Because of the constitutional difficulties in the way of military cooperation, proportionately higher hopes are being placed in Japan's economic strategy.

For example, this fact can be seen from the hopes expressed by Mr. Eugene Black, Special Adviser to the American President and former president of the World Bank, who arrived in Japan last September for a brief visit, during his meetings with Prime Minister Eisaku Sato and other Japanese leaders. In spite of the fact that the United States had not yet fully contributed its special fund of $200 million to the Asian Development Bank, Mr. Black requested that Japan double her contributions to the special fund from $100 to $200 million. He also requested that Japan play a more positive role in the Mekong River Development, a key project in the economic development of the Indo-China region after the conclusions of the Vietnam war.

While such economic cooperation and assistance must fall within the limits of Japan's national strength, she must also fully realize that her responsibility and role in the maintenance of security in the Far East in the future will become

310 MODERN JAPAN'S FOREIGN POLICY

increasingly greater. Thus, Japan must endeavor to discover and to implement the most effective measures.

Confrontation and Dialogue

Although there are criticisms that the Japan-United States security system implies "confrontation" and "provocation" against the communist bloc, I wish to stress that nothing could be further from the truth. This charge is mainly leveled in connection with Japan's relationship with Communist China, but such a claim must first be considered against the background of the type of comments and news about Communist China disseminated by Japan's mass communication media.

Generally speaking, the mass communication media in Japan voices critical views of the United States, but appears to go out of its way to be frightfully understanding of Communist China. For instance, even in the face of the overbearing attitude of Communist China, the mass media not only shows no signs of anger but also painstakingly attempts to recognize the validity of the Communist Chinese claims, even being critical of Japan's attitude and policy.

In trying to explain the causes for this extraordinary attitude, it is not enough to say that the United States is a close friend with whom Japan can be frank.

While it appears that the Great Cultural Revolution in Communist China is finally subsiding, the inflexible foreign policy based on dogmatic ideology and judgment shows no sign of changing.

As far as Japan is concerned, there is no indication of any letup in the charges that she is working hand in glove with so-called American imperialism.

Beginning from 1962, the general trade between Japan and China has retrogressed into a trade regulated by a memorandum and limited to a period of one year as from 1968. Moreover, in addition to the renewal of trade for the coming year being uncertain, the Communist Chinese have completely disregarded Japan's request for the release of thirteen Japanese news reporters and businessmen now detained in Peking.

The antisecurity treaty forces, such as the Socialist Party, are placing the blame for the hard-line policy of Communist China and the resulting "confrontation" on the existence of the Japan-United States Security Treaty. At the same time, they urge that the security treaty be abrogated and diplomatic ties be established with Communist China, but this is nothing less than putting the cart before the horse.

The conclusion of the Japan-United States Security Treaty originally resulted from the signing of the Sino-Soviet Treaty of Friendship, Alliance, and Mutual Assistance in which Japan was the hypothetical enemy, and in order to thwart the ambition of the communist countries to communize the world either by direct or indirect aggression.

To meet such aggressiveness and expansionism, it is necessary to state in no uncertain terms that Japan does not intend to budge an inch from her basic stand in support of freedom and democracy.

The bitter lesson of recent history, in which the failure to clarify this basic stand led to dire consequences, can best be seen in the debacle resulting from the so-called appeasement policy adopted by Great Britain and France in dealing with the aggressive and expansionist policy of Nazi Germany.

Since Japan and the Chinese Mainland are geographical neighbors, sharing strong historical ties, it is naturally desirable that Communist China enter the international society of nations as quickly as possible and establish diplomatic relations with Japan.

To achieve this objective, the need for an understanding "dialogue" with Communist China is stressed, but before this objective can be attained it is necessary to fully recognize Japan's basic position. It is only on this basis that a really meaningful "dialogue" can take place.

However, it would be naïve to accept the contention of Communist China that the Japan-United States Security Treaty represents a provocative policy of "confrontation." To entertain such a stand would not only invite the contempt of Communist China but also "induce" direct and indirect aggression. A foreign policy based on what we call flexibility does not, of course, countenance such an attitude on the part of Japan.

Appendix

Chronological Treaty Highlights

1855 Russo-Japanese Treaty of Amity   *defines territorial limits of both countries*

1882 Triple Alliance (Germany, Austria, and Italy)

1902 First Anglo-Japanese Alliance

1905 Portsmouth Treaty (Russo-Japanese Peace Treaty)

1905 Second Anglo-Japanese Alliance   *offensive and defensive; recognizes Japan's paramount interests in Korea*

1908 Root-Takahira Agreement (U.S.-Japan)   *reaffirms "open door" principles*

1911 Third Anglo-Japanese Alliance   *third-party arbitration clause*

1915 Triple Entente (Great Britain, France, and Russia)

1919 Versailles Peace Treaty

1921 Four Power Treaty (Japan, U.S., Great Britain, and France)   *maintains Pacific islands* status quo

1922 London Naval Reduction Treaty (Japan, U.S., Great Britain, France, and Italy)   *reduction of naval armaments*

1922 Nine Power Treaty (Japan, U.S., Great Britain, France, Italy, China, Belgium, Netherlands, and Portugal)   *defines open door and equal opportunity*

1940 Japan-Germany-Italy Axis Treaty

1941 Soviet-Japanese Treaty of Neutrality

1945 United Nations Charter

1949 North Atlantic Treaty

1950 Sino-Soviet Treaty of Friendship, Alliance, and Mutual Assistance

1951 Japan-United States Peace Treaty

1951 Japan-United States Security Treaty

1952 Japan-Republic of China (Nationalist China) Peace Treaty

1953 United States-Republic of Korea Mutual Defense Pact

1954 United States-Republic of China Mutual Defense Pact

1954 Southeast Asia Treaty

1954 Mutual Assistance Agreement (Japan and U.S.)

1956 Japan-Soviet Union Joint Declaration *normal diplomatic relations resumed*

1957 Kishi-Eisenhower Communique

1959 Geneva Agreements *Vietnam question*

1961 Soviet Union-North Korea Mutual Assistance Treaty

1965 Japan-Korea Basic Treaty *stipulated the conditions under which relations between the two countries would be normalized*

1966 Manila Declaration *proclaimed the four points to be relevant in Vietnam and in the Asian and Pacific areas*

1966 Japan-Soviet Union Trade Agreement

Bibliography

Coudenhove-Kalergi, Richard Count: *Pan-Europa*, Pan-Europa Verlag, Vienna, 1923

Kajima, Morinosuke: *Sekai Taisen Genin no Kenkyu* (The Study of the Causes of World War I), Kajima Institute Publishing Co., Tokyo, 1920

————: *Genzai no Gaiko Mondai* (Current Problems of Japan's Foreign Policy), Kajima Institute Publishing Co., Tokyo, 1964

————: *Tomen no Juyo Mondai* (Major International and Domestic Problems Facing Japan), Kajima Institute Publishing Co., Tokyo, 1965

Kajima Institute of Research and Japan Institute of International Affairs: *Nippon no Anzen Hosho* (Problems of Japan's Security), Kajima Institute Publishing Co., Tokyo, 1964

Kirby, S. W. B.: *War Against Japan*, H.M.S.O., London, 1957

Lin Piao: "Praising the Victory of the People's Liberation War," *People's Daily*, Peking, 1965

Mao Tse-tung: *The Problems of Guerrilla Warfare . . .* , Frederick A. Praeger, Inc., New York, 1961

Otaka, Shojiro: *Dai Niji Taisen Sekinin ron* (On the Responsibility for World War II), The Jiji Press, Tokyo, 1958

Roosevelt, Franklin D.: *On Our Way* (Warera no Michi o Yuku), *Asahi Shimbun* (Japanese edition), Osaka, 1934

Socialist Party, Central Executive Committee: *Nippon no Heiwa to Anzen* (For Japan's Peace and Security), Tokyo, 1966

Takigawa, Masajiro: *Tokyo Saiban o Sabaku* (A Trial of the "Tokyo Trial"), Towa Sha, Tokyo, 1952

Welton, Harry: *The Third World War,* Philosophical Library, New York, 1959

Yoshida, Shigeru: *Sekai to Nippon* (The World and Japan), Bancho Shobo, Tokyo, 1963

List of Abbreviations

ABM	anti-ballistic missile
ANZUS	mutual defense treaty among Australia, New Zealand, and the United States
ASA	Association of Southeast Asia
BIAC	Business Industry Advisory Committee
CACM	Central American Common Market
CDU	Christlich-Demokratische Union
COMECON	Council for Mutual Economic Assistance
DAC	Development Assistance Commission
DAG	Development Assistance Group
ECAFE	Economic Commission for Asia and the Far East
EEC	European Economic Community
EFTA	European Free Trade Association
EURATOM	European Community of Atomic Energy
GATT	General Agreements on Tariffs and Trade
IAEA	International Atomic Energy Agency
IMF	International Monetary Fund
LAFTA	Latin American Free Trade Association
MLF	Multilateral Force
NATO	North Atlantic Treaty Organization
OAEC	Organization for Asian Economic Cooperation

OAS	Organization of American States
OAU	Organization of African Unity
OCAM	L'Organisation Commune Africaine et Malgache
OECD	Organization for Economic Cooperation and Development
OEEC	Organization of European Economic Cooperation
OEECD	Organization for European Economic Cooperation and Development
OPEC	Organization for Pacific Economic Cooperation
SEATO	Southeast Asia Treaty Organization
SPD	Sozialdemokratische Partei Deutschlands
UAMCE	L'Union Africaine et Malgache de Coopération Economique
UN	United Nations Organization
UNCTAD	United Nations Conference on Trade and Development